GOD&
Human
Suffering

GOD&

Human&

Suffering

An Exercise
in the Theology
of the Cross

DOUGLAS
JOHN HALL

AUGSBURG Publishing House • Minneapolis

Library of Congress Cataloging-in-Publication Data

Hall, Douglas John, 1928–
    GOD AND HUMAN SUFFERING.

    Bibliography: p.
    Includes index.
    1. Suffering—Religious aspects—Christianity.
2. Suffering of God. I. Title.
BT732.7.H27   1986   231'.8   86-7964
ISBN 0-8066-2223-7   ISBN 0-8066-2314-4 pbk.

Manufactured in the U.S.A.   APH 10-2641

For my Kate

Contents

Preface 13

Introduction 19

Basic Affirmations of the Tradition
The Importance of the Context
The Ordering of the Discussion

1. The Reality of Human Suffering 31

A. Biblical Faith Confesses the Radical Reality
   of Human Suffering
B. Ideological Presuppositions of First World Apathy
C. The Incapacity to Suffer
D. The Question

2. Creation: Suffering as Becoming 49

Introduction: What *Should* Be?
A. Struggle Belongs to the Created Order
B. The Circumscription of Suffering in
   Creational Theology
C. The Human Vocation: Stewarding Life
D. Transition: The Great Risk

3. The Fall: Suffering as Burden 73

Introduction: Suffering that Should Not Be!
A. Sin and Suffering: Connections?
B. The Irony of Sin
C. The Tragic Dimension
D. Understanding and Changing

4. Redemption: Conquest from Within 93

    Introduction: Redemption as "Point of Departure"
    A. Not by Might
    B. Intimations of an Alternative: The Theology
       of the Cross
    C. The Conquest from Within
    D. Acceptance and Transformation

5. The Church: Community of Suffering and Hope 123

    Introduction: Faith, Religion, and Suffering
    A. The Courage to Become
    B. Suffering as Participation and Transformation
    C. We Rejoice in Our Sufferings: Suffering and Hope

Appendix: Dialog and Conclusions 149

    1. Harold S. Kushner, *When Bad Things Happen To Good
       People*
    2. C. S. Lewis, *The Problem of Pain*
    3. Diogenes Allen, *Traces of God: In a Frequently
       Hostile World*
    4. George A. Buttrick, *God, Pain and Evil*
    5. Leslie D. Weatherhead, *Salute to a Sufferer*

Notes 199
Indexes 219

Soyen Shaku walked past a house where he heard much crying because the master of the house lay dead. He entered, being well known in the locality, sat down, and cried with them.

Said one of those present, "Master, how can *you* cry? Surely you are beyond such things?" Soyen Shaku answered gently, "It is this which puts me beyond such things."

—*A Zen tale*

I know the things that happen: the loss and the loneliness and the pain. . . . But there's a mark on it now: as if Someone who knew that way Himself, because He had travelled it, had gone on before and left His sign; and all of it begins to make a little sense at last—gathered up, laughter and tears, into the life of God, with His arms around it!

—*Paul Scherer*

Preface

God . . . and human suffering! Perhaps the most difficult combination of words in the Christian vocabulary—in the *human* vocabulary!

The subject has been disturbing my peace of mind for 30 years—perhaps from the beginning of my conscious life. I don't know why I should have lighted upon this particular problem. Like most of my fellow citizens in this First World—at any rate, most males who are white and middle class—I have not suffered especially. Not, at least, in obvious ways. But two things, I think, have pushed me, unwilling, into the orbit of this issue.

One is that I have been conscious since my adolescence of living at a time when much of human experience has been of the kind denoted in the word *suffering*. To be concrete: I belong to the age of Auschwitz and Hiroshima. . .and of the decline of optimism in North America. Beyond that, I sense on the horizon, as do many of my contemporaries, still greater forms of suffering. About these I cannot be blasé: I am a father. Through my children (to one of whom this book is dedicated) I have been granted that special grace (sheer grace!) that allows, sometimes, the members of one generation, having had a good part of its day, to reflect existentially on the fate of the generations to come. I wonder: will my children have to know a nuclear winter? Other people's children have already in our time known fates that may be just as bad, and I am no better than they, nor my children than theirs! Where can one find the courage to face all that?—or even to think about it?

That brings me to the second catalyst of my preoccupation with this subject: God! For some reason—sometimes I think it was in spite of the church!—I began rather soon in my life to suspect that God, the biblical God at least, is also preoccupied with human suffering. That is why, in spite of the route taken by so many of my contemporaries who found it simpler, I could not follow their lead and leave "God" out of the above-mentioned combination of words. Like them, I could not retain a "God" who was all thunder and lightning, a sort of Christianized Thor, or Mars perhaps, show-ing a slightly compassionate side in the little Lord Jesus asleep in the hay! The "Almighty God," the great Father-figure of Chris-tendom, simply begged (for me and for us) the question Why? If "He" *can*, why doesn't "He"? But in any case that particular Why?—the Why? of classical theodicy—no longer interested me or my generation very much, because already two centuries of secularism had been preparing us to dispense with the psychic need for Thor (though, as our century testifies amply well, Mars fared much better!).

With a minority of postmoderns, however, I have not been able to rid my soul of another kind of Why? that comes from the con-templation of another kind of God. I mean the God who is not much interested in regular displays of "His" omnipotence, appar-ently, but (as I have just said) seems even more preoccupied with human suffering than I am! Wouldn't it be ironical if all these centuries Christian and other religious defenders of God's honor have been trying to show how God and suffering do go together after all, are somehow compatible, while *God* has been personally appalled by the combination and has been trying—at enormous cost!—to do something about it! So long as such a prospect, *such a God*, could claim my attention (and the more familiar with the tradition of Jerusalem* I became, the more I felt that it had to do with precisely such a God!) I could not leave God out of the contemplation of human suffering and conclude, with the disillusioned humanists of my epoch, that it would no longer be profitable to entertain the particular combination of words that form the title of this book.

But that left me—as it left Rabbi Kushner, whose work I shall consider in the Appendix—with the need to understand the Why? and the How? of that combination of words. Just because one dispenses with Thor and Mars and Jupiter (and the "Almighty" of Christendom) in favor of a *Theology* that takes the compassion of God more seriously than God's alleged "power," and wants to give more than a glance in the direction of "the little Lord Jesus," it doesn't follow that this particular combination of words all of a sudden becomes easy! For one thing, the expulsion of the thunder-and-lightning gods as models of deity does not by itself rid the biblical tradition of its need to reflect on the meaning of divine omnipotence. More importantly, the positing of a God who is also appalled by human suffering and "trying to do something about it," leaves us with the responsibility of elaborating such a strange hypothesis—strange even to Christendom, despite its accumulated centuries of devotion to. . . the cross!

I do not have the gall to claim that in this little study I have addressed that other Why?—even to my own satisfaction. This is not a statement of false modesty (I am not especially modest); it is just a statement of fact. Finally, I think, *no one* can say *why* God is merciful, or *how*, in Christ, God has articulated that mercy. In this respect, the Why? of the present inquiry is far more difficult to answer than the old Why? of classical theodicies. Love is *always* harder to explain than power. Writers who think that they have explained love (*any* love!) satisfactorily have probably stopped experiencing it. Where the *agape* of the "crucified God" is concerned—and that is what this discussion is all about—theology can

---

* I shall use the term *tradition of Jerusalem* throughout to refer to what I regard as the *whole* Christian tradition, which in a fundamental way includes the Hebraic faith as this is expressed supremely (though not exclusively) in the Scriptures of the older Testament. The term should thus be heard against the historical backdrop of empirical Christianity's repeated attempts to avoid or transcend its basis in the faith of Israel.

only, finally, lose itself in wonder . . . and in the service of others, of sufferers.

But the wonder and the service, doxology and liturgy, should not be offered as *substitutes* for disciplined thought, for theology! There is a need—a real *drive!*—and it belongs to faith itself, and without it faith is not faith which insists upon understanding (*fides quaerens intellectum*). If we are going to make such perfectly outlandish statements as that God is preoccupied with human suffering, then we had better be prepared to back them up—if not always with reasons that the (empirically trained) head can follow, at least with reasons aimed at the still-human heart!

In this book, my basic aim is to present (for both head and heart) a reasoned elaboration of the thesis that I have flung out rather brazenly in this preface, that God in fact *is* preoccupied with human and creational suffering, or, to put it in a more scholarly way, that the response to human suffering coming out of the tradition of Jerusalem is nothing less than the suffering of God.

The adjective *reasoned* in that last sentence assumes, in some real sense, the risk of faith (*faith* seeking understanding): I am writing mainly for Christians—clergy, students, laity—who feel something of this drive to understand what they believe. But unlike some of my coreligionists, I make no *absolute* distinction between believer and inquirer and nonbeliever. There is a doubter in every believer, and the doubt has an almost wholly *positive* function, for it keeps faith from degenerating into credulity. There is also, for the most part, an openness to something akin to faith in every nonbeliever, and that openness also functions positively, for its keeps disbelief from degenerating into cynicism.

I wanted my statement about God and human suffering to be "reasoned" also in this sense, namely, that it takes seriously the fact that this subject is part of a larger body of teaching and belief—though a very central part. As Christians, we inherit a tradition (we did not invent it!) and we are obligated to listen to this tradition, from the Scriptures onwards, and to attempt to work through the particular problems and themes to which we must address ourselves in the light of it. Too many studies of God and human suffering, it seems to me, confine themselves too narrowly to *some aspects of* the theological tradition of the church—chiefly, of course, to God and the human condition, with sometimes (but not always) a certain auxiliary concern with Christology. In order to achieve an account of the subject that is "reasoned" in the sense of being an attempt at comprehensiveness, i.e., seeing this particular issue against the backdrop of the *whole* tradition, I have considered human suffering not only in relation to the doctrines of God and humanity (theology, anthropology) but in relation to creation, fall, redemption, the doctrine of the church and (throughout) eschatology. If this lends to the discussion an air of conventionality, being the *structure* usually followed in systematic theologies, I trust that the *content* of the discussion will offset the fears of any who might deplore conventionality in form.

At the end of the text proper, I have included a rather extensive Appendix in which I describe and dialog with the works of five other authors. I have done this for two basic reasons: first, since theology is a communal undertaking, I felt that my readers would like to pursue the questions involved in this topic as they are handled by other writers with whom they might or might not be familiar. Hopefully, it will encourage the reader to engage in further research—at least to read some of the books in question. Second, it seemed to me that one of the ways in which I could test and expand—or further elucidate—the basic ideas advanced in the main part of my work would be by engaging in a sort of conversation with other points of view. For this purpose I have chosen five familiar, in some cases very popular, treatments of the subject. The choice was determined by the scope of the book, the need for a certain variety in points of view, and by what I felt was just the right admixture of agreement and disagreement with my own position. Works on the subject with which I could feel no common bond, or, on the other hand, works which seemed too close to my own position (Dorothee Sölle's fine book, *Suffering,* * is a good example of the latter) were for that reason not included.

The manuscript in its final form evolved over approximately a three-year period, and I am grateful to the many persons who, along

---

* Philadelphia: Fortress, 1973.

the way, have contributed to its unfolding. (Theology really *is* a corporate exercise!) First, my thanks are due to the Protestant and Catholic clergy of the Canadian Atlantic Provinces who invited me to speak on this subject in the spring of 1983 in Truro, Nova Scotia. The next hearing of my lectures on this subject occurred in Colorado about a year later, when I was asked to address a conference of Lutheran clergy, who were both sympathetic and thoughtful contributors to the project. I am especially indebted to the eight Doctor of Ministry students who spent two very intensive weeks with me at Candler Seminary, Emory University in Atlanta, during the summer session of 1985, working through this theme. I appreciate very much the invitation of Augsburg Publishing House to publish the results of this research, reflection, and dialog, and I thank especially the director of book development for his encouragement and help in this connection.

Introduction

A voice says, "Cry!"
And I said, "What shall I cry?"
All flesh is grass,
   and all its beauty is like the flower of the field.
The grass withers, the flower fades,
   when the breath of the Lord blows upon it;
surely the people is grass.
The grass withers, the flower fades;
   but the word of our God will stand for ever.
                                        —Isaiah 40:6-8

Basic Affirmations of the Tradition

The tradition of Jerusalem* takes its stand on two basic affirmations concerning the human condition: the first is that suffering is real and is the existential lot of "fallen" humanity—"All flesh is grass. . . ; surely the people is grass." The second is that suffering is not the last word about the human condition and therefore that it need not and must not become our preoccupation, the object of

---

* See footnote on p. 15.

19

our *ultimate* concern, for ". . .the Word of our God will stand forever." Both of these affirmations must be sustained if we are to be faithful to this tradition.

It is not easy to sustain them both! For there is a profound tension between them. It is hard enough to articulate this tension; it is harder still to live within it. Common human spirituality would prefer to resolve the tension once and for all. One could in fact say that the two poles of spirituality between which the human soul characteristically ranges—cynicism and credulity—are posited upon the false resolution of precisely this tension. Cynicism resolves the tension by affirming only the one side of it: suffering is real—period. Credulity, which is not to be confused with faith even though it is almost always a "religious" response to existence, resolves the tension by taking up only the positive side: suffering has been overcome by the enduring Word; it is fundamentally illusory. Faith, as distinct from both poles of the spirituality to which the human psyche is "naturally" prone, knows that it must live *in* the tension; that to espouse only one of these affirmations is to invite the lie.

It is a lie if one fastens solely upon the reality of suffering. For there are moments of almost pure joy, pure pleasure. Beauty, goodness, and truth belong to our experience of life, and most of us know whole seasons of merriment. Pain cannot erase the memory of shared laughter, and death itself grows pallid in the presence of true human love and courage. In view of these and similar realities, the decision of the cynic that "life is suffering" can only be maintained if all such things are intentionally forgotten. That is the price that cynicism pays for its theoretical resolution of the tension. Committed in principle to the melancholy conclusion that all that is real is futile, cynicism must consign to vanity everything that is not obviously negating, thus in the process providing justification for many evils which could have been averted had a different outlook on the world been brought to them.

The prophets and apostles allowed themselves to move very near to the habitat of the cynic: "All flesh is grass, and all its beauty is like the flower of the field." But they could not in the long run indulge the lie of the cynic's resolution of this tension. Truth, for them, had to account not only for the fading of the flower but for its blooming: "Consider the lilies, how they grow; they neither toil nor spin . . . ." That created things cease to be and are vulnerable in the extreme the representatives of the tradition of Jerusalem knew—and they knew the pain of that knowing. But that things *are* in the first place, that there is something and not nothing—this enduring mystery of the life-giving Word prevented even the most sensitively realistic among them—even Koheleth—from embracing the way of the cynic.

It is also a lie, however, if, with the credulous, one courts this or that ideology which is blind—and which to sustain itself *must* be blind—to the actual suffering of human beings and human communities. The world fairly hums with the speculations of those who would demonstrate that suffering is unreal, temporary, illusory, a mere cultural lag, technologically containable, progressively being overcome, a figment of the imagination, etc. Every drugstore book counter abounds in paperbacks which illustrate in the most graphic terms how to avoid every sort of suffering (reminding us of Alfred North Whitehead's dictum, "Seek simplicity . . . and distrust it!"). The purveyors of electronic religion urge us to submit to their gods and their formulas, all of which promise slightly differing versions of the same pain-free life. But however "successful" all these theories and messages may seem to the affluent and basically healthy persons to whose quest for "peace of mind" they are obviously directed, they are reduced to dust and ashes by the cry of one child dying of cancer, one woman tortured until she betrays her friends. The tradition of Jerusalem can be jubilant, even triumphant, in its declaration of the victory of the enduring Word over all that destroys. But it will not join its voice to the chorus of this world's triumphalizers at the expense of the truth concerning that one child, that one woman (see Matt. 18:12-14; Luke 15:1-10).

Thus the task that Judaic and Christian faith always assumes when it attempts to be faithful to its sources is how to be entirely realistic about the actuality of human suffering and at the same time affirm that the end (*telos*) of existence nevertheless transcends suffering. To put it in the form of a question: How can faith avoid on the one hand a shallow optimism which to maintain itself intact must close its eyes to the data of despair, and on the other hand an equally shallow pessimism which refuses to perceive even mystery, let alone meaning, in and beyond the fate of mortal flesh whose beauty fades, whose life withers like the grass?[1] Or, stating the matter in the most direct language available to us: How shall we express plausibly— with our eyes wide open!—the meaning of *hope* in this tradition of Jerusalem?

The Importance of the Context

The attempt to articulate a theology of suffering, complex as it is in theory alone (and of course it never *is* "in theory alone") is further complicated by another, unavoidable factor, namely, the historically conditioned character of all thought—what is today called "contextuality."[2] In our time, Christian theology is at last beginning to take seriously that the search for truth—for "gospel"— has to reckon not only with what is contained in Scripture and tradition, but also with what is occurring externally and internally within the culture in whose midst the community of belief is called to make its witness. If the truth is to be faithfully investigated and communicated, then faith and doctrine must become, ever anew, conscious of the questions, attitudes, values, fears, aspirations, and the like, which dominate the milieu to which the gospel is to be addressed. Theological truth is not static. It must always be discovered afresh. For while truth is no doubt "one," as the medieval thinkers insisted, life is forever in flux. Truth, therefore, to preserve precisely its unity, its integrity, must always readjust itself to the changing circumstances of time and place. What is eminently true in one social context may in another context constitute precisely *a way of avoiding the truth.* The search for a true theology (*vere theologia*) is thus a never-ending vocation of the church. The gospel, far from being the steadfast, unchanging, and rather obvious "proclamation" that it is frequently assumed to be, is in fact always in need of restatement; for its principal object is to address, engage, convict, and make new; and this can be attained only through a difficult struggle with the spirit of the age (*Zeitgeist*). It will be *gospel* (*good* news) only if and insofar as it confronts the quite specific problematique* (if you like, the *bad* news) of the *hic et nunc*.[3]

By way of anticipation, we may note that this inherent and un-avoidable requirement of theology, viz., that it entails an ongoing struggle to "discern the signs of the times," constitutes a vital aspect of the suffering *of the church*, a subject to which we shall have to turn in the course of this discussion. To ask about the theology of suffering is, in part, to reflect upon theology *as* suffering. For when the Christian community takes to itself the task of comprehending and engaging the culture which is its worldly context, it is not assuming a merely intellectual investigation; it is entering into the deepest darkness of its world. It will only discern the truth of God that is light for that darkness if and insofar as it exposes *itself* to the darkness. As Helmut Thielicke wrote out of the abyss of a devastated Germany at the end of World War II:

No man (*sic*)** will ever come to the truth and thus to a trustworthy bridge over the abyss of Nothingness who has not faced doubt, despair and shipwreck. . . . He who knows what faith is must also have stood beneath the baleful eye of that demonic power against which we fling our faith. Faith is either a struggle or it is nothing.[4]

In relation to the particular aspect of Christian theology that concerns us here (especially here!), we must take careful stock of our own context. Who are we, who have determined to consider

---

* I am aware of the fact that in recent theological and other literature the word *problematique* has been overworked and is by many relegated to that unfortunate category of jargonese. It is, however, a useful and in some ways irreplaceable term, because it refers to a reality—so characteristic of contemporary social analysis—in which a whole battery of interrelated and mutually complicating "problems" work together to form a kind of network of "problematic" reality. For instance, in environmental studies one may speak of a "problematique" involving issues of demography, ecology, pollution, and other matters complexly interacting one with another. Even to comprehend this complexity, a science has to be created (environmental studies) in which researchers with different kinds of tools and expertise relate to each other in an interdisciplinary manner. Thus the wholistic connotations of this term render it particularly suitable in theological discourse, e.g., in hamartiology.

** Throughout, while I shall attempt to avoid noninclusive language in my own text, I shall reproduce quotations from the works of others as they are written.

once more this ancient question of God and human suffering? Whom do we represent? To whom are we called to communicate whatever truth we are enabled to glean in relation to this question? What do we find in our cultural milieu by way of presuppositions, expectations, biases, and assumptions which have direct or indirect bearing upon this question? To ask about God and human suffering is, to be sure, to renew a discourse which is as old as religion itself— as old, probably, as human self-awareness. It is therefore tempting to ask this question (as it is so often asked) as though it were a purely theoretical one, the same yesterday, today, and forever—to ask it, for example, in this familiar form: How can one believe in God, a God who is at the same time good, loving, and powerful, in view of human suffering?

Such a formulation of the question, however, obscures its most existential dimension, which is the identity and condition of the one who asks it. The poem of Job is a paradigmatic and unforgettable grappling with the problem of God and human suffering because it is *not* theoretical, but a drama in which the identity of all those who put the question, especially Job himself, is revealed in detail. It is because Job is who he is that the question is put in the way that it is put, and that "the answer" must be given in the form in which it is given.

No human question is ever asked (and no answer given!) in a historical vacuum; it is asked in a specific time and place by specific persons. With certain kinds of questions this contextual dimension may not be so significant; but with our present question it is of primary importance. The aspects of the problem of suffering which we shall hold up, as well as the responses that we shall give to them, will be determined in great measure by the particular circumstances, openly acknowledged or silently assumed, in which we find ourselves.

Perhaps I can make this methodological observation more transparent by drawing on a certain distinction that has become part of our theological vocabulary today, as it has become part of the vocabularies of the social and other sciences. We speak about various "worlds": the First World, the Second, the Third—sometimes a Fourth. The nomenclature is not wholly satisfactory; perhaps North and South, East and West are better designations in some respects. However we achieve it linguistically, the purpose is to attempt to do some minimal justice to the painful but real distinctions that exist today on the surface of this small planet, this *one* "world": distinctions between political entities that vie with one another for military superiority, distinctions in economic conditions, distinctions of race, sex, class, culture, and language. The social sciences as well as certain theological movements (especially liberation theologies and feminist theology) have helped Christians to begin to comprehend that it is not the same thing to tackle a theological question—*any* theological question—in the Third World as in the First, in the affluent North as in the economically depressed South, etc.

This general observation is conspicuously—almost notoriously— true in the case of the question that we are asking in this study. In El Salvador, Ethiopia, South Africa, and many other parts of our "one" world where human suffering is so very close to the surface of existence, where it is indeed the most conspicuous social fact, a fact not only of individual life but the primary *political* fact—in *such* contexts it is hardly necessary for Christians to accentuate the side of our particular theological question which insists that suffering is *real*. Life itself has made this reality all too prominent. No one could possibly avoid it! As a rule, in Third World contexts it becomes the task of the theologians to *speak to* this reality of which everyone is immediately aware. In their work, consequently, Third World theologians address themselves to that second basic theme of our faith, which insists that while suffering is certainly real it is not ultimate; that in, through, and beyond this so conspicuous human suffering there emerges a meaning and a hope; that this meaning and hope can even now be approximated; and that nothing in the world can finally annul the *liberating* power of that meaning and that hope.

What about *our* context? How does the fact of our being part of the First World, the still-affluent peoples of the northern hemisphere, affect our handling of the age-old theme of God and human suffering? What are the influences brought to bear on our treatment of this theme by the facts that:

- we belong to the have-nations rather than to the have-nots;
- we are part of the 6% of Earth's population which consumes 40% of the planet's natural resources;
- while approximately 53¢ out of every tax dollar in the United States goes towards military spending, citizens of this continent can go about for years on end without ever seeing the bodies of slain or starving persons in our streets;
- those who suffer most conspicuously in our society—the aged, the dying, the poor, the socially or psychically "abnormal"—are for the most part hidden from everyday view, sequestered in places which effectively insulate them from public notice; and
- the oppressed in our own midst—racial minorities, sexual minorities, the unemployed, and others—can still *seem* to the majority of us to be well and wisely treated?

One could go on enumerating such data of our social context, but the point, I think, will have been made: the dimension of the problem of suffering which has to be emphasized in our particular context, as distinct from most Third World situations, is quite obviously the *first* of the two affirmations to which I referred in the initial section of this Introduction, namely, that suffering is real, is intense and ubiquitous, is not easily overcome, and is the lot of humanity under the conditions of existence.

This at least is where I think we have to *begin* in our First World situation, more particularly in North America. To use Paulo Friere's term, the "conscientization" of the nonpoor[5] must mean our coming to a radical, informed, and sensitive awareness of the depths of suffering—particularly the massive corporate suffering—of those who cannot camouflage their pain, as we do, through the diversions of Dives. This conscientization of the nonpoor is vital, not only because the diversions of rich Dives are killing poor Lazarus at our gates, but also because it is indispensable to the healing of our own First World soul, whose dis-ease is far more complex than the malaise of the world's obvious victims and is indeed a "sickness unto death" (Kierkegaard). The great temptation amongst us as we try to articulate a gospel that speaks to the human condition is that we shall indulge once again, as Christendom has so often done, in

the sin of reductionism, i.e., that we shall minimize or even tri-
vialize the actuality of human suffering, including our own subtle
and repressed suffering, and so end with religious "answers" that
are premature and shallow. Our temptation as Christians of the First
World is not that we shall fall into cynicism as we confront the
overwhelming dimensions of this ancient problem of religious
faith—though our failure really to confront them may well disguise
not only cynicism but a covert nihilism! Our temptation is that we
fall into superficial belieffulness—credulity—healing the wounds of
the people lightly and degrading the hope that belongs to the gospel
of the cross. In short, our temptation (and if one subjects oneself
for five minutes to almost any media display of the tawdry religious
bravado that claims the attention of this continent one knows that
it has gone well beyond the stage of temptation!) is: *cheap hope.*

It is on account of this (as it seems to me) *dominant* factor in our
apologetic situation that I have chosen to begin this modest study
with a discussion aiming to show that the tradition of Jerusalem
regards the fact of human suffering very earnestly. It would not be
an exaggeration of the earnestness of this tradition's commitment
to realism to say that the reality of human suffering is the thing to
which biblical faith clings most insistently. If that faith must let
go, now and then, of one of the two affirmations named in the
opening sentences of this Introduction; if, in the attempt of the
community of belief to live *within the tension* created by these two
affirmations, it becomes impossible to sustain both of them at once,
then it is characteristic of the *Hebraic*-Christian tradition that it
will drop its hold on God's enduring Word before it will betray
God's creature with a religious exaggeration. There is in this tradition a commitment to humanity and the earth which not even
loyalty to God must usurp. For instance, the psalmist voices many
expressions of utter and almost blind trust in the Lord; but, when
this trust is tempted to protect itself by turning a deaf ear to the
cries of the oppressed and suffering, it changes to *lament*—and even
to accusation—for it will not abandon those whom *its God has taught
it* to befriend. To certain forms of piety—indeed to much avowed
Christian piety—this commitment to creation and to honesty concerning the creaturely condition seems almost blasphemous! There

is in fact very little in traditional Christian liturgy to reflect or parallel the language of lament and struggle with the Divine which dots the classical worship of Israel. But Christians who are offended by Israel's readiness to wrestle with God beg the question of their own foundational event, at whose center there is One who on account of *his* commitment to and full identification with "crucified" humanity not only had to *endure* the absence of God but was made bold to *express* this absence openly. There is nothing in Job or Lamentations to equal, in its context, the full impact of the cry of dereliction on Golgotha.

The point is this: Only if we are ready to begin our contemplation of this problem by reaffirming Jerusalem's commitment to the creation and its dogged honesty about the creaturely condition shall we be able to work our way through to a hope that is not cheap. Costly hope (to borrow a leaf from the notebook of Bonhoeffer) is hope that is hammered out on the anvil of historical actuality. Costly hope is never a completed and undialectical statement of the positive. Part of the cost of this hope is that it has to *go on* dialoging with its antithesis. The dialog is never ended, because the dialog is history, is life itself, and life keeps presenting data for which the past articulations of hope are inadequate. Such a hope can be taken seriously, however, only by those who are unwilling to take the shortcut of the credulous; for this costly hope, which submits itself anew each day to the data of despair, dares to speak—to whisper—only in the presence of real suffering. It is this costly hope that belongs to the faith of which I wrote earlier, when I said that, unlike either cynicism or credulity, faith does not seek to *resolve* the tension between the two steadfast affirmations about suffering held by this tradition, but rather seeks the courage to live within the tension.

The Ordering of the Discussion

After the initial chapter dealing with the reality of suffering as confessed by faith, our discussion is ordered by a wish to honor the general movement of theological reflection that is given within the

Christian tradition. This means that we have to do with three fundamental foci, or rather with a three-dimensional focus; in one way and another this focus is brought to bear upon all the basic issues of Christian belief, including the present one. The dimensions of this focus or perspective are named creation, fall, and redemption. They are not the only aspects of the total perspective that our tradition offers, but they are rudimentary because (whatever nomenclature may be used) they stand for three different-but-related questions that must be put to the various themes with which biblical faith has to occupy itself.

The focus called creation asks the question: What according to this tradition is *intended?* In the ordinary language of faith and piety, creation theology inquires about "the will of God." Regardless of what *is,* what is *willed?* Despite what actually *exists,* what is *essential?* The importance of this focus for our present considerations is obvious as soon as we ask ourselves (and how could we avoid asking this?) whether according to this faith-tradition human suffering is intended, is "of the essence," is the will of the Creator God?

Second, the focus upon faith's deliberations which we name the fall in the mythopoetic language of our doctrinal tradition asks the question: What according to this tradition is the primary problem— the *problematique,* * the predicament that must be overcome, the evil that must be undone, the negation that must be negated if what is *intended* is to be realized or approximated? What is the thing that is "wrong," and what is the cause of it? How can we speak about this "wrong thing," how understand and account for it? In the present instance this means asking whether suffering, according to our tradition, is wrong, and if so to what extent or in what sense. What is the source of this "wrong" suffering? If, according to the tradition of Jerusalem, suffering is in some way bound up with the sinful "fall" from divine intentionality, how shall we understand and articulate this connection between sin and suffering?

The third dimension of the threefold perspective on the reality of suffering given in our tradition is the decisive focus called redemption. From this vantage point on experienced existence, faith

---

* See the footnote on p. 23.

asks after the nature of the *overcoming* of what is not "intended" (creation), what is "wrong" (fall). In the present instance, this means that as Christians we are obligated to ask how, according to the gospel of the Christ, human suffering is met, addressed, engaged, altered, redeemed. At the outset we affirmed that one of the two constants in the biblical treatment of God and human suffering is the confession that while suffering is real it is not *ultimately* real, not the last word. Obviously, this confession implies the perspective of salvation or redemption.

The internal logic of this discussion, treated in Chapters 2, 3, and 4 respectively, will lead to a fifth chapter in which we shall ask about the role of the church in relation to our topic. We must do this, not simply as a practical application of the theological reflection that we shall have engaged in throughout the preceding chapters, but as a necessary continuation of that reflection. For in particular the Christian understanding of redemption, as it applies to the questions implicit in this topic, leads inevitably (as is evidenced in the scriptural sources themselves) to the positing of a community in which the redemptive event is extended. The church, in other words, is part—a very vital part—of our tradition's response to "the problem of suffering."

Finally, as explained in the Preface, we shall examine in the Appendix several rather popular attempts to enucleate a theology of suffering, with a view not only to enriching our own treatment of the subject but also of relating our discussion to the wider discourse of the Christian community at this stage in its pilgrimage.

1

The Reality of Human Suffering

Hear my prayer, O Lord;
  let my cry come to thee!
Do not hide thy face from me
  in the day of my distress!
Incline thy ear to me;
  Answer me speedily in the day when I call!
For my days pass away like smoke,
  and my bones burn like a furnace.
My heart is smitten like grass, and withered;
  I forget to eat my bread.
Because of my loud groaning
  my bones cleave to my flesh.
I am like a vulture of the wilderness,
  like an owl of the waste places;
I lie awake,
  I am like a lonely bird on the housetop.

—Psalm 102:1-7

A. Biblical Faith Confesses the Radical Reality of Human Suffering

Biblical faith does not flinch or cloak in pretty phrases its assumption that being human means suffering. One of the foremost characteristics of the faith of Israel in particular is the forthright nature of its language of lament. This faith does not beat about the bush, but comes right to the point: We are hurting! Nor does it appear before God cap in hand, gently pleading, suggesting, wheedling; it speaks its mind directly. It asks for help without apology. There is even an edge of command in its plea: "Answer me speedily in the day when I call!" One can only stand in awe of this directness. Christians, hearing such demands expressed by their pastors in prayers of petition and intercession, would be properly astonished!

This openness about suffering belongs not only to occasional works of the collection of writings that we call the Bible. It is to be found not only in Job, Ecclesiastes, Jeremiah, Lamentations, and many of the Psalms; it informs the whole story. What is, from one vantage point, the history of Israel's providential deliverance from evil, oppression, and extinction is, from another, the story of Israel's continuous degradation and suffering. When Peter Abelard wrote up the sad tale of his life, this greatest teacher of the Middle Ages called his autobiography *The History of My Calamities.* It would not be accurate to assign such a title to the biblical story—the story told in the continuity of the two Testaments—because that would be to ignore the other side of the dialectic of this history: deliverance, liberation, redemption. But whoever tries to read the Bible without taking serious note of the "calamitous" nature of the history to which it bears witness and whoever makes of it a success story with predictable, Horatio Alger-type motifs will have misunderstood the Bible in a truly fundamental way. Its account of existence is, to be sure, not a tragedy in either the classical Greek, the Shakespearean, or the Ibsenian sense; for, as we noted in the Introduction, the last word is not a word about the fatal or futile nature of human existence but about the enduring *logos* which lends to history, for all its apparent vanity and absurdity, a permanent worth and meaning. But while the tragic dimension is not the ultimate one in the biblical story, it is certainly present there, and profoundly so. What-ever may be the relation between Jerusalem and Athens, these two foundational spiritual traditions of Western civilization can dis-course with one another at the point of their common understanding of the tragic element in human life and history. Greek *drama*, es-pecially, bears affinities with Hebraic-Christian anthropology and, as Reinhold Niebuhr frequently pointed out,[1] it is precisely at this point that *modern* assumptions about the human condition conflict with both the traditions of Athens and Jerusalem. We shall return to this observation later.

While empirical Christianity has manifested a strong propensity to suppress or downplay the human awareness of pain (partly, as we shall see, on account of its questionable theological triumphal-ism, and partly because it has functioned so consistently as the "positive religion" of empire), the newer Testament at its core is not less forthright when it comes to realism concerning the pain of historical existence. For Christian spirituality, the suffering that inheres in existence under the conditions of "the fall" is given primary symbolic expression in the life and death of Jesus, the Christ. It has many times been remarked—with historic insight—that in both of the historic creeds of the early church (the Apostles' and the Nicene Creeds), the only word that depicts the *life* of the Christ as distinct from his birth, death, resurrection, and kingly reign, is the word *suffered*: ". . . suffered under Pontius Pilate." Whether in full consciousness or not, this was the primitive Chris-tian way of saying that in order fully to identify himself with the human species it was necessary for the incarnate Logos to become a broken man. If it is the object of the divine *agape* in the advent of the Son to identify completely with broken human being, then (as the Synoptics' predictions of the passion keep insisting relent-lessly, the protests of the disciples notwithstanding) "the Son of man *must* suffer. . . ." The inner logic and rationale of this famous scriptural "must" is not to be found in some inexorable and vin-dictive type of divine justice but in the human condition "with" which God would now enter into full communion. The Christ *must* suffer because suffering is the condition of those in relation to whom God would be "Emmanuel" (God with us). Suffering, to put the matter in contemporary *koiné*, is "where it is at" with "us"; therefore, a God who would achieve solidarity with us *must* become a suffering God.

This suffering, moreover, is not to be conceived in physical terms only. It is not only the suffering of the flesh that is intended; that, in fact, may be the least of our suffering, if we take the incarnation and humiliation of the divine Word seriously as our criterion for understanding what suffering is. It is perhaps more than coincidental that Jesus did not live into old age, to face the infirmities, the protracted illnesses, the humiliating failure of the flesh that belongs to the long process of aging. Not that these are insignificant; but the more significant suffering to which the incarnate Word "must" be subjected is the suffering of the human spirit—and *that* suffering, as we can see in the faces of our own youth today, can be experienced long before one has reached threescore and ten. The young man of Nazareth, still no doubt strong of limb and certainly in possession of all his mental faculties, experiences the apex of human suffering, in fact, long before his body is broken at the Place of the Skull. As one who must endure the fickleness and weak loyalty of his closest friends; as one who knows loneliness and alienation from family and society; as one who finds no haven from the *Sturm und Drang* of daily existence, no home, no place to lay his head; as one driven by a destiny, the rationale of which he is by no means certain; as one rejected by his kindred and race; as one frustrated by the continued failure of others to grasp even his best and simplest insights; as one seeking the kind of absolute sense of meaning that Providence neglects to provide; as one, in short, "tempted in every respect as we are tempted"—as such a one Jesus of Nazareth, long before his brief physical torment, enters into the passion and pain of human existing. And this is required. It is a condition of his messiahship. It is a "must"—because, given the logic of incarnation and cross, only through solidarity with humankind in all the reality of its suffering is God able, from within, to affect the healing process.

Of that healing we have yet to think. But not too soon! For only those who are ill have need of a physician. Unless we are willing at least to begin to entertain, in existential awareness, the reality of our dis-ease, we shall not be able to receive the "costly grace"

(Bonhoeffer) by which the pain of our existing has been, is being, and shall be met. For "there is no Christian hope except that which is born at the resurrection out of the darkness and travail of being crucified with Christ. Those who do not know that defeat do not know that hope."[2]

That the *suffering* of human beings should be taken this seriously by God, who would be God even without such compassion—this is where Christian faith and theology have to begin when they reflect on the *problem* of human suffering. To enter into the deepest communion with us, to be "Emmanuel," God (who as such, according to our theistic tradition, does not suffer inevitably or "naturally") must nevertheless *become* the suffering God. God must become indeed the *crucified* God (*der gekreuzigte Gott*), as Luther did not shrink from saying. So earnestly does the theology of the Judeo-Christian heritage look upon the *fact* of human suffering.

There is a polemic in this (there is usually a hidden polemic in theology, even when it sounds irenic). The polemic hidden beneath the biblical determination to be entirely honest about human suffering, to the point of insisting that God has to participate in it if God would be with *us,* is that this tradition rejects every Weltanschauung, secular or religious, which minimizes, ignores, or too easily resolves the complex problematique of human suffering.

One of the ways in which human beings and societies have tried to cope with suffering is by denying its existence or relegating it to the status of the ontically unreal, the merely apparent. A perennial theme in the religious history of the race has been just this docetic motif: pain, whether physical or spiritual, is fundamentally unreal, insubstantial. Or it is only as real as we, subjectively, allow it to be.

While this approach to suffering has important antecedents in ancient religion and philosophies, especially those which denied in the first place the reality of matter, it has flowered in modern civilization, and particularly in North America. Typically, New World religionists do not occupy themselves overmuch with the metaphysical foundations of such a view, but concentrate chiefly upon techniques for its application. Various cults of positive thinking and personal growth advise their followers that if they concentrate on the positive, pain will disappear. Like dietary prescriptions and fads, techniques for such concentration multiply phenomenally in our society, reflecting on the one hand our rather recent discovery of the mysteries of psychosomatic medicine, and on the other hand our accelerating preoccupation with ourselves and our repressed anxiety.

Christian Science, which in some ways may be regarded as a forerunner of contemporary cults of this type, is nevertheless more responsible than are most of the latecomers on this scene when it comes to the provision of a theological-philosophical rationale for its conclusions and techniques. In rather obvious continuity with Neoplatonic, Gnostic, and other movements of the period coinciding with the formation of early Christianity, Mrs. Eddy's rudimentary philosophy was an ontology which grants reality, in the strict sense of the term, only to spirit, matter having no actual existence. God, who is absolute good, is spirit (as the founder of Christian Scientism could claim with a scriptural warrant that she always coveted); and God has neither created nor consented to any sort of evil, illness, or death. God's laws provide only for life. Sin, sickness, and death are thus abnormal conditions of the mortal mind and have no existence outside of carnal thought. Disease is a belief, not a reality. The way to the healing of physical ills, then, is through the renovation of the spirit. The more the spirit grows and is strengthened, the less actual (existential?) will be the mortalities of the body. Mrs. Eddy insisted upon the "scientific" nature of her interpretation of Christian belief (she eschewed all trickery, such as she believed hypnotism, mesmerism, spiritualism, theosophy, faith-healing, and the like to be), and the basis for this insistence lies in her metaphysic, which denies the very reality of suffering.[3]

It is, however, not only avowedly religious denials of the reality of suffering that biblical faith takes on. In truth, many of these ostensibly religious denials are little more than stained-glass versions of the secular worldview in whose bosom they have been nurtured. Christian Science may be in some respects at least a primary instance of this religious mirroring of cultural faith. While, as I have acknowledged, it can claim a positive linkage with Hellenic and Hellenistic religion and philosophy, and can also draw upon certain emphases in newer Testamental writings, it would be inconceivable, I think, outside the world that we call modern, and specifically outside the American appropriation of modernity. It is not the only religious development—though it is an especially interesting one—that reflects the modern spirit of progressive redemption, the refusal to entertain negation, the quest for a pain-free life and the imaginative unfolding of techniques for the achievement of such a life. If in the 20th century Christian Science has given way to ever more shallow, how-to orientated, or plainly irrational and emotive versions of this same quest, it is surely indicative of the degeneration of the modern vision. Mary Baker Eddy's spirituality was shaped by an age which could still regard both social and personal progress as factual, and would happily entertain as rational and even "scientific" any theories grounded in and extending the scope of that fundamental fact. Today, progress is no longer an assured doctrine—though we are hard-pressed to admit it and incapable, it would seem, of finding any article of faith with which to replace it. Consequently, "rational" explanations of the unreality of that which negates life contain for many an unwelcome and unintended sting: what claims rationality for itself is always vulnerable to the critique of those who are ready to demonstrate its rational flaws; and in an age that has been visited by greater outbursts of the irrational and the absurd than thought possible in Mrs. Eddy's 19th-century New England, the flaws are legion. Hence the "scientism" of such brave visions as hers has been superseded, on the whole, by technique-conscious cults of the positive, and by wild, apocalyptic, or frenzied faiths which partake of the absurdity of the epoch and are therefore immune to the inquiries of the reasonable.

To ask about God and human suffering in our sociohistorical context is to encounter very early in the discussion the implications for this question of modernity and its waning. The modern vision conflicts with Christian faith at many points, but none is more transparent than the issue concerning the reality of suffering. As Christians in the North American situation we are obligated to consider this issue very carefully; for, being a society whose foundational assumptions are those of modernity—whose fundamental "religion" has been identified as "the religion of progress"[4]—we

must face the prospect of there being a radical incompatibility between our cultural presuppositions and the ancient faith-tradition
we blithely claim as our own.

B. Ideological Presuppositions of First World Apathy

There are many different ways of characterizing the nature of the
modern worldview and of the civilization that has resulted from it,
but one of the most straightforward would be that the modern
experiment is based on the assumption that human suffering can
be overcome—can be, is being, and shall be! In other words, suffering is not a necessary or inevitable dimension of human existence,
but represents rather a challenge to human ingenuity and inventiveness. What has been experienced as suffering in the past, it is
frequently claimed in our society, has been in great measure a consequence of human ignorance, indecisiveness, superstition, and lack
of scientific knowledge, initiative, or resourcefulness. It was taken
for granted by past ages that the various ills by which the race is
haunted—hunger, infant mortality, the great social diseases and
plagues, poverty, war, and even many of the things that seemed to
be "natural" catastrophes—were inevitable. One simply had to ad-
just one's thinking to them, to endure them. The modern mentality,
commencing with the Renaissance and expressing itself most grand-
ly in the Enlightenment of the 18th century and the industrial-
technological revolution of the 19th and 20th, challenged this entire assumption, and set to work to create a world from which
suffering of every sort would be banished. The modern age entertained the prospect of Utopia, no longer as an impossible dream
but as a blueprint for society. Through scientific and technological
genius, through the rational ordering of life in society, through
superior organization of corporate energies, through universal education, and simply because the world was unfolding that way, all
suffering—perhaps finally death itself—could be conquered.
    This attitude is for North Americans far from a merely theoretical
one; it is the primary spiritual-intellectual vision by which our so-

ciety has been nurtured, almost from its outset. Presidents can still be elected to office in the largest nation of this continent by promising to restore the national faith in just this vision. Even in Canada, which by comparison with the United States is conspicuously skeptical of visionaries, people can be moved by the rhetoric of the pale Canadian version of "the American dream."

Now the element of truth in this vision should not be gainsaid. It is certainly the case that humanity has the capacity to avert, eliminate, alter, or turn to good and useful ends many kinds of suffering that our forebears regarded as inevitable. None of us would want to return to the mentality of those ages of the world which took it for granted that plagues were sent by God or that the average life-expectancy could not exceed 27 years or that slavery or serfdom simply belonged to the divine order of things. We are children of pioneers, many of us, who had the courage to determine that they did not have to wait about in old Europe for famines and other forms of dismal fate to nip their lives in the bud. These ancestors of ours—the Third World of their time—took their destiny into their own hands, faced hardships and bitter perils they would not have known had they resigned themselves to dying quietly as pawns of the Industrial Revolution, and fiercely hoped that they could change their lot in the forests of the New World. And they did! Their blood still runs in our veins. We as a people, insofar as we have not capitulated to luxury, are still motivated by a determination to change the world, to challenge fate, to exchange suffering for winning. Nothing stirs our emotions so much as the decision of an underdog or someone handicapped by forces greater than herself to strike out in the direction of life—like a Terry Fox, defying cancer and setting out with one good leg to run from Halifax to Vancouver.

We need not be ashamed of such emotions! But in the process of the decades and centuries this important modern emphasis on the possibilities of change and the rectitude of human initiative was turned into an ideology. What was right and good in the New World insistence that many forms of "inevitable" suffering were not at all inevitable became in turn an exaggeration. The undeniable fact that *so much* could be changed led to the promethean assumption that *everything* could be changed, that there was nothing that human rationality and mastery could not achieve—and especially seeing that history itself was on our side! Thus the rightful discovery of human responsibility and stewardship was transformed into the concept of human mastery; and this sense of our lordship was ontically undergirded by the "religion of historical progress." It is the most powerful faith at work on this continent. It is the very substance of our thinking. "We *are* technique," as George Grant has incisively put it. The religion of technocratic mastery and historical progress is a direct assault on the ancient human experience of the tragic. In Rolf Hochhuth's play *Soldiers*, one of the characters remarks that in America the word "tragedy" does not exist: "they call it migraine."[5] While (as I shall argue in a moment) such an assessment is somewhat dated, it is still true of the *image* that we project officially and publicly. We are a society which still attempts to build a world in which the tragic is obsolete. We want to believe that with the appropriate "faith," a positive outlook, and technical know-how *everything* that negates can itself be negated. "Has technology brought some problems?" ask advertisements in our magazines that are placed there by big industry. "Well, technology can also solve them!"

Yet this "faith" is increasingly difficult to sustain. Time, resources, isolation from Old World conflicts, and, above all, our collective will to believe have enabled the peoples of this continent to live out of this faith in the overcoming of suffering for an exceptionally long period of time, and to amass a truly impressive accumulation of "evidence" for the truth of our view of the world. The chief executive of the United States can still fly over suburban Washington, D.C., in his private helicopter and point (Russians, take note!) to the neat rows of houses, *worker's* houses, and find in this experience all the evidence required for the truth of his progressive assumptions. But in the meantime some other people, including social scientists, artists, and others who are less programmatically dedicated to the rhetoric of progress, have been looking *inside* the houses. What they have seen there are forms of pain of which the founding fathers did not dream. There are many ways, again, of describing this pain; but in keeping with our theme let us name it the incapacity to suffer.

C. The Incapacity to Suffer

Every worldview, every system or meaning or image of the human runs the risk of insulating its adherents, at the level of intellect and spirit, from some dimension of reality. In our theoretical attempts to account for and order existence—in other words, in our ideologies—we human beings regularly truncate, simplify, or falsify reality. Life is always more mysterious and less manageable than our theories about life—including our religious theories and systems of theology. Freud, who was himself the inventor of what is virtually a worldview, nevertheless had sufficient self-knowledge to realize that all theory at some point lies about reality. He was fond of quoting the dictum of Jean-Martin Charcot, a 19th-century French physician: "La theorie c'est bon, mais ça n'empeche pas d'exister" (Theory is fine, but it doesn't prevent things from existing).

The modern Weltanschauung attempted to eliminate the negative, but the negative does not admit of being dismissed easily. Sickness, death, anxiety, the demonic, human failure, and all such negating elements of our experience may be called unreal in theory, but the theory does not prevent them from existing. "There is only one alternative to life with failure," wrote Tillich, and "that is lifelessness without failure."[6] The forms of human suffering may be changed, and even changed significantly; but theories which leave the Nihil out of account, or minimize the magnitude of suffering, relegating the tragic to dark ages of the species' past, give the lie to life. What is still more dangerous is that such theories tend to produce societies which, in order to continue giving credence to their foundational ideologies, must blot out their knowledge of actual pain.

Much of the literature and art of North America for the past several decades has to do precisely with this repression of pain and the incapacity to suffer that is its consequence. Arthur Miller's modern classic The Death of a Salesman,[7] which was recently revived on Broadway with Dustin Hoffman, is a good example of this genre. Willy Loman, the salesman, is a pathetic figure, not because he suffers but because he is incapable of confronting and appropriating the reality of his suffering. Moreover, the suffering that he cannot

face—just *because* he cannot face it—spills over into the lives of
those around him, especially his two sons; for, as every pastor and
counselor knows, repressed suffering must be paid for by those in
proximity to it! Willy, says Miller of the character he created,
"cannot bear reality; and since he can't do much to change it, he
keeps changing his ideas of it."[8] Even when he is confronted with
the ultimate failure of his scheming and dreaming, Willy grasps at
the final straw (and one that is not untypical of Homo sapiens,
North American style): his *insurance policy* will make it possible for
his family to realize, after his death, the success that in life he could
not acquire. "When the inevitable arrives, when he has lost his
job, when it is clear that his sons have been ruined by his belief
that success is just a matter of concealing the needle of sharp practice
in a hand gloved by fraudulent gladness, his suicide is only in part
dictated by despair. There is this insurance policy. . . ." "Miller's
people," comments the drama critic of *Time*, "are first and second
generation Americans who have yet to achieve a perfect-pitch imitation of standard American brag, bluff and bluster; their language
is thus a precise and moving metaphorical expression of the uneas-
iness with which they live in the American Dream they have not
quite assimilated."[9]

The repression of some dimensions of our experience is necessary
to sanity and survival. The human psyche, as Paul Tillich has said,
"cannot stand naked anxiety for more than a flash of time."[10]
Christ's cry of dereliction from the cross should be interpreted in
connection with this insight. Only this One—only *vere homo/vere
deus*—is made to suffer *utter* abandonment. The rest of us are shielded by the common grace of God, the grace of forgetfulness, of sleep,
of repression. God clothes our psychic nakedness, as God clothed
the pair in the garden, pathetically hiding from their own, newly
acquired self-knowledge. Repression is to human beings, said Ernest
Becker,[11] what instinct is to animals: it is how we cope when we
know that we cannot cope.

But when the repressive instinct becomes a whole way of life,
and there are vast areas of experience upon which we dare not
reflect consciously even for a moment, then the instinct has gone
awry and, instead of being a protective device enabling our survival

"in spite of" self-knowledge, it becomes the greatest threat both to our sanity and to our survival.

This is as true of societies as it is of individuals. Robert Lifton, the Yale psychologist who studied the psychic reactions of persons who experienced the bombing of Hiroshima and Nagasaki, today applies the insights that he gained from this original research to our own society in its *anticipation* of nuclear disaster. He names the collective spiritual state of our dominant culture "psychic numbing." "Psychic numbing," he writes, "has to do with exclusion, most specifically the exclusion of feeling."[12] Sensing in advance that we cannot cope with the complex and horrendous data of nuclear warfare, with the question mark that it scrawls over all our personal and societal pursuits, we turn off our feelings. The data about war and violence becomes for us mere data, information that does not elicit an emotional response. But of course it is not possible to turn off one's feelings in relation to one phenomenon alone, especially a phenomenon as far-reaching as the nuclear threat. A society which "handles" nuclearism through the massive psychological effort of ignoring its impact upon our emotions finds it difficult to achieve depth or openness of feeling in any area. Our programmed indifference to the world; our ability to listen without emotion to the most shattering "data" about genocide, mass starvation, widespread political torture, and violence of every kind; our frantic, narcissistic pursuit of private "happiness"—how much of this is a direct result of our incapacity consciously and *feelingly* to absorb reality, with its real and anticipated suffering?

The social consequences of the repression of suffering are devastating and, given the fact that our society is a very powerful one technically and militarily, they are also patently *dangerous*. Three types of consequence of the incapacity to suffer as this is evidenced in our society may be noted. In the *first* place, it is unusually difficult for most persons in our society to accept or articulate their own personal suffering. This can be documented in many ways—for instance, through the various studies that have been made concerning the North American way of handling death, terminal illness, or great personal loss. Contrary to some popular opinion, the covering up of negative experiences and the accompanying suppression of emotion typical of our dominant culture is not simply a contemporary extension of Anglo-Saxon (WASPish) stiff-upper-lip-ism, nor has it "always" been the case. Some of us are old enough to remember when death was still called "death," when funerals were held in people's parlors, when the mentally handicapped were cared for at home and allowed to participate in village or town life, and when schoolchildren were caused to read stories and poems in which innocent maidens were drowned and lovers (like Evangeline and Gabriel) did not walk off into the sunset![13] One of the most interesting ways of calibrating our present inability to handle personal grief was put forward in a paper by Jean-Francois Beaudet, one of my French Canadian graduate students.[14] In the premodern Catholicism of Quebec—the almost-medieval Catholicism that predated "La Revolution Tranquille" of the 1960s—one found in that province symbols of suffering everywhere: the suffering of the Christ, of the Virgin Mary, of the saints and martyrs, of holy persons recently deceased, like Brother André of St. Joseph's shrine in Montreal. For Protestants these symbols seemed particularly unacceptable, even gruesome. Part of the activity that, somewhat puckishly, is dubbed "The Quiet Revolution"—that is, the entry of Quebec into the dubious grandeur of the modern secular world—consisted of the jettisoning of precisely these apparently outmoded and morbid religious symbols. Quebec Catholicism, numerically decimated but proud of its new look, entered the modern era, complete with its concentration on city culture—its skyscrapers, its large industrial projects, its many symbols of the human triumph over nature.[15] But, Beaudet notices, while his grandfather, a devout Catholic of the Old School, could accept and speak about the various experiences of suffering that came his way, his father, an enthusiastic advocate of the new secular approach, seems locked into a gospel of success and, like the secular Protestant and Jewish Willy Lomans, has no point of reference on the basis of which to articulate his own pain. The symbolic images of success which in Quebec as elsewhere have replaced the wounded Jesus and the tormented saints—the smiling young people of TV commercials—do not permit the admitting of one's pain, failure, or anguish.

A *second* consequence of the incapacity to suffer is the inability of so many in our society to enter imaginatively into the suffering of *others*. We probably have more data about human suffering than any generation before us. Every news broadcast deluges us with more information about the Nihil than we can absorb, even at the intellectual level. Vietnam—as it has frequently been observed—was the first war to be fought right in the living rooms of America. But just as at the personal level people in our society find it taxing to visit their own sick and dying relatives in hospitals and nursing homes, so they appear incapable of absorbing at the level of feeling, compassion, or (in its deepest sense) sympathy the plight of the world's hungry, politically oppressed, or war-ravaged—including the degradation and dehumanization of minorities within our own midst. Our response to the starving in Ethiopia is a species of the sympathy that begets charity (and that is not to be discouraged), but it seldom leads to deeper sympathy (*sym* + *pathos*)[16] which is the recognition that the pathetic condition of "the other" is also our own fundamental condition—that we share a common lot, *mutatis mutandis*. Especially, citizens of our culture repress the emergence of any deeper feeling when it concerns those whose victimization must be traced in an all-too-direct manner to our own vaunted way of life. The suspicion that we may be the *cause* of the suffering of others, that the very freedom from pain and want for which we have striven and are willing to fight may be a source of gross injustice for others—this seems to be a conclusion that few of our contemporaries permit themselves concretely to entertain.

The *third* consequence of our cultural incapacity to suffer is perhaps the most alarming of all. It may be called the search for an enemy. For it belongs to the psychic state of a people which cannot consciously confront its own suffering, yet cannot avoid absolutely the shock of nonbeing ("future shock," for example), that it is driven to look elsewhere for the source of its trouble. Just as individuals who are ill but cannot face their illness often rail out at persons around them, seeking to locate the cause of their malaise outside themselves, so societies which will not or cannot confront their own internal problems manifest an extraordinary need to blame their condition on external agencies. The Western—and especially the American—attitude towards the Russian bloc today surely has its genesis in something like a collective paranoia of this order. (Perhaps a similar argument can be made concerning the Russian attitude towards the West; *our* concern, however, is chiefly the beam in our own eye!) This paranoia is only further complicated by the sociopolitical needs of empires. Every empire needs its "enemy" in order to avoid facing up to the internal flaws in its own triumphant self-image.[17] Neither of the two superpowers in today's world seems to manifest the public courage that is required to analyze in an imaginative way the suffering inherent in its own history and pursuits.

Thus we have come upon a moment in history in which not suffering as such but the incapacity to suffer—including the incapacity to acknowledge, accept, and articulate suffering—may be the most terrifying social reality, the thing that determines the fate of the earth. Driven by what Ernest Becker called "obsessive denials of reality," our society insists upon the rightness of its priorities in spite of the clear evidence that its priorities *could* lead to civilizational oblivion. Looking at the faces of our leaders and the dominant classes of our nations, says Becker,

> We are reminded of those Roman portrait-busts that stuff our museums: to live in this tight-lipped style as an average good citizen must have created some daily hell. Of course we are not talking only about daily pettinesses and the small sadisms that are practiced on family and friends. Even if the average man lives in a kind of obliviousness of anxiety, it is because he has erected a massive wall of repressions to hide the problem of life and death. His anality may protect him, but all through history it is the "normal, average men" who, like locusts, have laid waste to the world in order to forget themselves.[18]

Today I must conclude—even more adamantly than I felt it necessary to do a decade ago[19]—that nothing is more needful in our culture than a forum for the open expression of the experience of negation that as a people we darkly suspect but do not, seemingly can not, allow ourselves to admit, to voice, to feel. There could, I believe, be no more responsible public activity on the part of persons of understanding and good will today than working for the creation of such a forum. What is needed is a vantage point, a frame of reference, a "place," a system of meaning through which people in this repressive society could experience a certain *permission* to tell themselves and one another of the suffering they dumbly sense and labor to forget.

D. The Question

Certainly it is not a matter of trying to get back to some pre-modern sense of the reality of suffering. The sheer acknowledgment of the tragic dimension of human existence, such as one had in the Middle Ages, or such as some of the romantics and existentialists proffered, could only *worsen* our condition by convincing more people of the sheer inevitability of suffering. In the nuclear age, this could only mean giving *a priori* victory to the annihilators!

On the other hand, to continue blindly in this postmodern era to embrace the platitudes of an outmoded optimism is tantamount to endorsing the repressive infrastructures and cultic positivism of our official culture, and thus by another route to court oblivion.

The question therefore becomes: *How can one at the same time acquire sufficient honesty about what needs to be faced, and sufficient hope that facing it would make a difference, to engage in altering the course of our present world towards life and not death?*

I began by insisting that the tradition of Jerusalem take human suffering very seriously: it is real, it is not illusory, it is the common lot of fallen humanity. But, unlike some other views of the world (Stoicism, for example), our tradition does not regard as an end in itself realism about that which negates. It is a means to something else—to acceptance, yes; some things must be accepted; but also to change, to the altering of conditions which make for meaningless suffering, to the mending of creation. The mere acknowledgment of suffering would suffice only for a religion that was finally indifferent to the fate of the earth and human life upon the earth. Acknowledgment of the reality of suffering is only the first step. It is a necessary step, for without it there can be no depth of understanding and no will to press on to the second phase.

Even to take that first step, however, there must be some anticipation of the prospect of going farther, some intimation, however intangible, that *understanding* suffering can lead to a new plateau of *being* in relation to it. It is with this in mind that Hans Küng has asked, "Can it not be said that only if there is a God is it possible to look at this infinite suffering of the world at all?"[20] The admission of the reality of suffering, in whatever *form* it may be expressed or felt, requires some sense of that other side of the dialectical tension to which I drew attention in the Introduction: belief that the Word of the Lord endures even though the people is as grass (to employ Isaiah's imagery). To put it otherwise, the trust that something—the life process or Providence or God—something "enduring," as Isaiah puts it, is able to take into itself all that does not endure, even things that are not, and give them a future that infinitely transcends the bleak promise of their past.

It is to the exposition of that enduring "something," understood in specifically Christian language and symbol, that we now turn our attention.

2

Creation:
Suffering as Becoming

Introduction: What *Should* Be?

In conspicuous ways, the central focus of theology today has become the doctrine of creation. After a period of neglect, during which (understandably enough) neoorthodox preoccupation with sin and salvation dominated the church's concern, we are witnessing a renewal of Christian interest in creation theology. The reason for this is no doubt many-sided, but I do not think it particularly obscure. In the first place, a number of things have conspired to make all of us newly conscious of the vulnerability of the created order— and of its unique and precious character. Without ceasing to occupy ourselves with matters of salvation (for this primary thrust of the gospel cannot be altered without forsaking the Christian faith as such), we are led under these contextual conditions to inquire more insistently than in the past whether salvation is a *this*-worldly category. So long as redemption theology is content to explore the prospects of an ultimate salvific state transcending this world, the doctrine of creation holds at best a secondary interest for Christians; and since the tendency towards otherworldliness in redemption theory has never been *very* far away from the heart of Christian discourse and spirituality, creation in much traditional doctrine and

49

liturgy has almost seemed the very thing that had to be overcome—
a sort of failed experiment of the Deity, incapable of being righted,
thus leaving rescue from it the only alternative. As the evangelist
Dwight L. Moody stated the matter (in exaggerated but not untypical form): "I look upon this world as a wrecked vessel. God has
given me a lifeboat and said to me, 'Moody, save all you can.' "[1]
Fortunately, this fatalistic assessment of the world has been challenged by many Christians in our time, especially since the advent
of the nuclear age 40 years ago; and responsible theology now asks
about redemption *for* the world, not *from* it. This brings the doctrine
of creation to the fore, and in a way that is perhaps unique in the
whole of Christian history.

Related to this, but from a rather different perspective, is another
factor arising from our sociohistorical context which gives creation
theology a new prominence. Life in the latter fifth of the century
that was supposed to have been "the Christian century" has become
complex and uncertain. We have lost our bearings. The familiar
moral, spiritual, and even intellectual signposts which guided previous generations are down. While our civilization has produced
astonishing feats of science and technology, it has lost touch with
sources of wisdom through which it might direct the very energies
unleashed by its technical genius. The famous dictum of Einstein
even suggests that we may never have had sufficient *wisdom* as a
race to cope with the forces that our know-how (*scientia*) has made
accessible: "The splitting of the atom has changed everything save
our mode of thinking, and thus we drift toward unparalleled catastrophe."

The difficult status of earth at this juncture causes the sensitive
in every field of human endeavor to ask—and with an existential
urgency—What then *should* be? As the Latin American theologian
Juan Luis Segundo has put it, the fundamental experience that
moves all thinking persons in our time and must be the point of
departure for every responsible theology is that "the world should
not be the way it is."[2] This sense of the present wrongness of the
world inevitably leads the mind to ask after what the right way
would be. What should be?

And that is surely the *principal* function of the doctrine of creation in Christian theology. One of the many things that is objectionable about making creation doctrine into a supposedly scientific theory about the world's beginnings—as has been happening again in our time under the impact of a shallow and reactionary "evangelicalism"—is that it detracts from this basic function of the Christian confession concerning creation. Creation is not a theory of how the world came to be—not a *cosmogony* (though there are certain almost accidental cosmogonic elements in the Genesis creation sagas). It is faith's confession concerning *what* came to be, and *why*. That is to say, it speaks about the *essence* (*esse*) and the *end* (*telos*) of creaturely life, of what is essential, and of what is intended. Doctrines are more or less formal, if fluid, statements of faith which speak to existing human questions; and the question addressed by creation theology is an aboriginal one. It is to be found in every culture and clime, whether in the sophisticated forms of the ancient Greeks or the concrete and oblique forms of tribal societies; for it is *the* human question. It is as such a two-pronged question, but its two aspects are inseparably linked. From one perspective it asks: What *is*? What is basic? What is really real? What is *fundamental* (*fundamentum* = foundation)? But this *ontological* form of the question already contains, implicitly, what is perhaps the still more basic aspect of what is being asked, namely, the *teleological* question: Is there *meaning* in what *is*? Is being as such *purposeful*? If so what *is* this purpose? What in particular is *our* (human) purpose, our "chief end" (to use the Westminster Catechism's memorable formula)? Thus, in what is perhaps the most famous literary formulation of this very human question, Shakespeare's prince of Denmark is not only asking after the nature of "being" as such but, having encountered the *pain* of being in such dramatic fashion, he wants to know whether there is sufficient *telos* in being to warrant the decision to affirm it, to refrain from seeking refuge in oblivion. "To be, or not to be: that is the question." And this double-edged question is precisely what informs creation theology from its inception.

In the preceding chapter, I claimed that the tradition of Jerusalem affirms the reality of human suffering. Suffering is not regarded by this tradition as mere appearance, a state of mind, something to be sloughed off lightly. It is real, and its reality has to be taken with utter seriousness. The God of this tradition takes suffering so seriously that God's *self*-manifestation can only occur through suffering. But now we must put this in the context of creation theology. Does this tradition's acknowledgment of the reality of suffering mean that suffering is inherent in creation as such? Is human suffering *foundational?* Is it built into the *fundamentum*—the very scheme of things? Are the creatures of the biblical God "programmed" to suffer? If so, then this would seem to add to our actual suffering as human beings a heavy weight of ontic melancholy; for it would mean that suffering is simply inevitable, and that the only answer to it is the acceptance of its inevitability.

That, of course, is one of the answers that human beings have in fact given to the actuality of suffering; it is indeed the essence of Stoic courage. But is it Christian? Christianity and Stoicism have very often been comingled in Western religious history. Stoicism was an influence on Christianity from the earliest days of the latter's spread into the Graeco-Roman world. The Stoic doctrine of the acceptance of suffering—resignation— has its origins in the ontological assumption that suffering is indeed inherent in the very foundations of the world. In certain circles, there has always been a strong tendency to identify Stoic and Christian courage at just this point. Today, for instance, there seems to be a propensity to equate Stoicism and Christianity in some of the pastoral theology and psychology which is geared towards helping the terminally ill to "accept" death. There is a fine but very important line between the Christian acceptance of what cannot be altered and the "cosmic resignation" which dominates Stoicism. Of Christian acceptance of the suffering that cannot be changed we shall think at a later stage in this discussion. At the present juncture, we need only observe that acceptance for Christian faith is not a program, a generally applied spiritual technique. It is, rather, a possibility that must always be worked out in the concrete situation in dialog with the other alternative—change, transformation. This is an aspect of the tension about which we thought earlier—the tension of faith, which in contrast both to credulity and cynicism tries to sustain simultaneously the reality of suffering and the challenge of grace to its *ultimate* reality. Stoic resignation does not deserve to be castigated as cynicism, but it does come closer to cynicism than does Christian courage, at least in its decision concerning the nature of created being. *Ontologically*, it believes that to be is to suffer; but it escapes cynicism because at the *teleological* level it affirms that through the acceptance of suffering meaning can be found. Stoic resignation is therefore not a simple capitulation to fate, but a spiritual program for coping with fate. It was this that caused Paul Tillich to consider Stoicism the one truly admirable alternative to Christian courage.[3] It shares with biblical faith the determination to be entirely honest about the reality of suffering. It does not seek the consolation of easy answers nor does it gloss over pain. It therefore meets the test of courage, which is always based on exposure to truth.

But while Stoic courage is in many respects admirable, it is not the same thing as Christian courage. The reason for this is both simple and basic: Stoic courage, unlike Christian faith, is grounded in the assumption that suffering as we know it is inherent in the creaturely condition. Biblical faith on the contrary, while acknowledging that creaturely being implies *certain forms* of suffering (or the conditions under which certain forms of suffering are likely) contains at the same time a fundamental and ongoing polemic against the deterministic assumption that suffering as we experience it under the conditions of historical existence is built into the process, that "whatever will be, will be."

I am now anticipating the development of a rather complex argument, which must become the primary material of our reflections in this chapter. Biblical faith, it seems to me, gives a profound but paradoxical answer to the question whether suffering in any way inheres in the structures of our creaturehood. I want to develop what I understand of this answer in four stages.

A. Struggle Belongs to the Created Order

For complex but perhaps, finally, understandable reasons, the human imagination throughout the ages has insisted upon positing a Golden Age, a time when the world was "as it should be." We find satisfaction, it would seem, in the contemplation of a perfect world. Such perfection, variously conceived, functions both as a critical judgment upon our imperfect present world and as a mental, mythopoetic escape from it. And what again and again constitutes the great distinction between our imperfect present world and the perfect world of the mythic Golden Age is that in the latter there is "no suffering," "no pain." Thus in many popular Christian articulations of it, "the Garden of Eden" is held up to faith as a place in which there was no sort of suffering.

But if we reflect carefully on the mythology of Eden as it is given in Scripture (not only in Genesis, but implicitly elsewhere as well), and if in our reflections we refuse to let ourselves be carried away by the long associations of this story with what we may call the paradise syndrome, we shall have to admit, surely, that it is hardly accurate to represent Eden as a sphere entirely devoid of suffering. There are at least four conditions in the saga of creation—especially in the older of the two versions of creation, viz., that of the Yahwist—which constitute, if not suffering as such then the stuff out of which some types of human suffering are made.

(1) *Loneliness* is one such condition. *Adam* ("the earth creature," as Phyllis Trible imaginatively designates this speaking animal in order to avoid the traditional sexism associated with the saga[4]) is "alone." Not only so, but this creature becomes acutely conscious of its solitude. This is not the filled, positive solitude that we experience as a part of the goodness of life, but a sense of incompleteness and of loss—loss without knowing what is lost! The created being of this creature, along with that of all the other creatures, has already been evaluated by its Maker in a definitive way: it is "good . . . *very* good!" Yet the creature must also discover—yes even *the Creator* must discover, apparently—that there is something "not good" in the midst of this goodness: "It is *not good* that the *Adam* should be alone" (Gen. 2:18, RSV alt.). So concludes the Creator, learning, it would seem, from the creature's own behavior. Yet, had *Adam* not been alone; had this emptiness of solitariness not been a strong dimension of the earth creature's experience, neither would it have been possible for the creature to experience the ecstasy that he so obviously does experience at the discovery

of the appropriate counterpart: "This at last is bone of my bones and flesh of my flesh" (2:23).

(2) Suffering emanates not only from loneliness but also from the experience of *limits*. At every turn human being has to encounter the limits of its existence, its powers, its intelligence. There are many things that we can do and ought not to do, and we know the suffering that belongs to that genus of activity. But there are also many things that we *cannot* do—we are not big enough or strong enough or wise enough, old enough or young enough, agile enough, versatile enough; and much of what we call suffering stems from the frustration which results from this circumscription of our powers. Yet limits are also presupposed by the tellers of the creation narrative. Much is permitted in that garden; but there, in the very center of it all, stands the living, fruit-bearing symbol of the limitations of creaturely existence which must not be transgressed.

(3) A third condition evocative of suffering in the creation saga is that of *temptation*. Temptation belongs already to the situation of Eden in this story. The serpent, a creature of God (for there is no *ultimate* dualism here), makes certain that the human beings become conscious of the thought that they might employ their wits and *exceed* the limits of their creaturehood. How much of the suffering that belongs to our personal and collective life is the consequence of reaching beyond our potentiality—of seeking to become gods? We reach high and fall low! Yet this temptation appears to be given with creaturehood as such; one cannot avoid concluding that temptation, according to this tradition, is an aspect of what "should be." The tempter cannot easily be separated from the Creator. As someone once put it, "There are more cordial relations between God and the devil in this tradition than are usually imagined!"

(4) Finally *anxiety*: clearly anxiety does not, in this biblical myth, pertain only to the situation *east* of Eden! It is the anxiety of the creaturely condition that opens Eve—obviously the more sensitive of the two!—to the subtle admonitions of the serpent. The anxiety of ignorance: How can one know what tomorrow will bring? The anxiety of dependency: How can one trust the One upon whom we are dependent? The root cause of *sin*, in this biblical tradition, is

certainly just such anxiety. Christian theology has always insisted that sin is not our *created* state.[5] It is precisely for this reason that theology makes the distinction between creation and fall. The human creature is not *created* sinful. Yet one must admit that the *potentiality* for sin is certainly already present in the creaturely condition and, apparently, as a matter of divine intention. This potentiality is visible in the creaturely *Angst* that is so vulnerable to the suggestions of the tempter. It is the same point that is made in the myth of Babel, that story which depicts the human fall in corporate terms. Anxious *Homo sapiens*, with its awful and poignant awareness of the insecurity of creaturely community, attempts to assuage its fears of being "scattered abroad" by creating a city.

Loneliness, limitation, temptation, anxiety: these are not the only forms of human suffering, to be sure; but they do describe dimensions of suffering, and they do belong to the foundational *ontos* of human being as this is symbolically articulated in the mythology of Genesis. Beyond that, we can discover the same insistence that certain forms of suffering belong to essential humanity if we turn to that other—and, for Christians, primary—criterion of divine intentionality to which our Scriptures and theological traditions point us: the man Jesus who is "true humanity" (*vere homo*).

Jesus too, to reveal the "truth" of our nature and vocation as human beings, must experience *loneliness*. Only, since he is made to bear also the consequences of our *distortion* of our creaturehood, there is no resolution of his loneliness. Surely it is not incidental that in a culture which prized marriage and family life as much as Israel did and does Jesus of Nazareth must be and remain a bachelor. Jesus can only participate in the human condition—he too—as he is made to know the *limitations* of human creaturehood. All that belongs to the power and glory of the divine must be "emptied," relinquished (Phil. 2:7). Death itself must be tasted. But, since Jesus has to assume not only our created but also our fallen estate, he must taste not only death but also "the sting of death" (1 Cor. 15:55). Of *temptation* it is hardly necessary to speak in this connection: the temptations of the wilderness, the temptations of the garden—that other garden, the garden of sorrows, where the temptation of the First Adam is recapitulated . . . and magnified.[6] Nor is the fourth dimension of creational suffering excluded in the case of *vere homo*—*anxiety*. If anything, it is intensified, since Jesus not only reveals true humanity but also must participate in the real condition of "existential manhood" (Tillich). What else could the cry of dereliction from the cross mean, or the prayers of Gethsemane with their accompanying sweat, like great drops of blood? If Jesus is the pattern of authentic humanity, then, without overlooking the fact that his suffering is also the consequence of *our distortion* of human creaturehood, we must pay strict attention to the suffering to which, simply as a human being in God's intention, "a man pure and simple" (Bonhoeffer), Jesus is necessarily subject.

What I am contending is that there are, in fact, forms of suffering which belong, in God's intention, to the human condition. Not *all* of what we experience as suffering is totally absurd, a mistake, an oversight, or the consequence of sin. There is something about a significant portion of the suffering through which we pass that belongs to the very foundations of being—something without which our human being would not and could not be what it is meant to be. There is, as it might be said, a certain logic—a *theo*-logic—in at least such dimensions of human suffering as we have adduced in the foregoing discussion. The kind of logic that I have in mind can be reinforced, *via negativa*, if we ask ourselves what sort of life would be possible if none of these forms of suffering were present.

(1) Imagine a life without the experience of *loneliness*. How, in that case, would one ever come to know the joy of human fellowship, of union with the other, of ecstasy at the discovery of the appropriate counterpart—of love? As it is, far too many of the human relationships in which persons stand occur without a sufficient knowledge of the antithetical condition—of being alone. The relationships are taken for granted, assumed as a kind of birthright, a "natural" condition. From one point of view Christians must certainly defend the belief that it is right and natural for human beings to exist in relationship; for relatedness is of the essence of our being itself. Being is a matter of being-with, *Mitsein*.[7] Yet, unlike nonhuman creatures, which also exist in relationship, the highest expression of human *Mitsein*, that is, love, presupposes the element and experience of separation. The discovery of love therefore always

contains a strong dimension of grace or givenness over and above the dimension of the natural. If many of the relationships in which human beings in fact find themselves are superficial, unsatisfying, or even burdensome, it is surely in part because they are posited on personal and social expectations from which the dimension of grace is sadly lacking. If the sense of the undeserved, the gift-quality, is missing from a relationship, then something vital to its depth and mystery is missing. Pure nature, including the needs of the body and of individuals to cooperate in order to achieve certain ends, may sustain such a relationship; but there will be neither joy nor mystery in it. Depth of human relatedness presupposes something comparable to the Adamic experience of loneliness. Not only once, but continuously—as a kind of descant of every loving relationship—it is necessary for us to know that this love *might not have been*, and will not automatically continue to be. That is, the sense of its contingency must be there, just beneath the surface; for without that half the wonder of the thing could not be. (Sometimes I think that it would cut the divorce rate in half if human beings were forbidden to marry until they had given sufficient indication of understanding deeply what it means to be alone!) Thus loneliness, which is certainly a cause of much human suffering, is all the same a kind of prerequisite of what Paul in 1 Corinthians 13 names as "the greatest" of all creaturely capacities, the capacity of love.

(2) Imagine, secondly, a life without the experience of *limits*. You could have wild strawberries whenever you wanted them! Nothing would be inaccessible, nothing forbidden, nothing out of reach, no unfulfilled dreams or wishes, no "thus far and no farther!" But how could human beings under such conditions ever experience wonder, surprise, or gratitude? As it is, part of our spiritual problem in the First World especially is certainly that we know far too little about the ordinary limits of creaturehood, the limits that most of the people in this world both in the past and still today were and are caused regularly to encounter. We have created a society, a very shaky city culture, based on the fiction that there are few if any limits to growth. We are annoyed—and many of the economic and industrial leaders of our society are incensed—when representatives of a wider geographical and chronological outlook like that of the

Club of Rome insist that there are, in fact, limits to growth. Our institutions of business, industry, and government behave for the most part as if the earth were infinitely productive and resilient; and as citizens we have become blasé, indifferent, picking up straw-berries from our supermarkets in January as if they were a natural right—so predictably "natural," indeed, as to go entirely unnoticed by us. Nothing speaks so eloquently of the beneficial character of the experience of limitations as does the "way of life" in societies which court the illusion of limitlessness!

(3) *Temptation* is certainly a source of human suffering; but imag-ine a life free of every temptation. Suppose the human being were simply programmed to be good—to do the right thing, always, and for the right reason. But in that case what would "good" and "right" mean? Such distinctions depend for their meaning upon the pros-pect of their antitheses. Alternatives, significant and even radical alternatives to righteousness, justice, truth, obedience, and so on, must be present if human beings are to be capable of freedom, decision, sacrifice, restraint, and most of the other qualities which constitute whatever grandeur we as a species possess. As it is, one of the more pathetic aspects of the so-called permissive society which may have reached its zenith in the 1960s is that when every-thing is permitted nothing any longer requires the effort that belongs to this grandeur, and so the human spirit drowns in a sea of sensual gratification and apathy.

(4) *Anxiety* produces untold suffering, for it often leads to despair. Yet who, under the conditions of a life entirely free from anxiety, could ever know comfort, relief, or joy? More than that, who would achieve any real depth of being? Depth either of being or of thought is certainly bound up with anxious awareness of one's condition: "*De profundis*"—"Out of the depths I cry to thee, O Lord!" (Psalm 130). Hope, when it is real, presupposes an ongoing dialog with despair (as the common Latin root for both words, *spes*, bears out so instructively). Only a chatty cheerfulness could result from a humanity in which no anxiety were present. We do not have to speculate about this, for all around us today we can encounter persons who for the sake of achieving peace of mind have effected, with or without the help of medical or pharmaceutical technology,

an ersatz freedom from anxiety. But they have purchased this alleged freedom at a very high price: the price of authenticity and depth, the price of passion and of feeling. Passion and feeling and sensitivity stem from the same sources as do less desirable qualities. At the end of Peter Shaffer's play *Equus*, the psychiatrist Dysart decides to "cure" the boy Alan whose illness has led to the bizarre act of blinding horses (a symbolic reference to great sexual confusion). But the psychiatrist knows that the "cure" will also rob the boy of the hidden springs of his passion for life:

> All right! I'll take it away! He'll be delivered from madness. What then? Do you think feelings like his can simply be re-attached, like plasters? Stuck on to other objects we select? . . .
> With any luck his private parts will come to feel as plastic to him as the products of the factory to which he will almost certainly be sent. Who knows? He may even come to find sex funny. Smirky funny. Bit of grunt funny. Trampled and furtive and entirely in control. Hopefully, he'll feel nothing at his fork but Approved Flesh. *I doubt*, however, with much passion! . . . Passion, you see, can be destroyed by a doctor. It cannot be created.[8]

"The basic anxiety, the anxiety of a finite being about the threat of non-being, cannot be eliminated. It belongs to existence itself."[9]

What we are admitting, surely, in such reflections as these, is that life without any kind of suffering would be no life at all; it would be a form of death. Life—the life of the spirit like the life of the body—depends in some mysterious way upon *the struggle to be*. This presupposes, as the condition necessary to life itself, the presence of life's antithesis, that is, of that which threatens or negates, circumscribes or challenges. This is where evolutionary theory and creational theology *do* converge, and in a provocative and unusual manner. Both evolution and creation presuppose that there is a struggle involved in existence, and that this struggle is basically positive, even though it contains strongly negative dimensions.

Another illustration from the world of literature will help to establish the point. Tennessee Williams, in a thoughtful essay on

his most famous play, A *Streetcar Named Desire*, describes his attempt, after writing this play, to escape from the creative urge into
a kind of comfortable stupor (a temptation with which, as we now
know, he never fully came to terms). In the wake of his failure to
achieve the nirvana for which he thought he was longing, Williams
wrote:

> Once you fully apprehend the vacuity of a life without struggle you
> are equipped with the basic means of salvation. Once you know this
> is true, that the heart of man, his body and brain, are forged in a
> white-hot furnace for the purpose of conflict (the struggle of creation)
> and that with conflict removed the man is a sword for cutting daisies,
> that not privation but luxury is the wolf at the door and that the
> fangs of this wolf are all the little vanities and conceits and laxities
> that success is heir to—why then, with this knowledge you are at
> least in a position of knowing where danger lies. [10]

Shakespeare, in *Macbeth*, states the matter more succinctly:

> And you all know security
> Is mortal's chiefest enemy. [11]

As in evolutionary theory, the struggle that creational theology
presupposes is a struggle for survival; only here it is a struggle for
the survival not only of physical life but for the survival and full
realization of our potentiality for spirit. As such it is a battle with
death. But while death is the enemy it is also a useful, perhaps even
a necessary enemy. In this tradition, as we have already observed,
even death must be God's servant, serving God's project, namely,
the blossoming of the *life* of the world. With its limiting and its
questioning of every supposed security, death introduces a dimension of profundity into our life which could probably never be apart
from it. The most wondrous of all our human capacities—that same
capacity for love upon which we have just reflected—is deeply qualified by the reality of death. Instinctively we realize this. As Martin
Heidegger has insisted, it is because we are being-towards-death
that we are capable of a *compassion* (German, *Mitleid*) towards one
another, i.e., of a sympathy (suffering-with) that transcends mere
passion. Thus death itself can be life-serving. This is why biblical
faith is thoroughly realistic about death—not only because "death

occurs to all the living," but because it belongs to the essence of
the life-process itself. Death too is . . . intended! What is *not* intended, in the tradition of Jerusalem's interpretation of the matter,
is not death as such but what we may call death-serving death, that
is, death which draws attention *to itself* instead of drawing us the
more fully into life. This is the death that Eve darkly suspects when
she is confronted by the wiles of the tempter—and she was right
to suspect it!

Summarizing the argument so far, then, we may say that suffering
belongs to the order of creation insofar as struggle is necessary to
the human glory that is God's intention for us. Like any good parent,
God does not want to protect God's "children" from challenge,
risk, or the anxious awareness of that which negates; for God knows
that the full potentiality of the creature for the *gloria* appropriate
to it can be actualized only through the facing of many trials. "Man,"
as Johannes Metz has written, "must learn to accept himself in the
painful experiment of his living. He must embrace the spiritual
adventure of becoming a man, moving through the many stages
that lie between birth and death."[12]

Even in its creational theology, therefore, our tradition distinguishes itself from all those views of the world, including the modern
one, which eliminate the negative in favor of a monistic positive.
Biblical faith is not, of course, ontologically dualistic. It does not
give to the negative (to death, the demonic, evil, or sin) a permanent reality that is independent of the positive. There is, however, a *provisional* dualism, as we may call it, in this tradition, in
that it acknowledges a sufficient antithesis between God and the
demonic, life and death, good and evil, righteousness and sin, to
permit the negating dimension an independent role *in the service of
the positive.* Like Satan in the poem of Job, that which threatens
and negates life is intended, in the wisdom of the Creator, for the
service of a more abundant life.

B. The Circumscription of Suffering in Creational Theology

We have affirmed that suffering-as-struggle belongs, according to
the tradition of Jerusalem, to life's foundational basis and goodness.

It is a significant dimension of the *becoming* that is implicit in the creaturely being of all that is, especially of the human creature.

There are, however, definite limits placed by the tradition upon the logic which leads to this conclusion. A degree of pain, it would seem, is necessary to evoke the human potential for nobility, for love, for wisdom, and for depth and authenticity of being. A pain-free life would be a life-less life. But this counsel cannot and must not be exaggerated to the point of celebrating or cultivating pain.

The elevation of pain to the status of the essential—even the quintessential—has been a popular conception of many societies, including some societies reputedly Christian. Victorian and Wilhelmian morality made much of this principle. "Spare the rod and spoil the child!" The work ethic! Duty! The woman was regularly made a conspicuous victim of such doctrine, as were slaves and members of the lower economic classes. The *reductio ad absurdum* of the 19th-century glorification of pain was the military training characteristic of imperialist societies. Like Sparta of old—and now strengthened by pseudoscientific applications of the Darwinian principle of survival of the fittest—it was assumed that excellence could only be achieved through excruciating programs of training: struggle raised to the status of a religion. Significantly, Adolf Hitler called his famous autobiographical statement and program *Mein Kampf* (My Struggle)!

Unfortunately, the fervor which made a religion out of suffering and the kind of power to which it gave access cannot be divorced from empirical Christianity. Throughout the ages, ascetic and triumphalistic forms of the Christian religion turned the biblical insight that suffering belongs to life and can be life-serving into a religion of heroic struggle. Hitler was not attracted to classical Jesuit discipline for nothing! And between the Jesuitic and other Catholic forms of heroic religion and various Protestant forms, such as Puritanism, there are only shades of distinction. Rudi Wiebe's powerful novel *Peace Shall Destroy Many*[13] depicts a situation that is not uncommon either in literature or in life: the destructive power of an ideology of self-denial and restraint, religiously adhered to by authoritative personalities. It is no wonder that, reflecting upon much of the history of the Christian religion, some members of other faiths have been moved to ask: "Are not you Christians *too interested* in suffering?"[14]

The question that such observations as these put to us is of course: Where do you draw the line? Creation theology, we have said, affirms the goodness of finite conditions in which, inevitably, certain forms and degrees of suffering are present. But where does biblical faith draw the line between suffering that is part of creation's goodness and suffering that is harmful? How does it distinguish the kind of struggle that is essential to human becoming from struggle of the sort that simply detracts from life's fullness and constitutes something like the "cursed" estate depicted by the Creator in the closing verses of Genesis 3?

The answer is, of course, already implied in the question. So far as the Hebraic-Christian tradition is concerned, the line must be drawn at the point where suffering ceases to serve *life*.

To elaborate: Consider again the four conditions inherent in creation—conditions which, as we have said, while they do not constitute suffering in themselves at least provide a context in which certain types of suffering are likely to occur: loneliness, limitations, temptation, and anxiety. In each instance, what interested us primarily about these conditions was their potential for evoking from the human spirit qualities or experiences to which it would otherwise remain a stranger. Thus the function of the "lonely" state of the creature is not to elevate loneliness as though it were good in itself, but to provide a background against which relationship with another might contain a dimension of wonder and ecstasy. Similarly, limits as such are not to be lauded; but without encountering any limits the human being would be a victim of endless illusion; for what, from one perspective, are limits to our creaturehood are, from another, graceful boundaries within which we may discover our genuine possibilities for the attainment of the grandeur appropriate to our kind. We are not gods, and to pursue life as though we were is to court perhaps the greatest unhappiness. Our mortality constantly betrays our pretensions of omnipotence. Camus' Caligula, whose futile attempts to transcend his humanity end in destruction, offers as his concluding philosophy of existence: "Men die; and they are not happy."[15] Again, temptation as it is presented in both of the great temptation stories of the Bible—the temptation of the first pair and of the Christ—is intended positively. For without temptation the human being would lack the challenge that is necessary for the development both of its rational powers of discernment and its moral capacities for goodness. Finally, anxiety, while it is undoubtedly questionable as a permanent state of being (hence Jesus admonishes, "Be not anxious. . ."), as a background awareness of our finitude makes possible a depth of reflection and compassion without which neither wisdom nor art nor courage would be likely.

In each instance, in other words, factors which no doubt make for a species of suffering—at least for struggle—are at the same time conditions without which we should be deprived of fullness of being. As we wrestle with the antinomies contained within these conditions, we become (what otherwise we should not become) *active participants* in the life process. Because of this struggle, life is no longer something merely "provided," "laid on." It does not simply happen to us; it becomes our own. We make life ours as we confront the alternatives present in these conditions, discern the consequences of these alternatives, and through trial of spirit and body make our choices. In the course of struggling with the conflicting elements that are present in all four of these conditions (and others that could certainly be described), we *become* the beings that (in essence) we are. This cannot be done without pain. There is a measure of pain in every sort of growth known to human science. *Becoming* is suffering. One must "suffer" one's becoming—whether this means the transition from childhood to adolescence, or the disciplined self-denial that belongs to every art and profession. But suffering thus understood is nevertheless meaningful and good because through it—and *only* through it—our lives are integrated. We become more truly whole, unified, and centered persons. Such suffering is a means—an indispensable means—to our greater appropriation of the *life* that is our birthright as covenant partners of the Lord and Giver of life.

All of this is premised on the assumption that suffering is a means. It is another matter when suffering and struggle cease to serve life, when they become independent of the life process, when they become interesting in themselves, when they become ends (or almost-ends) in themselves; or when suffering is turned into a law, a principle, a soteriological technique: Suffering is beneficial! Suffer; it will be good for you! Suffering as such is hardly ever simply "good." The goodness that may come of the experience of suffering depends on something else. It depends on the felt presence of an end which both transcends and incorporates the suffering. That end, which suffering as such must never be allowed to usurp, is the goal that Jesus announced as the very heart of his mission: life. "I came that they may have life, and have it abundantly" (John 10:10). Such an end would necessitate Jesus' own suffering; but in his case too—and supremely in his case—the end of the matter was not the humiliation, the rejection, the abandonment, the cross, but rather the "eternal life" that through all this exposure to life's antitheses might be made possible.

There can be no doubt, then, that what distinguishes the suffering inherent in creation from the suffering that "should not be" is the criterion of life. Suffering which integrates us into life and makes us more fully and truly "alive" (Irenaeus) is not only *acceptable* to this tradition, but essential to it. There is no interest here in an effortless, struggle-free, and placid sort of existence. There is also, however, no flirtation with masochism.

The question that remains is how, concretely, it is to be determined what makes for life. It is clear enough that suffering which leads to life and its enhancement receives the approval of this tradition (see, e.g., Rom. 5:3); but while there are numerous criteria for what the Judeo-Christian tradition understands by life and the fullness of life, there is no fixed enunciation of the types of human suffering that can contribute to the life-giving process or, conversely, of those that cannot. Is it perhaps assumed that any and all kinds of suffering may be occasions for becoming? That the integrative principle lies not in the suffering itself but in what is made of it? That a specific experience of pain may lead, therefore, either to integrative or disintegrative ends, depending upon what other influences are brought to bear upon it?

Just here is where it may be most instructive to consider the role of that creature who certainly—though not without qualification—dominates the creation theology of our tradition.

C. The Human Vocation: Stewarding Life

There are of course numerous ways of addressing the question of the nature and vocation of human being; but the present discussion affords us the opportunity of emphasizing a dimension of human being and calling that has not always been accentuated in Christian anthropology. In our zeal to stress the creatureliness of the human, we have frequently neglected the special kinship of this creature with its Creator. This neglect is no doubt understandable, because, for one thing, Christian anthropology has had to view humanity from the vantage point of its distortion of its essence and its vocation; for another, particularly during the modern epoch, responsible theology has been obliged to combat the unwarranted Prometheanism of secular versions of human grandeur. Nevertheless, neither these longstanding needs nor the present-day necessity of presenting Homo sapiens in solidarity with (and not opposition to) the other creatures should blind us to the fact that our tradition, in terms of its creational theology at least, assumes that the human creature is both capable of exceptional accountability and appointed to a place of high responsibility in the scheme of things created.

To state this responsibility in terms continuous with the foregoing discussion, we may say that it is the vocation of this thinking, speaking, making creature, created for covenant with its Creator, to participate in the process of giving, directing, preserving, and enhancing life. The gifts that have been given to this creature equip it for the task of fostering, from within the process and as part of it, God's creational enterprise, namely, the unfolding of the "abundance" that is creation's potential.

Making this human calling even more explicitly related to the course of our deliberations here, we may say that it is the vocation of this creature to address its skills to the fine distinction to which

we have been alluding, namely, the distinction between the suffering which is necessary to creaturely becoming (integrative suffering) and suffering which detracts from life (disintegrative suffering). The special gifts assigned to the human creature—the gifts of
rationality, of freedom, of speech, of manual dexterity, and so on—
are not for the purpose of elevating this creature ontically above
all the others, but in order that there may be in the midst of the
created order a *discerning* being, who is able to distinguish what
makes for life and what makes for death, what builds and what
destroys, what enhances and what detracts. This being, who is
himself or herself part of the process and therefore, presumably,
immediately sensitive to its movements and moods, is able from
within to help to guide the process towards its goal—to be, as it
were, midwife to the abundance that is creation's promise. Being
itself creature, the human being cannot create the life process, nor
can it alter creation's fundamental patterns. We have said that one
of the patterns which seems inherent in creation is the manner in
which the unfolding of life entails a certain amount of struggle,
passion, and pain. The becoming of creaturely life, its growth towards maturity, is not without suffering. The human being cannot
alter this basic pattern. But—to state the vocation of humanity as
conceived in creational doctrine in at least one way—the human
being does have the capacity to assist in the orientation of the
creational process towards life. It can, if it will, do much to prevent
what is negating within the life process from becoming independent
of the goal of fulfillment. It is within the purview of the human
creature, as biblical faith envisages this unique being, to keep the
negative in the service of the positive, to keep death in the service
of life, to keep the struggle orientated towards integration and away
from disintegration. When, later on, the apostle Paul affirms that
the "groaning in travail" of the "whole creation" is linked indelibly
with the human fall, he is assuming this same capacity of the creature as intended by God, viz., that the human being has been called
to the awesome responsibility of discerning and directing, from within, the course of creation towards its fulfillment (Rom. 8:22).

This is how we should understand the biblical symbol of the
steward.[16] The steward neither owns nor controls the household

(*oikos*); the structuring of the universe is determined only by its Creator—it is God's "economy." The steward (*oikonomos*) must obey the laws inherent in the process. These laws include, as we have seen, the dimension of struggle: the lions seek their meat from God; the seed falls into the ground and dies; human beings age and grow weary. The disintegrative element is present, and it is never far from the surface of creaturely existence. But as the human priest of creation, the steward is called to tend the process, to enhance the life principle within it, to reduce the pull of death with which the life principle is necessarily bound up, to accentuate the integrative and thus diminish the power of the disintegrative dimension.

When the "earth creature" of Genesis 2 is called to name the other creatures we have a symbolic statement of just this role; for naming means not only giving a nomenclature to unspecified things but the attributing to them of an order and purpose—not by way of superimposition, for their fundamental identity and right to be are given with their being as such; but through the enunciation of their identity the namer of the animals gives visibility to the purpose that is inherent in the unnamed thing. The name evokes the potentiality for meaningful life that is present in the nameless one, and so preserves it from "anonymity," from the virtual oblivion of undifferentiated being.

What we must of course notice later from the perspective of Christian hamartiology (Chapter 3) is that the *sinful* decision and disorientation of the human creature in respect to its place in the creative process results in the fostering of a disintegrative suffering that spreads beyond its own being and infects the totality. Seeking its own *superfluous doxa* instead of being the responsible steward of the divine project of creation, the human creature introduces into the *whole* creation a tragic orientation towards death. At the present juncture, however, we are considering the perspective on the question of God and earthly suffering that can be derived from the doctrine of creation, i.e., of what *should* be. From this perspective, what the *human* role should be is neither that of mastery in respect to the life process (that would imply capitulation to *pride*) nor that of passivity (capitulation to *sloth*), but rather a stance which at the same time honors the divine ordering of creation and accepts a high degree of responsibility for implementing that ordering. In a word, the human vocation, expressed in the idiom of our present discussion, could be stated in this way: *the stewarding of life through a wisdom which comprehends something of the role of the negative in the perfecting of the positive.* If we are to use the beleagured term *dominion* at all, it is, it seems to me, in something like this sense that we should use it: that is, as the maintenance of a vigilance for the life of the creation which is both wise enough and modest enough to know that sacrifice, restraint, and suffering are necessary to the unfolding of creation's wondrous variety, abundance, and glory.

D. Transition: The Great Risk

While it is clear that the tradition in which we stand entertains a quite explicit intention for the human creature—an intention which calls for the willingness to accept the forms of suffering which accompany understanding and responsibility—it is equally clear that this theological tradition knows from the outset that the human creature is fully capable of thwarting the creational intention for it, and radically so. We could not comprehend the nature of suffering as biblical faith understands it without giving a prominent place in our thinking to this anthropological presupposition of the doctrine of creation, namely, that in terms of what *should* be the freedom of the human creature is central. Freedom is integral to the whole conception of humanity in God's intention. Freedom is of the essence of the human creature just as, and just *because*, love is of God's essence. For the Creator will have at the articulate center of creation a being—not better than the others, but capable of both representing and being responsible for them—with whom this outgoing, overflowing love that expresses itself in creation can enter into communion: a speaking animal to correspond to the speaking God (*Deus loquens*). Only a free creature can fulfill this vocation. Only a free creature could love; and love, the Creator's essence, is the human creature's vocation. A being programmed to love would be no lover. A being predetermined to act responsibly within creation would hardly warrant our using the adjective *responsible* in its description.

Yet the freedom to love presupposes the freedom not to love, and the freedom to assume responsibility willingly presupposes the freedom to renounce it, to become slothful, disobedient, or rebellious. Under such conditions, the suffering which (as I have argued in this chapter) is *inherent* in the creaturely status may become the very occasion for rejecting and seeking to transcend precisely that status. . . and inheriting, in consequence, a form of suffering that is infinitely more problematic.

This is the great risk taken by the biblical God. Here the creation theology of our tradition shows its Achilles' heel, the point of its greatest vulnerability. Here is the little opening in the tent of creation through which the camel's nose of sin may enter: sin bringing suffering that is no longer the suffering of becoming but disintegrative suffering, the "bondage to decay" (Paul), the "sickness unto death" (Kierkegaard).

How often and how fervently does the rational mind ask whether freedom is worth its cost! But biblical faith would not forfeit the freedom of this creature, even for a world order in which whatever suffering there were would always, automatically, serve the life process. It is the genius and the burden of this faith that it determines to resolve the problem of suffering, not through a creation theology which makes the suffering born of distorted human freedom impossible to begin with, but through a redemption theology which takes upon itself the consequences of distorted freedom, transforms them, and offers them back to the sufferer as healing grace.

3

The Fall:
Suffering as Burden

Introduction: Suffering that Should Not Be!

Our tradition considers the human condition from the vantage point of three broad thematic foci. In the shorthand of theology we name these creation, fall, and redemption.

From the focus of the doctrine of creation, which treats of essences and ends—of "what *should* be"—we have acknowledged that according to Judeo-Christian belief there is a form of suffering that belongs to the created order. It is not God's intention that the human creature should live out its days in an absolutely pain-free state but rather, in order that the potentiality of the creature for fullness of life might be realized, human being in the divine intention is called to live under circumstances in which an element of existential struggle inheres. We called this suffering as *becoming*, or integrative suffering.

But quite clearly the reality of suffering that biblical faith acknowledges to be the lot of humanity (Chapter 1) is not wholly accounted for by reference to this suffering which belongs to the life process as such. That our sheer creaturehood implies an aboriginal loneliness, natural limits, temptations, and anxieties—this we may gather from the perspective of the doctrine of creation, as it is testified to in the creation sagas of Genesis and, indirectly, elsewhere in the Scriptures. But the great *burden* of human suffering requires that we seek another focus on the subject. It may be the intention of the Creator, according to biblical religion, that the human creature should experience dimensions of deprivation, struggle, and insecurity in order to make good the deeper promise of its creaturehood; but by no stretch of the imagination could anyone accuse this tradition of positing a God who actually wills the massive, unbearable, or seemingly absurd suffering of the creature—any creature! A deity personally and directly responsible for all the agony of earth would be unrecognizable as God from the perspective of biblical faith.

When therefore we move, as we must, from the consideration of forms of human suffering which are necessary to human becoming, to forms of suffering which sap humanity of its creaturely *joie de vivre* and bend its head towards oblivion, then, if indeed we are adhering to the tradition of *Jerusalem* and not some other worldview, we must move from the focus on this subject provided by the Judeo-Christian conception of creation to that named by our theological progenitors "the fall." For in making such a transition we are no longer contemplating "what *should* be"; indeed, it is the most rudimentary presupposition of our whole confessional tradition that the magnitude and ubiquity of the suffering that we actually see about us in the world *should not be!* Everything in this tradition cries out that the gross suffering to which whole races are subject, and which befalls ordinary people with apparent arbitrariness, should not be: that Auschwitz should not have been; that the abduction and murder of young expectant mothers in Argentina so that their babies could be given to favorites of the state should not have been; that the cancer deaths of children and young people who did not have the chance to become who they might have become ought not to have occurred; that madness and suicide and senseless traffic deaths, and unrelieved, debilitating despair are simply wrong! Dostoevski's Ivan Karamazov himself is not more sensitive to the wrongness of all this than is the God of Sinai and Golgotha. Like Jesus regarding Jerusalem from a little distance, our

Scriptures bear witness to a God who weeps over the tragedies of earth—even over our little losses (Matt. 10:30, par.). This God will not rest until all the wrong of suffering has been righted—until death itself is defeated (Rev. 21:4).

Because God's own face is set against that which negates life, suffering does not and must not have the last word in this tradition. That, as we have insisted in the Introduction, is one of the two biblical fundamentals that must be sustained in any discussion of God and human suffering. But the other fundamental has also to be given its due: that suffering is real, and is the lot of humanity as we know it. And if we ask why this is so—why, beyond the suffering of becoming, there is a disintegrative and burdensome suffering—we are carried at once to this second aspect of the three-fold perspective on the human condition offered by our doctrinal tradition: the fall, sin.

A. Sin and Suffering: Connections?

Certain expressions of liberal religious and secular thought tried very hard to dismiss the connection between sin and suffering. One may still hear echoes of this attempt. There is in fact a general distaste in both society and church for interpretations of human suffering which make use of the idea of sin in a causative sense. One prefers that suffering be accounted for more "scientifically"—medically, physiologically, psychologically, or sociologically. This is to be explained, in part, by the simplistic reduction of the concept of sin to moralistic and personalistic dimensions—a reduction especially conspicuous in North American religion and society. But it was a loss to Christian and human understanding, all the same, when the connection between suffering and sin was rejected; and part of the task of responsible theology in our time is to attempt to recover something of the deeper significance of this connection.

To begin with, however, we must acknowledge that it was both understandable and right in some ways that liberalism questioned this relationship; because earlier forms of Christian "orthodoxy" had made the connection between sin and suffering all too explicit.

So explicit was the causal connection between sin and suffering in many forms of preliberal Christianity that every pious sufferer, under the influence of such stern and doctrinaire codes of religion, was driven to inquire after the personal wickedness by which that suffering must have been caused—often in the process, of course, vastly complicating the suffering itself by adding to it a gruesome weight of guilt. The belief that suffering is punishment for sin, inflicted by a God whose judgment or purgation begins already in this life, is firmly rooted in almost all the forms of empirical Christianity. As Dorothee Sölle points out in her thoughtful book *Suffering*, Protestantism in its classical phases is no exception to this norm:

There is little doubt that the Reformation *strengthened* theology's sadistic accents. The existential experience developed in [later medieval] mysticism that God is with those who suffer is replaced by a theological system preoccupied with judgment day. . . . The situation is not viewed from the standpoint of the sufferer; rather it is through God's eyes that things are seen and, above all, judged.[1]

Professor Sölle quotes Calvin in this connection:

Scriptures teach us that Pestilence, War, and other calamities of this kind are chastisements of God, which he inflicts on our sins.

Thus, comments Sölle, "All suffering is attributed to God's chastisement; 'the nations whom thou now smitest. . . the individuals who are receiving thy stripes. . . all who are bound in prison or afflicted with disease or poverty' must have sinned."[2]

Such religion is by no means defunct. Powerful and self-consciously "Christian"[3] movements on this continent can be found today affirming that nuclear weapons are God's response to "godless communism," or that the dread disease AIDS is divine punishment on homosexual persons. This "theological sadism" (Sölle) seems to be unacquainted with the Bible's own criticism of the assumption that suffering is chastisement, the vindictive justice of a "righteous" (and compassionless!) deity. In the poem of Job, in Jesus' flat rejection of his disciples' suggestion that a man's blindness must have been caused either by his own or his parents' sin (John 9:10), and in many other places and ways, the Scriptures take on precisely this assumption. They must do so, obviously enough, because just this assumption is a recurrent motif of "religion," and a kind of preoccupation of the human psyche. It belongs to that familiar tit-for-tat approach to both religion and life, which prefers jurisprudence to grace, and which Luther accurately and frankly named "justification by works." To the smug thought that one is being justified by one's "good" works there always corresponds, in this brand of religion, the (usually pleasurable!) sense that others are being damned by their wickedness; and it is seldom that such religious zeal is willing to leave the working out of its neat conception of divine justice to the last judgment!

Given the power of this religious assumption throughout human history, and given the damage done to so many human lives by this hoary attempt to explain suffering through direct reference to sin and guilt, the determination of modern forms of Christian theology to reject the connection outright is understandable.

But it is also premature and simplistic. As in so many other aspects of the modern critique of the various dogmatic orthodoxies of the ecclesiastical past, liberal Christianity had an unfortunate propensity to ignore the deeper insights which were often concealed beneath badly articulated and practiced dogmas of the tradition. Instead of dismissing the connection between sin and suffering altogether, liberal Christian scholarship might have attempted to search out the more profound nature of their relationship. This is of course in fact what—eventually—responsible Christian scholarship did do. It has resulted in a thorough rethinking of the meaning of sin—but one which, for the most part, has still not greatly influenced the mind of the church!

Ever since Karl Barth, Paul Tillich, Reinhold Niebuhr, and their contemporaries discovered—through bitter experience—the flaws in theological liberalism, theology has been attempting to recover something of the more penetrating meaning of the elusive term *sin*. It is perhaps the most misunderstood word in the Christian vocabulary. Most people in the churches seem still, despite half a century of serious and critical reflection on the subject, to think of sin in rather crudely moralistic terms—in terms, to be explicit, of *private* morality, with special emphasis on private *sexual* morality. No one is surprised, however repulsed the sophisticated may be, when abor-tion, lesbianism, or adultery are described as sinful. But how many of our fellow citizens would think of connecting sin with the arms race, or the greed of the First World, or ecological disasters created by high technology? Even the association of sin with humanity's reputedly "greatest" achievements and successes, and with what individuals are prone to consider their best and most honorable deeds—even such an association, though it is as old as the prophets of Israel, seems difficult for our contemporaries to grasp. When it comes to this profound category of biblical faith, most of us seem to have advanced little beyond the mental estate of that fictitious but representative character, Boso, the dialog partner of St. Anselm in *Cur Deus Homo?* who, evidently incapable of getting beyond the idea that sins are bad deeds, proposed that a mere declaration of forgiveness on the deity's part could remedy the situation. In re-sponse, Anselm uttered what may be the most penetrating insight ever stated in the area of hamartiology: "You have not yet considered the weight (*ponderis*) of sin."

In order to recover something of the weight of sin as it relates to the question of God and human suffering, I want to concentrate upon two dimensions of its meaning. I shall call the first the "irony" of sin, and the second (following the lead of Paul Tillich)[4] sin's "tragic element."

B. The Irony of Sin

Irony, as Reinhold Niebuhr has shown in many of his writings, is a much-neglected but important category of Christian theology.[5] Nowhere is irony more in evidence than it is in connection with the biblical understanding of sin. For the purpose of glimpsing some-thing of what is meant in this connection, it is necessary to remind ourselves of what we discovered to be implied concerning the nature of suffering from the perspective of the doctrine of creation.

We have affirmed that God's intention for human being, as this is understood within the theology of creation, implies that its being is dynamic—a matter not of possession but of becoming. There is a necessary struggle in the process. To realize the potential of its creaturehood, the human creature must accept and affirm this struggle; it must be ready to make the journey and pilgrimage of life. Its life is not given it all at once; life must be lived, risked, achieved. There are limits and there are commandments, possibilities and impossibilities. These must be faced. The human creature has not already "arrived" on day one; it is on the way. There is a beginning; the way forward is pointed out; but decisions are called for on the part of the creature, and it is *not* programmed to move inevitably and inerrantly towards its goal. Nothing is assured about the outcome—or, rather, one thing only is assured, and that is that the Creator will be *with* the creature as it moves into the future. From the creature's side, therefore, one thing above all is called for: *trust*. Trust that God will not desert it, that its requirements will be met as they are felt—in short, the kind of trust that Jesus was getting at in his famous sermon, "Do not be anxious . . . consider the lilies . . . the birds of the air. . . . Sufficient unto the day . . . ." Of the *human* creature it is asked (what is not asked of the other creatures; they simply do it naturally, instinctively) that it freely and continuously *decide* that it can and will open itself to the becoming that is life; that it can do this, and wills to do this, because it can trust the Lord and Giver of life.

So (as we may continue in this vein) the being of the creature *anthropos*, that is, its *becoming*, implies movement, openness, the readiness to exchange one moment for the next, one experience for the next. *Temporality*, in other words, is of the essence of this creature's being—and not only temporality but the awareness of its temporality. Unlike the Creator, to whom classical theological tradition attributes such qualities as omnipresence and immutability, the human creature is required by the conditions of its creaturehood to be subject to the laws of time and space—and to accept and welcome the change and flux that this implies, trusting that time is the moving edge of the eternal, is our human mode, in fact, of experiencing the eternal. Perhaps this is what the great Danish author Isak Dinesen meant when she said she believed that if anyone wanted truly to love God he or she would have to love *change*.[6]

Movement, waiting, readiness to let the past become the present and the present give way to the future, and so on and on: this belongs to the *creaturely* status. Luther, who like all perceptive thinkers within the tradition realized that between the Christian doctrines of creation and redemption there is an uncanny but not irrational similarity, captured the essence of this creaturely status when he wrote concerning the life into which we are being *redeemed* that it

> does not mean to *be* good but to become good; not to be well, but to get well; not being but becoming; not rest but training. We are not yet, but we shall be. It has not yet happened, but it is the way. Not everything shines and sparkles as yet, but everything is getting better.[7]

Whether we draw it from reflection upon creation or from the redeemed life into which as Christians we feel ourselves to be beckoned, life as God intends it, then, is a life of becoming. It is life "on the way" (*in via*) as distinct from having arrived—a dynamic, as differentiated from a static, conception of being. It is not for nothing that the earliest Christians were called the "people of the way" (*communio viatorum*)!

What we are depicting here, to employ the shorthand of theology and philosophy, is finitude. The human creature in God's intention is a finite creature, whose primary distinction from the other creatures is its knowledge of its finitude, and whose vocation is to accept and rejoice in just this finitude.[8]

It does not require a great deal of imagination, however, to realize that the condition of finitude contains within itself a conspicuous degree of vulnerability. The darker side of change is impermanence, and of movement the lack of a firm standing-ground. To the experience of becoming (as every adolescent knows) there belongs the sense of not-yet-being, not having achieved what one must achieve in order fully to be. This negating element—this not-yet-being, this impermanence, this state of no-fixed-abode—is, as we have already suggested, present within the creaturely condition. It is present, we have insisted, for positive reasons: not as an end in itself, but as the goad towards greater fulfillment of the promise of our creaturehood. But it is present—just as present as is the tempting serpent in the saga of the human fall!

What the temptation is all about, surely, whether we take our cue from Genesis 3 or from that other great biblical story of temptation to which we have referred earlier, the temptation in the wilderness with its sequel in the garden of sorrows—what the temptation is all about is the felt desire of the creature to have arrived, to possess a permanent abode, to transcend the precariousness of temporality. Who, traveling along "the demon-ridden pilgrimage of human life,"[9] does not understand that the children of Israel longed, in the wilderness, for the possession of a place, for a land "flowing with milk and honey"? The temptation of Adam and Eve and of the Christ, the temptation of Everyman and Everywoman is to *have* their being rather than having to *receive* it, daily, like the manna of the wilderness or the "daily bread" of Jesus' model prayer. It is the temptation to possess being rather than to trust the One who gives us our being, daily.

It is, in short, the failure of trust. In its freedom to accept, embrace, and rejoice in its finitude, the creature grasps instead after infinity. In its freedom to trust its life to the Lord of life, the creature instead covets a life that is independent of the act of trust, a security already possessed—such as that one desired, in Jesus' parable, who built greater barns. But this security is the ultimate insecurity. Seeking to negate the negating element within the creaturely condition, the creature only succeeds in activating the negative beyond its rightful, useful place, thus elevating it to a position of undue prominence in its consciousness. ". . . And they knew that they were naked!" (Gen. 3:7). Seeking to achieve a state above the conditions of creaturehood—above the loneliness, the limitations, the temptations, and anxieties of finitude—the creature falls victim to delusions of grandeur that can never be approximated, for earth and the life process will not support them. Between the agony of failed illusions and the *hubris* of false expectancy, the human creature thus introduces into history sufferings beyond anything willed by the Creator.

To be sure, not *all* excessive suffering can be traced to this agony and this pride; but much of it can be. What would be left of the long history of our race, we may well ask ourselves, or for that matter of our own personal histories, if we could remove from them the pain inflicted upon us by our own prideful pursuit of unworthy visions and our agonies of disillusionment? Consider the delusions of power—dreamt by successive "tragic empires," pursued by parents who felt it their right to control the destinies of their children, fought and died for by generals and tyrants, vainly striven after by the weak and pretentious, coveted in some manner by us all! Consider too the delusions of immortality and greatness, of influence, and of the pride of achievement—and the dismay of failure! How much of the awesome suffering of our kind owes its genesis to this grasping and this failing to attain what is grasped after!

And the irony of it: that it is born of the attempt to supersede the *genuine* struggles of creaturehood! Seeking to transcend the suffering of becoming, we inherit a far greater form of suffering—the suffering of reaching after a glory incommensurate with our creaturehood. The suffering of those who wish to be "like God" but, being human, only end in becoming "unhappy gods."

C. The Tragic Dimension

The second aspect of the Christian conception of sin which bears upon the question of God and human suffering is what Tillich named "the tragic element." Tillich believed—and with ample reason, I should say—that it is particularly important for North American Christians to try to comprehend the meaning of this dimension of Christian hamartiology. For not only are we the products of a worldview in which (as we have seen) the element of the tragic in human life is minimized or dismissed in favor of more Promethean or triumphalist assumptions about human nature and the progressive flow of history; we represent, besides, types of Christian doctrine and piety which have stressed individual decision and responsibility to the exclusion both of the corporate and the predetermined aspects of the human condition. When it comes to sin, it is not only the moral (not to say moralistic) element that we characteristically stress, but it is at the same time the personal—indeed the private—side. Sin is the thought, word, or deed for which the individual perpetrating it is personally and directly responsible. This is frequently combined with a strong, and often an implacable and unforgiving, sense of the freedom of the will.

Now the combined influence of the social sciences and the arts, with a good deal of help from recent history, has helped to blunt the razor-sharp edges of the moralistic righteousness that results from this fatal combination of concepts. But it is still possible to discern in the public mentality, both in its secular and its ecclesiastical manifestations, an excessive influence coming from this source. While psychiatrists, criminologists, and other analysts of our culture look for the causes of "abnormal" or offensive behavior in unfavorable familial or social conditions (often to the exclusion of personal responsibility), the average citizen still seems with great regularity and singleness of mind to blame the individual. If anything, this tendency is *more* conspicuous, rather than less, in persons strongly influenced by the church. For whatever reasons—whether because of our New World individualism in general, or because the forms of Christianity which have dominated on this continent have emphasized individual freedom and responsibility—the tragic element in the concept of sin seems very far from the consciousness of most North American churchgoers.

An illustration, taken from my own experience as a student minister, may help to establish the point. In my village congregation, one of the most prominent members was a professional person of the community. She was one of those saints of the Pelagian variety who, I am sure, never permitted herself consciously to entertain as personal traits any of the manifestations of deadly sin in which Jesus seems to have taken primary interest: pride, self-righteousness, hypocrisy, greed, ambition, or egotism. My parishioner was what is known universally—at least in all the Canadian and American churches with which I have any acquaintance—as a very "good" person. She was in fact outstandingly virtuous in the mind of the entire community. So often had she been told of her saintliness, especially now as she approached old age, that I think she truly believed it herself—though she of course turned aside modestly in the presence of such acclamation.

Naturally enough, being one of the pillars of our church, this woman frequently took it upon herself to instruct me, the young and inexperienced clergyman, concerning my pastoral duties. In this capacity she suggested to me one day that I should visit a "poor chap" in the hospital—an outsider, an alcoholic and (as one would have put it two decades later) a "loser." This man, so my parishioner informed me, was the son of a prominent doctor in a nearby city. The doctor was mortified over his son's failure and the dereliction of a life that had had "every opportunity."

Obedient, I did visit the hospitalized man. He was middle-aged and broken, a bundle of nerves and apologies, and pathetically grateful for my visit. Afterwards, my good parishioner asked me: "Well, what did you think?" I replied that I felt deeply moved by the plight of this poor human being; that everything he had said to me—and left unsaid—pointed to his victimization by a very strong and demanding father, and by a society which expected him, as an educated and privileged person, to compete, achieve, and succeed—while all that he wanted was to be loved.

My parish saint was visibly surprised at my report, and perhaps with some deeply repressed part of her soul she wished to concur with my assessment; but such concurrence would have involved her in a rethinking of everything that she had come to believe about the moral workings of the universe, and a rebuttal of most of it. Therefore she dismissed whatever stirrings of memory and emotion were conjured up by my statement and reverted, after only a moment's hesitation, to her standard preunderstanding of the world. This she articulated in one brief, angry sentence: "But why can't he *change*?" It was not a question; it was a declaration. We are masters of our own fate, captains of our own souls! What becomes of us is our personal doing! And there is no condition—none!—that cannot be altered by an act of will, by resolution, or at least by prayer. (Yes, for this mentality is happy to use prayer and every other spiritual discipline to support its predisposition to mastery. But it does not understand the prayer of Paul that the "thorn" be removed, or of Jesus that the "cup" be taken away—refused prayer.)

That there is a tragic element in sin should not be misread or misused. The *moral* dimension is also there! According to the tradition on whose basis we are trying to reconsider all this, human beings are not *simply* victims! There is such a thing as personal responsibility. Decisions are made, patterns are created, and destinies are affirmed, consented to, not protested against, and (in some sense, usually), accepted—if not exactly chosen. But if human suffering were restricted to the sin for which the sufferer is personally and directly responsible, how little of human suffering would one in fact account for! In one important respect at least, our human situation is *not* that of the pair described in Genesis 2 and 3: none of us is born into a garden, with only a future and no past, and with all of our decisions ahead of us. We are all born into a world that is already old with the history of sin, guilt, and suffering: the fathers have eaten sour grapes! Significantly, the one whom our tradition names "the second Adam" was not tempted in a garden but in the wilderness. For millions of people in our world (it is perhaps the basic *ontological* condition of the whole Third World!) the hour of decision never arrives. People are pushed into the future by forces over which they have no control. They do not decide upon their destiny! They do not even decide what they shall eat for breakfast that day—if there is breakfast that day!

Is not this element of the tragic, and of its cousin, the pathetic, there in all of our lives, in one degree or another, one guise or another? Our physical appearance, so very important for life in our kind of world; our skin pigmentation, black or white or red; our sex, and our sexual orientation; our aptitude, our native intelligence; our metabolism; our sense of cosmic insecurity as citizens of the nuclear age—our "future shock"; our daily determination by the fads, the fashions, the economic conditions, the general social fabric of our environment—all of these things, each of them exceeding the power of our will, constitute live ingredients in the suffering that we experience. The very fact that we find it so hard to admit and articulate our suffering—what I called earlier our incapacity to suffer—has something to do with our being modern, middle-class North Americans rather than (let us say) peasants of the Middle Ages or emotionally freer Eastern Europeans.

It is true that all of these things are mixed in an indissoluble unity with decisions that we ourselves make. We cannot simply blame everybody and everything else for what happens to us. We are responsible. Probably, like Kafka's "K" in *The Trial*, we are in some mysterious way responsible even for things we do not understand and did not (in the strictest sense) *do!* Yet we would be less than perceptive if we did not admit that even we, the relatively affluent of the earth, who can still *seem* to be in charge of so much, are also caught in patterns and constellations of influences not of our own choosing—including the well-rehearsed pattern of believing oneself to be "in charge"! Obviously, some of us are more conspicuously victimized than others. None of us in the dominant cultures of the First World can claim the dubious distinction of truly great oppression. Even our celebrated oppressions are luxuries by comparison with the truly oppressed of this world! Yet we all know something of this tragic dimension. Even when (like my parishioner) our established preunderstanding of reality prevents us from giving voice to it, and even when the official rhetoric of our society fails to provide us with the words and concepts and symbols for the expression of it, this dimension is there, just beneath the surface of our existing. In moments when our defenses are down, when some "tragedy" puts us off guard, when (as Kierkegaard so poignantly expressed it) "time . . . gathers itself for the attack and is called the future,"[10] this aboriginal sense of our fundamental vulnerability expresses itself in spite of us—in words or in sighs too deep for words.

In the classical traditions of Christian theology, this sense of the tragic used to be named *original sin*. The dogma of original sin, one of the dogmas that theological liberalism discarded (perhaps it had to), was meant in its better expressions to symbolize precisely this sense of sin and of the suffering caused by collective human sin. It spoke of the tragic sequence of sin. It picked up that scriptural motif that was variously expressed, directly and indirectly, in isolated statements ("the fathers have eaten sour grapes . . .") and in whole epics in which sin and guilt and revenge are passed from generation to generation—therefore in one sense in the whole long story that is told in the continuity of the testaments. The sins of the fathers (and, as we may add today, of the mothers!) are visited unto the third and fourth generations. And beyond—far beyond![11]

Unfortunately—and, given human prurience, perhaps inevitably—the dogma of original sin became so enmeshed with sexuality, specifically with the supposed transmission of sin through the sexual act itself, that its theological, psychological, and historical usefulness was permanently marred. But its presence in Christian intellectual history reminds us that when we speak of the tragic dimension of sin we are not inventing something new.

The same is true of the concept of the demonic. Earlier generations of Christians knew that sin is not to be equated with individual deeds, nor even with the sum total of all history's sinful deeds. The evil which is unleashed in the world through the continuous distortion of human freedom acquires a life of its own. There are "principalities and powers" which transcend the individual thoughts, words, and deeds through which they come to be enacted and are perpetuated. Contemporary faith is not able to use the nomenclature of the devil and all his angels, for this only trivializes evil for the majority of our contemporaries, reducing it to the level of slightly scary entertainment. Yet, without recourse to some transcendent sense of the *mystery* of evil and the suffering that accompanies it, neither is it possible to comprehend the contemporary world. From the standpoint of the medieval mind, which had daily discourse with demonic spirits, a world in which every major city is targeted for nuclear destruction must look like some kind of hell infinitely beyond the imagination and prospects of mere *human* wickedness. Do not the death camps, the massive political exterminations, the sophisticated torture of prisoners in almost every modern nation, the organized crime ruining more lives than medieval plagues, the famine deaths of millions—do not such phenomena require for their explanation, or even for their registration in our consciousness, some sense of mystery that is not accessible to our ordinary science? Regardless of our linguistic choices and capacities, human beings are realizing once more—and in a way that our liberal forebears did not—that the human situation is prone to sufferings whose sources and supports cannot even be easily understood, let alone controlled.

An instance: In the spring of 1984 a young soldier, a placid man of 25, an excellent and peaceable neighbor and father of a young family, walked into the National Assembly in the city of Quebec and opened fire, killing three men and wounding several others. Predictably, popular journalism put it down to personal lunacy: something snapped; it was a case of insanity. The thing being explained to everyone's satisfaction, life could go on as usual. In the process, few people noticed, I suspect, what the young man said about his shame and humiliation at being a French Canadian. Everywhere in Canada he has heard that French Canadians are "stupid," a backward people, inferior. He is calm, sensitive. He does not fight back. But the humiliation and rejection register in his brain. Finally, irrationally, he strikes out at "the source"—that is, at what he insanely believes to be the source of his racial humiliation—the government in Quebec City, whose separatist policies have fanned the ancient embers of "Anglophone" pride and resentment.

Such events cannot be accounted for solely in terms of personal disorder, let alone personal sin! How many of the violent acts that occur thousands of times daily in our cities must be traced to the subtle but effective public attitudes towards other races, language groups, sexes, generations, political parties, and the like—that is, to this kind of hate and revenge that seems to have a life of its own?

Certainly, liberalism was right in discarding the prescientific and often purely superstitious ideas that accompanied both the concepts of original sin and the demonic. But the mystery of evil and suffering which these ancient dogmas cloaked did not disappear with the terminology and the thought-forms in which they were packaged. Whatever may have been the case in that modern world to which our liberal forebears addressed themselves, our postmodern situation calls for a serious reassessment of the tragic dimension.

We shall have to walk between two false alternatives: On the one hand, we must reject accounts of the world in which human suffering is attributable simply to extraterrestrial agencies. On the other, we must question accounts of the world in which the human agency alone is conspicuously responsible for its own predicament. A strictly deterministic account of evil and suffering, whether it originates in religious faith or in fatalistic secular ideologies, begs the question of obvious human guilt. The napalm that burned Vietnamese children alive cannot be laid at the doorstep of forces wholly beyond the control of the Western World's military powers. On the other hand, a strictly voluntaristic explanation of evil and suffering flounders on the rocks of contemporary experience: Can poor, drug-addicted young men and women be held totally responsible for their addictions? Are the bored, unemployed, television-educated adolescents of our society simply to be blamed, each one personally, for the havoc they create in our cities and on our highways? Can we legitimately accuse our elected representatives of causing the high rate of unemployment in our increasingly automated Western societies? To comprehend ourselves and the suffering that we feel, even if we cannot articulate it, and to comprehend the suffering that individually and corporately we inflict upon others, we need to have access to an account of existence which can draw simultaneously on the dimensions of moral responsibility and the tragic. That, I believe, is precisely what the Judeo-Christian tradition intends to offer us when it turns our attention towards this ancient concept, *sin.*

D. Understanding and Changing

It is not the intention of our tradition to leave the matter of human suffering at the point of analyzing its cause. Understanding something does not mean mastering it. Indeed, the most penetrating forms of understanding include the sense of humility. As Socrates said, the wise one is the one who knows the depths of unknowing. To understand is to "stand under." Sin, like its companion mystery, grace, cannot finally be understood; it can only be stood under, contemplated, and *confessed.*

Nevertheless, in a society which has difficulty even *thinking about* suffering and its causes—which manifests an incapacity for confronting openly the reality of the negation that it darkly feels—it could be a step towards redemption even to participate in the act of seeking to understand something of the *why* of suffering. Analysis is not cure; but any cure that is worthy of the name presupposes a courageous analysis, and, as psychoanalysts have understood for a long time, the cure in some real sense already begins with the analysis.

Perhaps there could be no more responsible act on the part of the church in today's world than that it should seek in imaginative, concrete, and contextually pertinent ways to explore its theological tradition of sin. This is one of the most important reflective tools that Christians have for comprehending our incendiary world. On the basis of this tradition, it is possible for persons to discover a mental and spiritual frame of reference which gives them both the conceptual tools and the psychic permission that are needed to enter their dark night. It is no small thing that the church can still draw upon this long analytical tradition of hamartiology in a world whose cultural foundations lack any comparable frame of reference. Too many Christians seem to feel that their primary calling is to provide answers. Might it not be that our better service is to give a language and a spiritual vantage point from which to explore the great questions of our age? The trouble with most answers—including the answers that popular Christianity is ready to offer at bargain prices— is that they are usually provided by persons who have not lived long enough with the questions.

With the problem of human suffering it is especially true that answers are on the whole both inadequate and inappropriate. What is needed most, whether in the theological classroom or in the pastoral situation, is a place to which to refer the question—a forum, a body, a community in whose midst persons may feel that they are allowed, at last, to explore and express the anxiety, bitterness, anger, remorse, or fear which in the ordinary course of their lives they think they must hide.

But it is not enough, I think, that there should be a sympathetic *community* alone. Certainly, nothing can replace a compassionate body of persons who are sufficiently in touch with their own feelings to recognize the deepest needs in others. But there must also be a tradition, a body of experience and understanding and searching, by which that community itself can be guided. Thus in the church today we are called not only to fashion of ourselves a *koinonia* of compassion to which the hurting of the world may turn, but also to rethink in great seriousness the tradition that we have been bequeathed. The biblical concept of sin is an important part of that tradition. It cannot account for all the suffering that human beings are caused to experience; for instance, it is very questionable when attempts are made to relate sin and natural catastrophe. It may also well be the case that the word *sin* and its derivatives are so badly misunderstood that its use in pastoral and other situations is unwise. But if serious Christian ministers and laypersons are willing to explore this concept in its biblical and best historical expressions, they will be provided with resources of courage and wisdom which are very rare in a society which pursues instant "fixes" instead of depth of analysis, and techniques instead of understanding.

That being said, it is still not the end of the matter. The analysis of any malaise is the prerequisite of its cure, and the line between analysis and cure is, as we have said, a fine one. Understanding something of the suffering of human being, and its cause, is already to enter the realm of transformation. Comprehending even a little—even through a glass darkly, as Paul put it—can open us to alternatives to the status quo. But our tradition wants to carry us beyond the gate of understanding. It intends to change, not only our comprehension of the world but our way of being in it—and *its* way of being as well!

"The philosophers," wrote Karl Marx in his 11th thesis on Feuerbach (the words stand written on his gravestone in Hyde Park), "wanted to understand the world, but the point is: to change it." In a real sense, biblical faith echoes that sentiment—or rather, to be more accurate historically, Karl Marx echoed the sentiment of biblical faith! The tradition of Jerusalem does try, and with unusual tenacity, to *understand* the world. Has any human enterprise had a longer history than the attempt of Judeo-Christian religion to *understand* the enormous questions that are posed by the juxtaposition of the two primary terms in our theme, God and *human suffering?* By comparison with this long search for understanding, the attempts of scientists to understand the nature of matter or the workings of the human brain are short-lived indeed! The prophets, the historians, the wisdom writers, the apostles, the apostolic fathers and

apologists and theologians and rabbinical scholars of many generations have devoted their lives to questions, most of which in one
way and another revolved around this theme. They had to, because
(as St. Anselm put the matter succinctly) "faith seeks understanding" (*fides quaerens intellectum*)—it would not be *faith* if it did not
do so. Moreover, they knew that understanding is the prerequisite
of change, and already in some real sense itself change. Still, Christian belief and theology does not *rest* in understanding. Being wise
in the world may be the goal of the tradition of Athens, but it is
not that of the tradition of Jerusalem. The point is to change it.
"If you know these things," said Jesus, "blessed are you if you do
them" (John 13:17).

Unlike activists who think themselves and their deeds the answer
to worldly problems, Christians do not regard themselves as the
agents of change, nor do they believe that change-for-the-better is
automatic. That belief belongs to the religion of progress; it is an
expression of optimism, not of hope. Christians do believe, however, that there is at work in this world a grace, an influence, a
Spirit of transformation which is engaging both the moral and the
tragic factors in the human condition which make for earthly suffering. And they do believe that they are called and enabled by
this same Spirit of transformation to participate in this conquest.

4

Redemption: Conquest from Within

Introduction: Redemption as "Point of Departure"

In this brief attempt at a theological overview of the theme "God and Human Suffering," we turn now to the third focus of the three-fold perspective from which Christian theology considers this recurring and many-sided problem of human and religious experience: redemption. From the focus of the doctrine of creation we have argued that there is a form of suffering which is inherent in creaturely finitude, not as a flaw or a mistake of the Maker, but as a positive aspect of the being that God intends for humanity: the suffering of becoming. Then, from the focus our tradition has named "the fall," we have reminded ourselves that there is a suffering which is the consequence of humankind's distorted freedom, and which is present in our situation both as act and as condition, both as a reality for which we are humanly and personally responsible and as a tragic fact of our corporate existence and history. It is here that biblical faith places its *chief* stress with respect to the reality of human suffering—though, wisely, it does not indulge in attempts to demonstrate direct or obvious connections between empirical suffering and actual sin.

Now from the focus that our doctrinal heritage names redemption or salvation, we are to remember that the reality of human suffering (the first of our tradition's two basic affirmations in relation to this whole topic) is met by an even greater reality: the conquest of suffering by the God of "suffering love" (*agape*). There is, after all, according to the tradition of Jerusalem, an answer to suffering. But no, let us use our words judiciously from the outset: there is. . . *an Answerer!*

Before we attempt to amplify that perhaps enigmatic but all-important distinction, however, it is expedient at this point that we make a methodological observation. If it is not already clear, then at this juncture it ought to be made quite explicit that the vantage point from which Christian faith considers this entire theme is not neatly separable into three distinct aspects or foci. Rather, the three foci (creation, fall, redemption) belong to *a single perspective*, a seamless robe of belief and contemplation. Moreover, even though we have treated our subject in a sequential way, starting with the doctrine of creation (as is usual in most theology), *faith* as distinct from *theology* does not adhere strictly to this sequence. In fact, in a real sense the *basic* point of departure for faith is heavily informed by the substance of this third dimension of our threefold perspective—redemption. For it is this aspect of the total perspective upon the question of suffering, namely, the gospel's *engagement* of the reality of human suffering, that lends to faith both the courage and the wisdom that it needs in order to consider, with greater openness than would otherwise be possible, the reality of suffering as it is glimpsed through the foci of creation and fall. Suffering *is* real—so real that the human psyche can only bear to contemplate the depths of its reality if from the outset it is given some cause to believe that suffering is not the *ultimate* reality, not as such the last word about existence in this world. Apart from such a prospect, who would have the stamina to expose himself or herself deeply to the fact of human suffering? Without at least the hint of a promise that meaning might be found in, alongside, or beneath such suffering as human flesh is heir to, no doubt the better course would be (what in fact so many of our contemporaries do!) to avoid so far as possible any such exposure!

It is from the perspective of redemption that Christian faith derives this necessary promise. Accordingly, we have assumed that perspective throughout these reflections. But now we must attempt to make it explicit. "Christian faith," wrote Reinhold Niebuhr, "fully appreciates the threat of meaninglessness which comes into history by the corruption of human freedom. But it does not succumb to the despairing conclusion that history is merely a chaos of competing forces."[1] Our task now is to provide what we can by way of background to this kind of faith statement. On what basis does Christian faith, while remaining entirely honest about the reality of human suffering and the "meaninglessness" that it conjures up, both admit this reality and affirm that it is nevertheless only the penultimate and not the ultimate reality?

A. Not by Might

In the title of this chapter I have used the phrase "the conquest from within." I must begin these reflections on redemption and human suffering, however, by registering a warning about such language as this. Words like *conquest*—and conventional theology and liturgy abound in them!—too easily suggest the application of sheer power to any problem. To employ the word *conquest* for the gospel's approach to the problem of human suffering, and to do so without any critical commentary on such language, is to invite people to think once again (as nearly all religion has conditioned us to think) in terms of the divine attribute of *omnipotence*: God, whose power is infinite, takes on the sources of human suffering in much the same fashion as St. George takes on the dragon, or the forces of law and order in old-fashioned Hollywood movies takes on outlaws and criminals, or an imperial host takes on a rebel army. Feminist and other types of critical theology remind us, rightly, that the church's resort to power language, as well as most of the analogies, myths, and illustrations that we employ to back it up, is very much a culturally conditioned approach to Christianity. For one thing, it is a characteristically masculine approach. As masculinity has been defined in Western civilization generally and in the New World in particular, power is of the essence! It is certainly not the only conceivable way of describing the male being—in fact it is highly reductionist; for men, like women, are capable of compassion, gentleness, meekness, humility, and identification with weak and suffering things. But every little boy in this society knows that these are not the qualities he is expected to cultivate. He knows that his calling as a man, regardless of his vocation, is to accentuate whatever he can by way of physical, intellectual, and spiritual strength, and to approach life with its challenges and problems in a spirit of self-confidence, leadership, and conquest. On this continent, where until recently that kind of spirit could find its proper outlet only in the milieu of the deed, the masculine mystique has hardly even known the courage of thought. Meditation upon complex and technically insoluble issues of human experience has been regarded for the most part as an unprofitable pursuit for "real men"—with the consequence that work requiring such meditation (especially teaching—except where prestige could be gained!) has been relegated to women; and with the further consequence that in the present sociohistorical moment, whose complexity requires unusual powers of abstract reflection and renders most technical solutions and mere deeds questionable and even dangerous, many *men* especially are frustrated and disorientated. After generations of the kind of problem solving which called for quick decisions and decisive deeds, executed with dispatch and sure power, an age whose great problems are in large measure due to the very delusions of mastery created by the power mentality presents enormous threats to all—female as well as male—who still want to assume that might is right.

All the same, the language and posture of power has in fact informed whole segments of the Christian tradition. As C. S. Song has put it in his provocative study *The Compassionate God,* we have been handed a "high-voltage God" and a "high-voltage theology" by our tradition. "Power has been stored up, and we must be on our guard." Ours is "a highly charged deity, a dangerous God." Our theology, accordingly, accentuates power, and itself functions powerfully in the post-Constantinian situation:

> It provides the church with theological grounds for anathema and excommunication administered to those recalcitrant souls who want

to bring God away from ecclesiastical protection and let the world have a better look at God. Mission theology too has been, on the whole, a militant theology that defends God from pagan gods and draws a clear line between salvation and damnation. It is a very highly charged theology from which very few pagans could get away scot-free.[2]

The language of power is prominent in Christian doctrine as it relates to our present theme. It can be observed both in the conventional way in which the so-called problem of suffering is stated, and in at least one of the three major types of atonement theology through which evolving doctrine responded to human suffering.

Formulating the problem of suffering in its conventional statement revolves around the seeming contradiction between the divine power and the divine love. If God is *loving* and at the same time *all-powerful*, then why is there so much suffering in the world? The assumption is that the deity *could*, if the deity *would*, simply eliminate suffering. Why then does God not do so, if God is truly loving?

When the question is put in this way there is, I think, no satisfactory way of addressing it. The chance of there being a convincing response to such a formulation of the problem is at least severely limited; and the limiting factor is just this power assumption. When infinite power is posited as the primary and characteristic attribute of deity, then no one can be satisfied with an answer that is less than the abolition of suffering as such!

It is the power assumption itself that must be questioned. Behind it lies a whole preunderstanding of both God and humanity which does not belong to the tradition of Jerusalem, and which in fact may be the direct antithesis of that tradition, despite obvious linguistic parallels. The Judeo-Christian tradition does not *deny* the power of God, but neither does it *magnify* this attribute; moreover, and more to the point, it does not abstract the divine power from the divine-human *relationship*. The relationship qualifies—radically—the nature and deployment of power on God's part.

This can be appreciated at least in a rudimentary way if we remember what has been said concerning freedom at the conclusion of the discussion on suffering and creation. If suffering is inextricably bound up with human freedom (not that all suffering is a direct and obvious consequence of freedom's misuse, but it is nevertheless impossibly intermingled with it) then *through power* God could only eliminate suffering by eliminating freedom. But if freedom is of the very essence of the human creature, as the tradition has generally maintained and as we also insisted earlier, then the elimination of freedom would imply the virtual elimination of humanity.

A parallel to this prospect exists today within the human sphere as such. Because of the rampant freedom of individuals and societies, problems of population, pollution, distribution, violence, and the like, have multiplied in an alarming manner. Behavioral scientists like B. F. Skinner have a solution to the dilemma: condition human beings from birth to desire only what they should desire and to do only what they should do! Freedom and dignity are luxuries that the species can no longer afford; therefore let the power of science solve the problem by effectively eliminating freedom and dignity. *But,* reply Skinner's critics (and with reason), even if this could be accomplished it would not really *solve* the existing dilemma. It would only eradicate the problem by substituting something else, some other organism, for Homo sapiens. For without freedom and dignity there is no longer humanity.

There are, in other words, situations in which *power* simply does not work. Such situations are not foreign to any of us. Even the most macho of males (and females) experience such situations, and it may well be asked whether their resort to power and brute force is not frequently a consequence of their frustration over knowing in the depths of their souls that power does not change anything but usually only complicates existing problems. There are (if we are permitted to speak in such a way) analogies to *God's* problem of dealing with human suffering in every nook and cranny of historical existence, personal and social. Who, through power tactics, can eliminate the self-destroying habits of a son or daughter who has fallen prey to hard drugs? What nation, through power alone, can ensure world peace? We live in a world which attempts through the sheer show of military might to deter nuclear warfare—with the very real prospect that *this power play itself,* through design or accident, will trigger the very thing it is supposed to prevent! There is no *sword* that can cut away sin without killing the sinner.

Beyond that, there are connections—deep and mysterious links—
between our suffering and our grandeur that render power approaches to this question abysmally simplistic. Frederick Buechner
in his novel *Lion Country* poignantly discloses some of these connections. The protagonist of his story, Antonio, has a twin sister
who eventually dies of myeloma, "a fatal disorder which has to do
with bones." At the end of the story, Antonio makes the following
observation:

> When Miriam's bones were breaking . . . if I could have pushed a
> button that would have stopped not her pain but the pain of her in
> me, I would not have pushed the button because, to put it quite
> simply, my pain was because I loved her, and to have wished my
> pain away would have been somehow to wish my love away as well.
> And at my best and bravest I do not want to escape the future either,
> even though I know that it contains what will someday be my own
> great and final pain. Because a distaste for dying is twin to a taste
> for living, and again I don't think you can tamper with one without
> somehow doing mischief to the other. But this is at my best and
> bravest. The rest of the time I am a fool and a coward just like most
> of the other lost persons that in the end it will take no less than Mr.
> Keen himself to trace.[3]

To reiterate: there are situations where power is of no avail. *They
are most of the situations in which as human beings we find ourselves!*
May we not also dare to say that, from the standpoint of a faith
tradition which posits love, not power, as *God's* primary perfection,
they are most of the situations in which God finds God's Self too?

Not only has power dominated the articulation of the conventional statement of the problem of suffering; it has also functioned
as the principal metaphor of at least one of the three major types
of soteriological theory which evolved in the course of Christian
reflection on the meaning of Christ's suffering and death. I am
referring to the so-called ransom or (in Gustav Aulen's famous
analysis) classical theory of atonement:[4] Christ the Victor, cloaking
for the time being his divine omnipotence beneath the apparent
weakness of the flesh, deceives and finally destroys the forces of

evil that are responsible for human misery, and delivers the human victims from the bonds of sin, death, and the demonic.

There are, of course, times and seasons when such a theory can have something very important to say to both church and society. It can give courage to those who sit in darkness and the shadow of death, to the discouraged, the fatalized, the oppressed. Strategically, it can be the right Word in certain contexts—as it is again, in forms necessarily different from its classical expression, in some types of liberation theology. But to present such a strategically relevant message as if it were an ultimately satisfactory theological response to the question contained in our theme is to overlook many important and complex things about the human condition with which the redeeming God must contend.

One of these things (as we have just been reminding ourselves) is that it is virtually impossible to separate the sources of suffering from the sufferer, especially when the condition of the sufferer is understood, as it finally must be, in its total communal and historical setting. The "ransom" or "deliverance" type of atonement theology on the contrary finds the sources of suffering to be external to the condition and being of the sufferer. Classical expressions of this theology located the cause of evil in an objectifiable, transhistorical demonic power, separable from the human community or at least from the elect within it, so that the relief and deliverance from suffering could be effected by a powerful Christ figure, dealing the death-blow to Satan.[5] The temptation for liberation theology when it takes over this ancient motif of the deliverance of the oppressed, is to identify the source of earthly suffering with equally objectifiable enemies, only now within the mundane sphere: with certain classes, with the capitalists, with the multinationals, with the military-industrial complex. So the gospel becomes a statement and praxis of liberation from these oppressive forces.

In raising this critique, I am by no means accusing liberation theology of actually or consistently succumbing to this temptation; nor am I in the least denying that the evils named by most expressions of this theological movement are truly evil and must be challenged and rooted out. My point is only that the *temptation* of every theology or soteriology which capitalizes on the power motif is too onesidedly to locate the sources of evil and human suffering "out there," i.e., in some external, objectifiable, and separable entity; and thus on the one hand to exaggerate the ultimacy of those evil entities, courting in this way an unwarranted dualism, and on the other hand attributing to those who are "delivered from evil" too much innocence and goodness. If evil is located externally and the causes of suffering thus isolated, it is of course possible to develop versions of the work of the Christ in which the destroyer/oppressor is vanquished and the victim set free.

But, as Anselm of Canterbury knew (for all his own psychic and theological limitations), the causes of suffering cannot so readily be isolated from our own selves, collectively and individually. This is why Anselm, in *his* attempt to answer the question of how the Christ delivers us from suffering,[6] did not present his case as a struggle between God and Satan, but as a struggle between God and the human soul, whose cause was espoused by God the Son. The other principal atonement theology developed in the long history of Christian reflection upon the meaning of the cross (I refer to the theory that was given classical expression by Peter Abelard and was taken up by 19th-century liberal theology as the "moral influence theory") is even more adamant than Anselm concerning the location of the sources of suffering as being *within the deepest recesses of the human spirit.*[7]

Without buying into the whole story that is told in either one of these alternatives to the Classical/Ransom theory, we may nevertheless see in both the work of Anselm and of Abelard an implicit protest within the Christian tradition against overuse of the motif of divine omnipotence in the articulation of the gospel of the cross. Once faith has overcome the perhaps "natural" but nonetheless simplistic tendency towards a Manichaean separation of good and evil, it is necessary to employ concepts far more sophisticated than power to the interpretation of the redemptive event.

Power is in the long run an intensely limited mode of response for meeting the subtle questions present in our theme. The changes that need to occur if there is to be any real or profound "conquest" of suffering are mainly internal ones. I do not mean internal, in this case, to be heard as a synonym for private or personal. It is not a matter merely of altering individual souls, one by one, to make the world right. This approach, the perennially announced program of religious personalism and pietism, overlooks the corporate aspect of that "tragic dimension" to which we have drawn attention in the previous chapter. Individuals are conditioned by societal circumstances far greater than themselves; so that even to alter the condition of the individual "soul," if it is *seriously* intended and not just a matter of pious rhetoric, would drive any who attempt such a thing into the social arena. (As I was informed by one of my students who has made it her vocation to "take care of" a number of elderly women who are otherwise alone in the world: "If I follow one of my women carefully for one day only, I am led directly into all or most of the *social* problems of our society!") It is not only the spirits of private persons that must be reached and changed but the spirit of the collectivity, of the community—indeed of the species. A *metanoia* must be undertaken which is aimed at the anxiety that seeks security in the building of "greater barns," at the collective fear which is always busy fashioning images of the enemy (*Feindbilder*), at the false pride which sets race against race and sex against sex and generation against generation, and at the economic concupiscence which tries to find permanence and meaning in the amassing of possessions. How can power, as it is ordinarily understood, meet and transform this anxiety, this fear, this false pride, this concupiscence? Such spiritual qualities, which belong not only to individual persons but describe the spirit of our First World, can be altered only through encounter with a judgment (*krisis*) which convicts from within and an alternative which commends itself through forgiveness and love.

In stressing the *internal* or "spiritual" qualities which, in my view, the tradition of Jerusalem identifies as the core causes of the greatest human suffering, I in no way intend to minimize the evil of the external *manifestations* of these qualities. Who could not discover, looking about in our contemporary world of "have" and "have not" peoples, that the bulk of the great physical forms of suffering in this world is inextricably linked with the *institutionalization* of greed, the *legitimation* of lust and concupiscence, and the public *authorization* of a system which rewards the strong and punishes the weak? And who could not surmise, regarding such a world, that the external symptoms of its malaise must themselves be dealt with; that steps must be taken to remedy injustice and unequal distribution and the arms race and violence in our cities and pornography—the list goes on? Yet who could not also detect, given a little time for reflection, that these and similar phenomena *are* in fact symptoms, manifestations of a more deadly cancer that eats away at the collective human spirit? To despise the activists who treat the symptoms— some of whom devote their very lives to the treatment of the gross symptoms of our spiritual malaise—is a travesty of Christian wisdom and obedience. In such a time as ours we must *all* be activists, all giving our energies to the conquest of economic injustice, racial and sexual oppression, violence and war, and the other evident evils that bedevil our world. Civilizations, like individual organisms, can *die* of the symptoms of their diseases! Too many of the intellectuals and "spiritual people" among us maintain our safe distance from the world by telling ourselves that we are interested only in the root causes of our late 20th-century dis-ease. Thus, theology, preaching, the conversion of souls, and "pastoralia" become for us fences upon which to sit, while others risk their lives and fortunes to save human bodies and the body politic.

In pleading for a deeper understanding of the spiritual causes of First World disorder and the suffering that it begets, then, I do not wish to provide a rationale for ethical passivity. Yet surely, while actively participating in God's work of saving the world from death through the symptoms of its disease, Christians must at the same time give themselves to the more complex work of seeking under God to comprehend and to change the collective spirit which begets these symptoms. It is not only the actual *practices* of the rich nations of the world that must be changed, it is the spirit which incites these practices and sustains them; it is the goals, the values, the anxieties, and bogus hopes that make such practices seem necessary or natural. It does not require any special revelation nor an explicit religious faith to know that it is the invisible, intangible, spiritual core of human society that must be altered if what is visibly and tangibly wrong in the world is to be altered significantly. Much of the secular wisdom of our time has led to that very conclusion.

Faith, if we confess it, only adds to rationality at this point the courage to believe that the collective spirit *can* be changed—because faith believes that the God revealed in Jesus as Christ is committed to life, and without significant change in the human spirit the life of the world is sorely jeopardized.

B. Intimations of an Alternative: The Theology of the Cross

The change for which faith hopes, which it believes *possible* (not necessary or inevitable, but possible), cannot be effected through power, might, majesty, dominion, and the like, but only through a divine *modus operandi* that stands all such preconceptions of God's way of working in the world on their head. Perhaps we have come to a moment in our history as a religion, we Christians, when more of us can be open to the alternative to power-orientated thinking that is present in the depths of our tradition—in the declaration that "*Jesus* is the Christ."

This is no doubt a very optimistic assessment of the religious situation, especially at a time when the most *vociferous* forms of Christianity on this continent are given to even greater boasts than usual! But I make the claim on two grounds especially. On the one hand many sensitive Christians in our time have already for a long time sensed the inappropriateness of the power motif in an age so gravely threatened by a surfeit of power, and are therefore at least open to radical alternatives. At the same time, the church itself, where it is capable of self-knowledge, recognizes that it is no longer the powerful institution that it once was; this knowledge, which is debilitating to some, is liberating to others. Perhaps, since we do not have to play the role of the powerful any longer, we may discover another way of being in the world, another way of serving, and even another kind of message.

In other words, as we emerge out of the Constantinian captivity of the faith,[8] the need to think triumphalistically is replaced by a new seriousness about the meaning of the event which stands at the center of our confession, the sacrificial suffering and death of the Christ. Kosuke Koyama speaks, I think, for many thinking Christians when he voices the following critique of conventional Western Christologies:

> The name, Jesus Christ, is not a magic name which transforms the broken world into an instant paradise. Has not the true dimension of the glory of this name suffered since the faith associated with this name became the state religion of the Roman Empire? Has it not been difficult to maintain the quality of the stumbling block of this name when the church became the powerful social group? How could the prestigious church proclaim the crucified Christ? The name of Jesus Christ is not a powerful name in the manner of the imperial power. It is a "foolish and weak" name (1 Cor. 1:21-25)! . . . Jesus Christ is not a quick answer. If Jesus Christ is the answer he is the answer in the way portrayed in crucifixion![9]

Koyama is here drawing upon the alternative to theological triumphalism that Luther named *theologia crucis*. Luther contrasted the "theology of the cross" with what he called "theology of glory" (*theologia gloriae*), whose essential metaphor is that of power. The theology of the cross, which, as Jürgen Moltmann has so aptly put it, "is not a single chapter in theology, but the key signature for all Christian theology,"[10] does not altogether eschew the idea of power and such related terms as triumph, victory, or (our word) conquest. But it *does* eschew—and radically so—the *models* of power, triumph, victory, and conquest which Christian doctrine has all too consistently employed in its endeavor to interpret the meaning of the work of God in Jesus as the Christ. The theology of the cross does not intend simply to discard the metaphor of power, but it does want to transform it; for it is an adequate way of speaking about the redemptive work of God only if it is conformed to the image of God revealed *in the crucified One*. The models by which heretofore too much Christianity has permitted its theology and its Christology to be informed have been culturally determined. They have been shaped primarily by the triumphalist societies and successive empires with which from Constantine onwards the Christian church has cohabited. As Koyama suggests, a "prestigious church," the official cult of empire, can hardly afford to be known through the symbol of a crucified man—or a crucified God! It belongs to empire ("superpower"!) to establish itself and to subsist on power alone. To make the faith amenable to the imperial mentality and at the same time a fitting symbol for and reflection of imperial splendor itself, the church through the ages has permitted its message to be filtered through the sieve of worldly power and glory. What adjective do we use for God more frequently (especially in our prayers) than "Almighty"? Jesus, in our hymns and liturgies, turns out again and again to be the Victor, the Conquerer, the Warrior-prince, the Captain of souls, the Slayer of foes. The church is "like a mighty army," a powerful and glorious movement, a crusade, waging battle (mission?) against all comers. The life of faith, accordingly, is a fight, a conflict with unbelievers, a struggle against the flesh, and so on. The language of our religion has been so consistently informed by the spirit of might, winning, success, and related concepts that it is difficult to use any of the *scriptural* nomenclature of glory and triumph without conjuring up the whole ideology of empire.

For many self-professed Christians, on this continent particularly, the heritage of imperial imagery and the confusion of Christ with Caesar presents no problem. It is indeed a bonus. It can be aligned very conveniently with that same imperial mentality that at the secular level has not yet noticed the question mark that the nuclear age has written over the whole notion of empire. The "theology of glory"—possibly the most crass and decadent form of the *theologia gloriae* ever to have articulated itself in a very long history of religious triumphalism—is openly displayed as normative Christianity every day of the week! Yet, in more thoughtful quarters of the church catholic we are beginning, I believe, to realize not only that such Christian bravado gives the lie to existence, and is credible only to chauvinists and philistines but (what is worse) that it is a betrayal of the more subtle "wisdom of the cross" (1 Corinthians 1–2). That wisdom understands that the anatomy of human suffering is infinitely more complex than triumphalism of every variety conceives it to be, and that it defies the "answers" of the powerful. The only power that can address suffering humanity is the power of love, and that is a power "made perfect in weakness" (2 Cor. 12:9).[11] The only victory that is both real and credible in face of human suffering is a victory visible to faith, not sight, a victory *sub contraria specie* ("hidden beneath its opposite"—Luther). What Reinhold Niebuhr called "the logic of the cross"[12] (for there *is* a logic in it; it is not merely irrational) must interpret power in terms the world calls weakness, and victory in terms the world calls failure, because the thing that this power would overcome and this victory win is delicate indeed: it is the human spirit. The root causes of our suffering in its burdensome sense being inseparable from our very selves, the conquest of them *must* be an intensely subtle one—a conquest *from within*.

C. The Conquest from Within

It is not easy to speak about this conquest from within. Here, I think, more than at any point in the "modest science" (Barth) of theology, the language of dogma and doctrine is shown up as paltry and inadequate. The truth of the cross, if it is to be conveyed at all through words, must finally draw upon the language of art, of story, drama, symbol, metaphor, analogy. The cross of Jesus Christ is after all not a theological statement— not a soteriology! It is an event, a deed, an enactment. One walks very close to blasphemy when one attempts to put it into words!

We, too, shall turn presently to story. But in order to keep our minds fixed on the tradition that we are rehearsing here, with its perhaps stilted but sometimes convenient signs and guideposts, I should like first to remind the reader of two doctrinal concepts (traditionally they are for Christians the *central* doctrinal concepts) which for all their awkwardness have precisely to do with this conquest from within. I refer to the concepts of the incarnation and the triunity of God. Each of them has been, and could also be for us, the subject of endless discussion and debate. I mention them here, however, only to demonstrate their connection with our theme.

It is unfortunate that the doctrine of the incarnation of the divine *Logos* was so soon and so successfully coopted by non-Hebraic assumptions and priorities. Under the impact of a religious and philosophical worldview which distrusted matter and sought redemption in the realm of pure and disembodied spirit, the concept of the indwelling of the "mind and heart of God" (Logos) in historical existence was uprooted from its essentially Hebraic matrix and, in the decisive early centuries of doctrinal evolution, encumbered with the heavy, heavenly language of metaphysics and abstract mysticism. If, however, one gets behind all the mystifying terminology of the "two natures," the concept of virgin birth ontically rather than historically understood, the *homoousios/homoiousios* debate, the *theotokos* idea, and all the rest, one discovers an affirmation that is both simple (in the profoundest sense of the term!) and in striking continuity with the whole bent of Hebraic faith, namely, God *identifies with humanity.* God, who in the faith of Israel certainly transcends creation, but who in this same faith is from the outset orientated in love *towards* the creation, now enters into full solidarity with the creature. God, who unlike Aristotle's god will not be God in isolation but only a God who is with *us* and for *us*—who "will be your God and you shall be my people"—this same God of Abraham, Isaac, and Jacob, declares the apostolic witness, takes the final step and gives flesh to the Word (the *same* Word) that from the beginning God spoke through the Law and the Prophets. Through an impossible (certainly, impossible!) act of grace and self-sacrifice, God bridges the unbridgeable gulf between eternity and time. The One whose ways are not our ways, nor whose thoughts our thoughts, yet who is never mentioned in the Hebraic Scriptures except in conjunction with the world of human and other created beings—this earthward-yearning God of Israel becomes now "Emmanuel."

It is this movement of solidarity and identification, of full participation in the life of the world, that is fundamentally intended in the dogma of the incarnation, whatever the language may be. When this is forgotten; when religion or doctrinal rationalism develops a special interest in Jesus' *physis* (nature); when the important thing becomes believing in the divinity of Jesus (what does *believing* in Jesus' divinity mean, anyway?), then the point of Advent and Christmas is lost. For faith in the Incarnate Word (which is very different from "believing in Jesus' divinity"!) means confessing the unconditional and unreserved presence of God *with us.* Incarnation is our tradition's way of speaking about the divine *Mitsein* (being-with). It signifies the determination of the Christian community from now on only to think about God as it thinks about "us," God's creatures and God's world. It means the church's refusal to indulge in God-talk that is not at the same time world-talk. It means that theology is no longer just "theology"; it is "theo-anthropology" (Barth).

God has entered effectively and without reserve into the life of the world. That is what we mean when we repeat the Johannine statement ". . . and the Word became flesh and dwelt among us. . . ." God *freely* did this, our tradition maintains: God was not under some external compulsion to enter into solidarity with the creation. Yet in another sense there is a certain *necessitas* in this movement of God toward the world. Remember the passion predictions: ". . .the Son of man must suffer. . . ." "Must suffer"—not on account of *external* pressure, but on account of the compelling internal necessity that the apostolic tradition names God's love—*agape*. Behind the "must" of Jesus' passion there is the "must" of the divine *agape*—and it is visible all the way from Eden! The God depicted in that long and tortuous story that begins already with the wrong turning of human freedom *must* take the road that leads, at last, to Golgotha, because the sin and suffering by which God's beloved creatures are bound can only be engaged profoundly from within the historical process itself.

History is not by itself redemptive. Here Christianity and Judaism differ markedly from Marxism and from every variation on the theme of progress. Left to itself, our tradition strongly suspects (though it does not know this, for it has not witnessed a creation left entirely to itself!), the world would capitulate to the Nihil that it is always in some way courting. But while the tradition of Jerusalem rejects the idea that the historical process is itself redemptive, it also rejects the contrary belief (deeply embedded in Manichaean and many other religious traditions) that history is irredeemable. Between these two unacceptable alternatives, our tradition conceives of another possibility: *History has a capacity for being changed from within.*

In a very real sense, the whole story that is told in the continuity of the Testaments is an illustration and documentation of that theorem. Contrary to the logic of sin, the disobedience of the first pair does not end in shame and death; they are clothed, they are given a way into the future—with pain, but still a way. Despite the finality of his deed, the murderer Cain, marked, to be sure, by his desperation, is able to go on; and the parents, bereaved now of both their sons, are given another. At the end of possibilities in his native Ur, Abram and his family discover, through many trials and errors, another homeland. Sold by his brothers into slavery, Joseph after decades of exile and fame in a foreign country, is able to preserve his kinsfolk from extinction ("You meant evil against me; but God meant it for good," Gen. 50:20). Driven away from slavery and "flesh-pots," the children of Israel discover a route to safety . . . to the wilderness . . . to the land of promise . . . to exile . . . to return from exile. . . . We could go on, but the theme is well known.

History is not fixed. It does not move *inevitably* towards either perfection or destruction, paradise or oblivion, the fulfillment of dreams or their ultimate frustration. The continuing freedom of the human creature, though marred, gives it an openness to the future. Men and women, both individually and corporately, do things, say things, leave things undone and unsaid. Their words and their deeds are sometimes good, beautiful, and true; sometimes better intended than their results cause them to appear; sometimes confused and tentative, sometimes "meant for evil," sometimes truly evil. And out of this apparently chaotic welter of acts and words and thoughts *history* comes to be; that is, faith perceives patterns of meaning and direction. To speak more accurately, it sees the miraculous! Not crass and gaudy shows of supranatural power in which the laws of nature are ignored, but true miracles of the everyday sort: the miracle of life going on; the miracle of something and not nothing; the miracle of purpose—*sub contraria specie*. The dismal portents of the present become, miraculously, portals to an undeserved future. No truth is heard in the land and prophecy feels itself utterly alone, yet seven thousand have not bowed the knee to Baal. Israel is occupied by arrogant men, and in Jerusalem a puppet king of the Jews does their bidding, but in a village a child is born in a stable. The little band is scattered, their hopes dashed by the execution of their leader as a common criminal—and "we had hoped that he was the one to redeem Israel. . . ."

Our tradition names this *providentia Dei,* the providence of God. It also names it *grace.* Grace is not nature. As for nature— that is, as for what *we* do, and what is done by all creatures—it is not in itself terribly promising. Even when it is "meant for good" it can produce questionable and even devastating results. And much of it, like the dark deed of Joseph's brothers, is not meant for good! Faith, therefore, does not account for the redeeming patterns and directions that it sees in history by pointing either to human intentions or human deeds. Faith confesses rather that *God* is able and willing, using the raw stuff of our deeds and misdeeds in much the same manner as God used the primeval chaos to create a world, to alter the course of things, to provide a way into the future. Finitude as such does not provide this way, is not "provident"; but the finite "has a capacity for the infinite" *(finitum capax infiniti).* Touched by the eternal, time gives birth to wonders of which neither ancient astrology nor modern futurology can know. [13]

History, then, has a capacity for being changed from within; and for the Christian the incarnation is the seed of radical change, of the new. It introduces into the process of time a new future, so that the future of death and oblivion which has been bequeathed to the historical process by distorted and confused human freedom is challenged by a radical alternative: life instead of death. *Abundant* life.

The second doctrinal concept that we need to review as we consider the conquest of suffering from within is the doctrine of the Trinity. While this is not a biblical concept (the New Testament uses neither the term *Trinity* nor most of the technical language associated with the doctrine; it only leaves us with the *problem* of the Trinity, to which early Christianity had then to address itself), it is, in its best theological articulations, strictly continuous with the biblical message. For it is in the last analysis nothing more— nor less—than an extension and elaboration of the same scriptural insistence that the tabernacle of God is with humanity.

Jürgen Moltmann, more sensitively than most other theologians of our time, has spelled out the linkage between the Trinity, the incarnation, and the cross. It was never the intention of the incarnation dogma in its responsible expressions to claim simply that "Jesus *is* God"; this in fact was identified by the early councils as a heretical view, put forward especially by the modalistic Monar-chians. But it *was* the intention of incarnational theology to say that Jesus—precisely this human being (*vere homo*) in all of his earthly vulnerability—is truly God-in-our-midst (*vere Deus*), that God is not other than this, that God's nature and intention is not other than what they are declared to be in and through this One.

> When the crucified Jesus is called "the image of the invisible God," the meaning is that *this* is God, and God is like *this*. God is not greater than he is in this humiliation. God is not more glorious than he is in this self-surrender. God is not more powerful than he is in this helplessness. God is not more divine than he is in this humanity.[14]

The doctrine of the divine triunity, like that of the incarnation, is misconstrued as soon as it becomes interesting in itself. Had the fundamental matrix of the evolution of trinitarian theology con-tinued to be that of the Hebraic understanding of the divine Being, the kind of metaphysical-speculative approach which did in fact color its development could not have been dominant. For Hebraic theology manifests very little, if any, interest in the interior life of the deity. Its thrust is always towards God's relatedness with creation and, though the prophetic tradition of Israel is keenly aware of the divine otherness, its manner of treating God's transcendence is entirely different from the theme of transcendence pursued in the tradition of Athens. God's *discontinuity* with creation is not under-stood by Judaism in physical (spatial or even temporal) terms but in terms of righteousness, that is, ethically. It is part of the divine transcendence that Yahweh wills to be *so close* to creation, to be immanent, to be "your God," in short, to love. In contrast to the human reluctance to love, and fear of proximity—transcending pre-cisely our human attempt to be alone, autonomous, self-sufficient—the God of the Bible goes to unheard-of lengths to achieve com-munion with us, even *union*, in a covenant closer than marriage. Not God's distance but God's bridging of the distance—this is God's transcendence; in this is God *totaliter aliter*. As in the Zen tale cited at the outset of this study, it is God's weeping with us that constitutes God's being "beyond" us and beyond our expectations of God.

The Trinity, at base, is nothing more—nor less—than a doctrinal device or symbol for affirming just this good news of "the beyond in the midst of life" (Bonhoeffer). As Moltmann has stated the matter elsewhere:

> To recognize God in the crucified Christ means to grasp the trinitarian history of God, and to understand oneself and this whole world with Auschwitz and Viet Nam, with race-hatred and hunger, as existing in the history of God. God is not dead, death is in God. God suffers by us. He suffers with us. Suffering is in God. . . . God does not ultimately reject, nor is he ultimately rejected, rejection is within God. . . . When he brings his history to completion, his suffering will be transformed into joy, and thereby our suffering as well.[15]

The theology of Bethlehem and Golgotha—that is, of the enfleshment and the cross-bearing of the divine Word—directs us from the lonely and morbid contemplation of our own real suffering to the suffering of God in solidarity with us. Because God is "with us," our suffering, though abysmally real, is given both a new perspective and a new meaning—and the prospect of transformation. Not through power but through participation; not through might but through self-emptying, "weak" love is the burden of human suffering engaged by the God of this faith tradition. *Engaged* is, I think, the right word. It implies that God meets, takes on, takes into God's *own* being, the burden of our suffering, not by a show of force which could only destroy the sinner with the sin, but by assuming a solidary responsibility for the contradictory and confused admixture that is our life. God incarnate and crucifed bears with us and for us the "weight of sin" that is the root cause of our suffering, and that we cannot assume in our brokenness.

But here theology must go to art for help—a fact which is as much demonstrated by the stolidness of soteriological doctrine which does *not* turn to art as by the current trend to enucleate a narrative theology.[16] There are numerous tales both in classical and in contemporary literature which can enrich our understanding of Christology and soteriology[17] but when it comes to the conquest from within, I know of no more profound expression of the mystery of Christ's priestly act of solidarity with suffering humanity than the one presented by the Japanese novelist Shusaku Endo in his book *Silence*. [18]

Endo's work in its entirety, including his perceptive *Life of Jesus*, [19] is a protest against the power-orientated Western "gospel" that was brought to his native land by the Jesuits in the 16th century in the wake of Western armies and Western trade (the Dutch). On the positive side, Endo's art is an attempt to discern an alternative to the gospel of power; and it is not incidental that in this search he has been aided by various expressions of the *theologia crucis* tradition, that "thin tradition" [20] which has functioned like an antiphon beneath the high triumph song of Christendom. Although he is a Roman Catholic, [21] Endo's greatest contemporary theological influence seems to have come from the Protestant theologian Kazoh Kitamori. Kitamori, whose constant theme is "the pain of God," has provided many oriental Christians with an entree to the Judeo-Christian tradition that is accessible to oriental experience in a way that the Western *theologia gloriae* is not. "The pain of God," writes Kitamori, "this is the essence of God, this is the heart of God!" [22] In this vein, and (as oriental students of Endo's work have told me) in the tradition of the school of Antioch, which over against the Alexandrians stressed the *humanity* of Jesus, Shusaku Endo attempts in all that he writes to depict a deity whose primary attribute is "suffering love" rather than omnipotence.

> The God of love, the love of God—the words come easy. The most difficult thing is to bear witness in some tangible way to the truth of the words. In many cases love is actually powerless. Love has in itself no immediate tangible benefits. We are therefore hard put to find where the love of God can be, hidden behind tangible realities which rather suggest that God does not exist, or that he never speaks, or that he is angry. [23]

Endo's novel *Silence* [24] is set in the so-called Christian century of Japan (i.e., the mid-16th to mid-17th centuries C.E.) when Western missionaries in the wake of Western military and commercial invasions of that realm made a concerted effort to convert the as-yet ununited country to Christianity. A young priest, Rodrigues, leaves his native Portugal to take his Christ to the "swamp of Japan," and at the same time to trace, if possible, the fate of his revered teacher, a famous Jesuit theologian who had preceded him to the Orient and is reputed to have apostatized.

The priest Rodrigues exemplifies a genuine and high devotion to the Christ whose image dominates the popular Catholicism of the age. He spends his hours of prayer and meditation contemplating the face of his Christ: a face that is noble, serene, unearthly in its beauty, its strength of character—full of the very qualities that the young priest himself wishes, in imitation of Christ, to possess: conviction, total trust, certainty of aim, strength of spirit, the willingness to suffer and die for one's beliefs.

Yet the communication between the priest and his Christ is all one-way. The Christ remains for Rodrigues a *visual* image. He does not speak. He is. . . silent. And as Rodrigues, having reached Japan, finds himself in increasingly difficult straits, the victim of a national uprising against the Christians; as he becomes in the course of time the fugitive, the hunted criminal, the enemy, and finally the prisoner and potential martyr, this divine silence is increasingly deafening.

At last, finally cornered by the anti-Christian nationalists, he is asked (as was his famous teacher) to renounce his faith. Naturally he refuses, still hoping to emulate the glorious Christ of his meditations: hoping even for martyrdom, which will surely bring him into the very presence of God! But instead of a triumphant martyrdom, Rodrigues is routinely imprisoned. In the darkness of his cell, he learns that the distracting noises which have kept him from sleep and which he believed to be the drunken snoring of his guards are really emanating from the mouths of native Japanese Christians—people who have already apostatized many times—who are hung upside down over pits of excrement, their heads half buried, and so breathing only with the greatest difficulty and pain. They will be kept in this position, Rodrigues is told, until he renounces his Christ. The priest's still heroic, though battered, faith is being bought (as such faith has so often been bought!) at the expense of other human beings with little courage and no influence.

Under the impact of this awareness, Rodrigues is again invited to apostatize. The method is simple—it has always been simple, like the pinch of incense on the flame to honor the genius of the emperor, the method applied to the early Christians. In this case it is more interesting, though, and more direct: a metal image of the Christ, a sort of *bas relief* called a *fumie* is brought before the convict. He is instructed to put his foot upon the face of this Christ, to trample on it, to grind it ever so slightly with his toe.

The face of Christ as it appears in the *fumie* placed before Rodrigues does not at all resemble the face that the young priest has been trained in his seminary to adore and to emulate—any more, in fact, than it resembles, by now, his own haggard, hunted, prematurely aged face. The face in the *fumie* has already been trampled on many times, and it is horribly distorted from the grinding toes and the dirt of many feet. Still, the priest hesitates: to step on this face, even though it has been shaped by pagans and trampled on by the faithless, is for him to deny the whole bent of his Western piety. He recalls, however, the hanging prisoners, whose lives depend upon his decision, and it is in this agony of existential torment that suddenly, miraculously (but in that everyday sense) he hears the voice of the Christ, speaking to him out of the *fumie*: "Trample, trample, it is for this that I have come. Trample!"

The silence of God is broken. The triumphing Christ of Christendom could only function as a model—really, an impossible model of strength—by which the weak and failing priest could only be judged. Only a Christ upon whom the sufferer could cast the impossible burden of his suffering could break the silence of God.

In a statement about the suffering of the Christ which could be a commentary on this saga, C. S. Song has written:

> The suffering of Jesus the messiah has removed all human barriers. It makes God available to human beings and enables them to be part of the divine mystery of salvation. The depths of God's suffering ought to be the place where all persons, despite their different backgrounds and traditions, can recognize one another as fellow pilgrims in need of God's saving power. Religious traditions tend to alienate strangers. Ecclesiastical structures become walls surrounding faithful believers.

Doctrinal precision creates heretics and infidels. Even expressions of religious devotion in worship and liturgy make peoples alien to one another.

Suffering, however, does not need to be transmitted by traditions; it is present here and now, as well as in the past. It needs no ecclesiastical sanction; it comes and goes without anyone's bidding. It does not have to be defended doctrinally; it is our daily experience. It cannot be worshipped and adored by fine liturgy; it is to be endured and not to be idolized. To be human is to suffer, and God knows that. That is why God suffers too. Suffering is where God and human beings meet. It is the one place where all persons—kings, priests, paupers, and prostitutes—recognize themselves as frail and transient human beings in need of God's saving love. Suffering brings us closer to God and God closer to us. Suffering, despite all its inhumanity and cruelty, paradoxically enables humans to long for humanity, find it, treasure it, and defend it with all their might.[25]

God suffers because God would be *with us*, and suffering is our condition. Echoing Luther's last written words ("Wir sind Bettler, dass ist wahr . . ." [We are beggars, that is certain]), the Roman Catholic theologian Johannes Metz writes: "We are all beggars. We are all members of a species that is not sufficient unto itself. We are all creatures plagued by unending doubts and restless, unsatisfied hearts. Of all creatures, we are the poorest and the most incomplete. Our needs are always beyond our capacities, and we only find ourselves when we lose ourselves."[26] This being our state, God's redemptive work in our behalf is given its *modus operandi*, its way: it cannot be the way of the sword; it cannot even be the way of friendship, filial devotion (*philia*). Both of these ways are proposed by the disciples, notably by Peter; both must be rejected—and forcefully (Matt. 16:23f. and par.; John 21:15f.). It must be the way of the cross, "the Son of man must suffer . . . ."

Draw back, physician. . . . Healing is not for you. . . . Without your wound where would your power be? It is your very remorse that makes your low voice tremble in the hearts of men. The very angels themselves cannot persuade the wretched and blundering children of earth as can one human being broken on the wheels of living. In Love's service only the wounded soldiers can serve.[27]

Like Peter, who had finally to be told straightforwardly that his way was nothing less than satanic, there is much in us that would prefer it to be otherwise. We are attracted to the heroic, and to strong ideals like friendship, esprit de corps. This is even accentuated for all of us who belong to triumphant cultures.[28] As Koyama says, "A strong Western civilization and the 'weak' Christ cannot be reconciled harmoniously. Christ must become 'strong.' A strong United States and a strong Christ!"[29] A Christ trampled upon, "broken on the wheels of living," is not the Christ whose praises are sung by electronic religion or, for that matter, in the more bourgeois sanctuaries of our nations. Yet beneath our surprise and distaste for a "broken" Christ, beneath the skandalon of the cross, there is for us too—for the affluent, the wise of the world, the "have" peoples—a certain basic relief in meeting the broken Christ. If we let it, this relief can turn to gratitude and even joy. For we too know, in the depths of our souls, that we are lost and broken—that "We are all beggars."

The conquest of suffering begins just here, with this relief, this gratitude, this joy. To find oneself befriended in one's suffering is not only a more believable "answer" to the pain of suffering; it is also more profound. The world abounds in physicians who promise to heal every wound . . . from the heights of their personal and professional detachment. Of answers to the "problem of suffering" there is in fact no lack! Only, all of them flounder on the rocks of reality, at the cry of one starving or derelict child. The only satisfying answer is the answer given to Job—the answer that is no answer but is the presence of an Answerer. It does not matter that the Answerer brings more questions than answers; for the answer is not the words as such but the living Word—the Presence itself. The answer is the permission that is given in this Presence to be what one is, to express the dereliction that belongs to one's age and place, to share all of it with this Other: to trample! Faith is the communion of the spirit with this fellow sufferer, this One whose otherness lies in the fact that he will not turn away in the face of one's failure, or the failure of one's world.

This communion with the "pain of God" gives to the community of faith a courage which is not like the courage of the Stoic. For it does not merely resign itself to pain and walk on in silent, lonely nobility; rather, *it seeks out other sufferers.* For in the encounter with "the crucified God" this faith has learnt, is learning, that the *sharing* of suffering is the beginning of its transformation to wholeness and joy. The suffering *of the church,* the theme of our next chapter, has its foundations in this courage.

D. Acceptance and Transformation

"Give us," runs the famous prayer of Reinhold Niebuhr, "grace to accept with serenity the things that cannot be changed, courage to change the things which should be changed, and the wisdom to distinguish the one from the other."

The resurrection-courage that is given to faith in the presence of the crucified Christ is a courage both of acceptance and of transformation. Some things must be accepted. But Christian acceptance is not an easy resignation to the status quo. For in the ambiguous world where wheat and tares grow up together, where good and evil are impossibly interwoven, it cannot readily be discerned that a given experience or fact belongs quite simply to the divine ordering of things, the reality of creaturely existence, the suffering of becoming.

That death, for instance, inheres in the structures of finitude seems both reasonable and scriptural. But premature death? the deaths of hungry children? the deaths of persons on account of that dread cancer, 80% of which is said to be caused by environmental factors? the death of whole species of plants and animals on account of the increasing mechanization of life and the pollution of the biosphere?

Loneliness too, we have said, belongs to creaturely existence. It is in some real sense the *conditio sine qua non* of love, even the love of God. Rodrigues might never have heard the speaking Christ if he had not known the silence of God. Loneliness should be accepted. But the loneliness of the aged in our youth-orientated societies? of prisoners in our prisons? of people without work in our cities and towns?

Limits, too, belong to the creaturely condition. From another perspective they are, we said, not limits at all, but boundaries defining the possibilities of our legitimate glory as human beings. They should be accepted, and gladly. But the limits experienced daily by the two-thirds undernourished? the limits felt by women, by racial minorities, by the handicapped in a society which worships "fitness"?

To the suffering of becoming there also belongs a certain anxiety. It inheres in finitude. It has its place—even an important place. Without it we might not have war, but we would probably not have civilization either. A certain degree of anxiety in the adolescent does not worry the wise parent. Such anxiety should be accepted, even with gratitude. But the anxiety of a meaningless life which drives alarming numbers of young persons in Canadian and American societies to suicide? the anxiety of those who at 50 or 60 are told there is no longer any work for them to do? the anxiety of a civilization psychically numbed by "future shock"?

There is a danger in all theory, all theology. It is that the mind will find a sort of "sabbath rest" in the theory itself. This is understandable. The mind needs rest. Nothing is accomplished by a mind that is only restless, that finds no place to perch for a moment and contemplate the course of its flight. When it comes to a searing question like God and human suffering, a question that in fragmented and concrete ways touches most of us every day, we need to perch for a time on the resting place of Scripture and tradition, so that we can fly again.

But it is for the purpose of flying that we rest. Theology leads inevitably (if it is *true* theology—*vere theologia!*) to ethics, the gospel to the law, the indicative to the imperative. To contemplate the Christological doctrine of a God who identifies with us in our brokenness; to find this satisfying, even moving; and then to close the book of reflection and go on living as before—this is a travesty of theology. Encountering the crucified Christ (as Peter is supposed to have done on his way *out* of burning Rome!) must mean wrestling with decisions about the *actual* suffering we encounter in our world. What is to be accepted, what can and must be changed? Where is transformation possible?

. . . The call of the gospel to its proclaimers consists in discerning the signs of the times in word and action so that people within the circumstances of their own lives may respond to the impetus of the Holy Spirit and move life in the direction of its glorious destiny in the kingdom of God.[30]

The line between thought and deed is here invisible. It would be a misuse of the great privilege of theology if, befriended by a suffering God, we were to take refuge in the comfort of this gospel away from the actual suffering of the world in which we find ourselves, whose destiny is to become fully God's kingdom.

The gospel of Jesus as the cross-bearer, the bearer of unbearable burdens, introduces all who hear it to a process: the process of bearing the burdens of others. To *know* that God participates in human suffering—*really* to know this—is to do it! To *believe* that nothing can separate us from this participating love—*really* to believe this—is to accept the gracious invitation of this crucified God to participate in our Lord's participation. The church is—*we* are!—a vital part of God's response to human suffering. For how many will the adequacy of God's response depend upon who *we* are?

5

The Church:
Community of
Suffering and Hope

Introduction: Faith, Religion, and Suffering

There is more about the suffering of the church in the newer Testament's writings than about any other single ecclesiastical theme. Not only is the suffering of the church the specific motif of whole documents (notably 2 Corinthians, 1 Peter, and the Apocalypse of John) but it looms large in all the literature of the newer Testament. In this the specifically Christian Scriptures are only picking up a constant theme of Israel's sacred writings and regarding it from the vantage point of the cross of Jesus. Historically, the developing *ecclesia* determined that its peculiar "marks" were those identified by the four adjectives (one, holy, catholic, and apostolic) cited in the Nicene Creed's article on the church: unity, holiness, catholicity, and apostolicity. But, said Martin Luther, even if all of these authenticating marks are present the body in question will not really be the church of Jesus Christ unless it bears about it the one truly indispensable mark, namely, "the holy cross"—by which Luther certainly did not mean the presence of crosses, jewelled or rough-hewn, with or without the *Christus* figure, but some real evidence of Christian participation in the sufferings of Christ in this world![1] In claiming this, Luther reflected (as at so many other points in his thinking) his intuitive and disciplined grasp of the Scriptures. For it is impossible to have any genuine impression of the biblical picture of "the people of God," whether of Israel or of the Christian *koinonia*, without coming to terms with the recurrent theme of the suffering of this people.

The question is, of course: *Why?* What kind of logic is it that worked its way towards such an insistence? Are we perhaps dealing here with a kind of corporate masochism? A martyr complex? Or is it perhaps a case of a people finding a posteriori theological "explanations" for the indubitable fact of its historic sufferings, its rejection by other peoples? "Beloved," writes the author of 1 Peter, "do not be surprised at the fiery ordeal which comes upon you to prove you, as though something strange were happening to you" (4:12). Do such passages suggest that the early Christians, taken by "surprise" at their harsh treatment by their non-Christian neighbors and fellow citizens, now search about for a religious rationale?

Such an explanation does not seem likely. For the theme of Christian suffering appears to have been one of the major motifs in the teachings of Jesus, predating therefore his own final humiliation and death, which, as the most salient feature of the gospel records, then becomes the principal paradigm for the life of the disciple community. Given the predominance of the theme both explicitly in Jesus' teaching and implicitly in his own destiny as our "pioneer" (Heb. 2:10) and "the first-born among many brethren" (Rom. 8:29), it would have been astonishing had the discussion of the church's suffering *not* been raised to prominence in the Gospels and Epistles. A "despised and rejected" Messiah followed by a train of worldly successful and socially "acceptable" disciples would be, to say the least, a non sequitur!

As it happened, of course, something like just such a non sequitur is what all too soon took shape in and *as* "the church." In a way, that, too, should not surprise us. The prospect of such an eventuality is, after all, already entertained by the writers of the newer Testament—presumably also by Jesus himself. It is entertained, namely, as *temptation!* And why would it not be? For the same theme permeates the older Testament's story of God's "chosen" ones, and the same dialectic of obedience and temptation is its constant leitmotiv. Israel is chosen, and there is a profound blessedness in its election. But the blessedness is not of the sort that human nature usually cherishes; so the prophets must ceaselessly remind the people that its *shalom* is inseparably linked with a vocation within history which will lead it again and again into wilderness, exile, rejection, defeat, and other forms of suffering.

The suffering of the Christ may have come as a surprise and a scandal to those who were anticipating a conquering Messiah, a new and better David. The earliest Christians were Jews who, no doubt, had themselves entertained such a triumphant denouement to the wanderings and sufferings of the people of Israel. But they discovered, through experience and reflection remarkably in keeping with Israel's prophetic tradition, that not even the Messiah could achieve the world's reconciliation and peace apart from a deep and sacrificial participation in its pain. For "the enemy" that had to be overcome was no flesh-and-blood thing but a roaring lion prowling about within the collective spirit of humanity itself—"principalities and powers" greater than, but inseparable from, the very beings who were the object of the divine *agape.* If these Christian interpreters superimposed upon the figure of the expected, conquering Messiah the "wounded healer" of Deutero-Isaiah, was it then, after all, so novel a thing? Or was it not in fact the consequence of a long-acknowledged prophetic understanding, namely, the understanding of sin and evil as a reality so complex, so impossibly interwoven with the very fabric of the good in creation, that its separation from that good could only be achieved from within, as the begetting of a new and contrite spirit, a new heart, and so as a victory "hidden beneath its opposite"?

The cross, we have seen, could not be avoided by the Anointed One. It was the "must," the *necessitas,* inherent in this unlikely combination of a deeply alienated world and a yearning, determined, and compassionate Creator. The whole story of God's searching for the beloved, like Hosea's quest for his faithless wife or David's tragic longing for lost Absalom, involves this movement of the divine Being into the heart of the world's darkness. Thus, as Karl Barth aptly said, Israel's story is the story of a people "hastening towards Golgotha";[2] for all whom this searching God involves in the search must have a part in God's own suffering love for what is lost. This is the only *blessedness* that the people of God can expect. It is, however, truly blessed, because it is rooted in truth: the truth of the world's pain, the truth of the "pain of God," and the truth of God's free and loving determination to heal the creation through the solidary assumption of its pain.

This blessedness (the "beatitude" that Jesus describes in every one of his famous sentences in the Sermon on the Mount) is contrary to the kind of divine favor that religion courts all the way from Babel to the Crystal Cathedral. It is typical of "religion" as distinct from faith that it seeks to gain (by storm, said Jesus!) the kingdom of heaven without the poverty of spirit which is the prerequisite of such a search (Matt. 5:3); comfort without "mourning" (5:4);[3] the inheritance of the earth without the meekness of the dispossessed (5:5); the satisfaction of all senses without hunger and thirst for unattained righteousness, justice (5:6); mercy for self without compassion for "those who trespass against *us*" (5:7); the beatific vision without striving for purity of heart (5:8); status, eternally, without the struggle for earth's peace (5:9); the consolations of immortality without persecution, slander, rejection (5:10, 11). Given the biblical testimony to at least a thousand years of such religious longing, now complemented by almost two thousand additional years of Christian triumphalism, we ought to need no further reminder of the basic distinction between religion and faith. It is the propensity of religion to avoid, precisely, suffering: to have light without darkness, vision without trust, and risk, hope without an ongoing dialog with despair—in short, Easter without Good Friday. Always, in an infinite variety of forms but finally with the same monotonous motive underneath the forms, religion demands the *securitas* of those who "have arrived" and spurns "the Way." If in the fourth century of the common era the Emperor Constantine provided a method through which Christianity could achieve the status of "institution" and slough off the vulnerable condition of "movement," the blame ought not to be placed on the emperor alone. He was acting simply, pragmatically, for the preservation of the imperium. Constantine only did for Christianity what in less impressive ways other, smaller rulers had already been doing for Israel (see the whole dispute over the kingship!)—namely, give it a place in the scheme of things earthly which, with a little adjustment of its expectations, it could substitute for the "sabbath rest," the "kingdom of God," towards which in its historical infancy it could only hesitantly move. The religious *tentatio*, as we should know from the biblical testimony, is never far from the tentative faith of "the elect." Historical events like the Establishment of Christianity may provide occasions for this temptation to rise to the surface, but they do not have to provide the temptation itself. It is and always has been faith's fast companion. And the reason is obvious: the *doubt* that is part of faith is directed quite explicitly towards the suffering into which faith knows itself to be beckoned. Like Peter "the rock," whose spontaneous confession ("You are the Christ!") was immediately followed by an equally spontaneous rejection of the way of the cross, the church has always felt an enormous pull towards a comfortable and comforting religion free of suffering.

But why? Why is *faith's* way the way of the cross? Is it a purely arbitrary thing that this is so? Is the God of Israel and of the church of a mind with those who believe that suffering is a good thing— reducing human pride, presumption, and arrogance, cultivating patience and endurance, and making for great art?

Perhaps there is some truth in such assertions. From the perspective of a lax and permissive society that has seen something of the sloth and boredom engendered by affluence we are today less prone than were our parents to ridicule Victorian morality, which abounded in aphorisms supporting the beneficial nature of pain. But whatever practical insights there may be in such sentiments, they are finally not commensurate with the biblical message at its most basic. They may reflect, or even be lifted from, certain biblical literature (notably, the book of Proverbs) which is able to provide practical wisdom for daily life. But at bottom biblical faith has no sympathy for masochism. It is strictly for life and against death. "The cross is not to be loved!"[4] If therefore the people of God are called to suffer in the world, it is not because suffering as such is beneficial. It is, rather, because the "logic of the cross" presupposes as its *telos* (inner aim) precisely "life"—but a life of such abundance that it can be entered only by way of an encounter with that which seems to negate and really does negate life.

The explication of this hypothesis, however, must involve us in a more complex discussion. For that purpose we shall reflect now on the suffering of the people of God under two categories which will recapitulate and advance the discussion of suffering in the previous chapters of this study: suffering as the courage to become, and suffering as the soteriological *conquest* of suffering.

A. The Courage to Become

The life that the God of the gospel wills for human beings— "abundant," "eternal" life—contains as such no hint of ambiguity, no dialectic of light and darkness, yes and no. It is all light, all affirmative (2 Cor. 1:19-20; James 1:17). But the question is, how can *we*, who *are* full of ambiguity and duplicity, who *are* children of darkness, who *are* "being-towards-death" (Heidegger)—how can we come to this light, affirm this affirmation, enter this life? Clearly, it is not a simple matter: purity in exchange for sin, light for darkness, life for death—like Aladdin's "new lamps for old." The Scriptures know that it is much more difficult than that. There is a cost involved (Matt. 19:23), a narrow path to be trod (Matt. 7:14), an "impossibility" to be encountered (Matt. 19:26). This is not because the authors of the Scriptures, like strict disciplinarians, enjoy making things difficult. The difficulty of accepting the life that is offered resides in us:

> 'Tis ye, 'tis your estrangèd faces
> That miss the many-splendoured thing.
> (Francis Thompson, "The Kingdom of God," stanza 4)

To begin to move towards real life means, for us, to come face-to-face with that within and around us which bars us from life. Not because God is who—in biblical perspective—God is, but because we are who and what we are, ". . . facing the God who is really

God means facing also the absolute threat of non-being."[5] The good news that *life* is available to those who sit in darkness and the shadow of death has as its corollary the less enticing news that in order to avail ourselves of this life we shall have to know ourselves numbered among those who sit in darkness and the shadow of death! This prompted Kierkegaard to remark that

> Christianity is certainly not melancholy, it is, on the contrary, glad tidings—for the melancholy. To the frivolous it is certainly not glad tidings, for it wishes first of all to make them serious.[6]

The gospel calls us to a great and profound seriousness about our condition as human beings, and there are many who would prefer to avoid that seriousness. For to enter reflectively and earnestly into the reality of one's (fallen) creaturehood is certainly the first step in "taking up one's cross."

In order to delve a little more deeply into this first aspect of the suffering into which the Christian is initiated, we need once more to recall the earlier discussion of suffering as becoming. From the perspective of creational theology, we affirmed, suffering must be seen as pertaining not only to the burdensome moral and tragic predicament introduced into the human situation through distorted freedom, but also to the creaturely condition itself. There is, we said, a sense in which existence as such contains dimensions which human beings are likely to experience as suffering. Being called into creaturehood means to "suffer" these conditions—that is, to let them be, to give our assent to them, to affirm that they are both necessary and good, part of the essential *goodness* of creation itself.

Each of the four conditions of creaturehood that we named is in the service of the good and virtually indispensable to our greatest good: the exposure to loneliness is a necessary prelude to the discovery and joy of human communion; without consciousness of our finite limits we should be incapable of recognizing transcendence; temptation is the presupposition of freedom to choose what is good; and anxiety is a goad to inventiveness, making us dissatisfied with ease, but providing as well the necessary contrast to comfort, peace, and contentment. It is not in the spirit of our tradition to celebrate these creaturely conditions in a mindless, Dionysian way; for they represent genuine limits, and biblical faith knows them to be points of entry for the truly perilous. Neither, however, does the tradition of Jerusalem bid us simply to resign ourselves to the fact of our creaturehood as if it were a less-than-enviable state, and with stoic courage to accept these and all such "indignities." We are asked, rather, to affirm this creaturely condition with gratitude, to take upon ourselves knowingly the limits that it entails, and to find in those same limits the graceful boundaries that mark out the territory within which we may discover our authentic humanity. We are asked to say yes to the dynamic unfolding of life, to enter expectantly our pilgrimage from birth to death, and to find in each stage of this journey some new unveiling of its depth and its wonder. We are asked to savor life "daily" ("Give us this day our daily bread. . .")— neither to resent the swift passage of time nor to wish today to-morrow, but to enter into time with a willing heart, to *be* the creatures of time that we in fact are, that is, to *become*.

If there is a dimension of suffering in this (and at least from our existential position "east of Eden" we cannot see it otherwise), it is the suffering of change and growth, of movement, of going on and not looking back, of living in the Now. In short, it is the suffering of life itself. And it is precisely *life itself* that we fear and resist! It was nothing else than life itself—with its day-by-dayness, its risk, its call for absolute trust, its readiness to become—that prompted the pair in the garden to reach out for possession, per-manence, security, "knowledge"! Something in them preferred the known path that leads to death to the unknown adventure called life. They felt they were not up to it. The trust it required of them proved too great. So, wishing to *possess* their life, they lost its essence—which is gift, given daily.

"And they knew that they were naked"! Humanity in its retreat from life is humanity overwhelmed by the pathos of finitude. It does not find any gracious boundaries in its temporality, its mate-riality, but only circumscription, confinement, frustration. Time it sees as its taskmaster, the body as its tomb. Loneliness turns to alienation, the consciousness of mortality to a fixation upon death

(*Todestrieb!*), temptation to obsession with the self, anxiety to despair. And since humanity cannot exist wittingly under such a "weight of sin" it becomes the willing prey to illusion. Whoever can offer it half-credible alternatives to reality, on whose basis it can seem to possess its being without the pain of becoming, is sure to achieve a hearing among humankind in flight from life.

It is just to this humanity that Jesus the crucified one speaks. Unlike the false shepherds who lure us away with their promises of security, promises echoing always the whisperings of that primordial tempter of Eden, the Good Shepherd speaks his word of invitation only as one who has first assumed, fully, our condition. With us he is caused to experience loneliness (for him, forsakenness!); with us he must taste the limits of the finite (for him, a *kenosis*); like us he is tempted—and "in *every* respect"; for us he must know anxiety (and for him is it not "naked anxiety" [Tillich]?). Only from within, only as the Shepherd who "lays down *his* life for the sheep" does this one issue to us his invitation to life: "Come, follow me." "Come to me, all who labor and are heavy laden, and I will give you rest. Take my yoke upon you, and learn from me. . .for my yoke is easy, and my burden is light" (Matt. 11:28-30).

It is, we have said in the language of theology and exegesis, the invitation to discipleship; and that is true. But first it is simply an invitation to *life*. When it is repeated by us in our vocation as Christ's ministers and missioners, this invitation should not be rendered in a sacrosanct or merely pious manner; for it is not an invitation to heaven but to earth, not to church but to life in the world. It is an invitation and permission to take up in all consciousness, and in gratitude, the *creaturely* life that is our destiny. To become who we are.

If once it were grasped that Jesus' call to us is a call to follow him into *life*—an invitation to *creaturehood*—we could disabuse ourselves of much of the false piety and idealism that has been so consistently associated with the teachings of our Lord, notably the Sermon on the Mount. In all that it contains, this compilation of sayings amounts to nothing more nor less than an invitation to risk the life of the creature, to accept gratefully and joyfully its conditions, to enter into the life of the world despite its seeming antinomies and disappointments and terrors. It is an invitation to take on willingly and wittingly—to "suffer"—the conditions that the lilies and birds of the air inherit as a matter of course. Nothing is denied about the creaturely life. It *does* involve the experience of being alone; even in our prayer we must know this solitariness (Matt. 6:5f.). It *does* imply very definite limits: not "one cubit" can be added to the span of life (6:27), and possessions are all illusory (6:19). It *does* contain recurrent temptations—lust, hate, envy (7:1). And it *does* present, each day, the occasion for engrossing anxiety (6:34, etc.). Jesus the teacher is not an ideologue. The life to which he invites us is real life. Nothing is hidden from view or smoothed over. His own life is not the stuff out of which utopias are made, and his teaching is as sober as his life. No one can read the Sermon on the Mount seriously and come away thinking that it is just "a lovely ideal." The world that is depicted in it is the world in which we already live and move and have our being. We are not being offered a different world, a supposedly "better" world. We are only being invited to assume a different posture in relation to the world that is already there.

And because this invitation is being extended by one who, though teacher, is "more than teacher," it is itself more than a simple invitation. It is a matter of permission and not only of exhortation. It is gospel before it is law. The imperative in it (and there *is* an imperative in it!) is founded upon the indicative behind it. That indicative is the grace of which, through cross and resurrection, through Spirit and Baptism, through Word and Sacrament we are being made recipients. Through our gracious incorporation into the life of the one who submits willingly to death and through our dying with him—dying to what is false and pretentious in human self-seeking; dying to our own fear of living!—we are enabled to accept his invitation to life (Romans 6). That is to say, we are being given the grace to become the creatures that we are; to trust the Lord and Giver of life in place of the futile attempt to *possess* life. Through our proximity to this one, who did not grasp at transcendence but found all the glory that he needed in obedience to his creaturely "sonship," we are learning the courage to become.

To employ now that other term by which the invitation to life is known, we are learning to live the life of the disciple community.

To the creaturely suffering of becoming, Christian tradition juxtaposes the grace and challenge of discipleship. Discipleship is the working out of our humanity within the freedom of the gospel and under the guidance of the divine Spirit. As such, the call to discipleship is not a summons to some exceptional, unearthly, or supraworldly rigor. We are not asked to become gods or angels or even (in the popular sense) saints, but only human beings. *Truly human!* Discipleship means the cultivation of a disciplined acceptance and exploration of the conditions of our creaturehood. It means responding to the grace that permits us to become who we are—that is, to cease pretending to be the more-than-human or less-than-human beings we are tempted to be.

There is, therefore (as Bonhoeffer long ago instructed us) a *cost* involved in discipleship. It cannot be undertaken without suffering. But the suffering is not more than we can bear as friends of the crucified one who continues with us and in our midst. It is not a heroic suffering to which we are called, but only a suffering that belongs to our creaturehood. We have long been acquainted with it—though we have avoided, repressed, and resented its reality. To be obedient to this call, all that we have to do is to let go of our vain ambition to be more than human (pride) and our equally vain flight from responsible humanity (sloth). We have only to become honest, to allow ourselves to become real. Discipleship means sacrificing all the little defenses and strategems by which we shield ourselves from life, and accepting freely and gladly the gift of life *as it is given to us.* If it is costly it is because we, of course, want to have life on our own terms still, want to retain our hard-won securities, our habitual detachment from time. "Do not be anxious about your life . . ." says the one who invites us to participate in the fullness of living daily; but we continue to prefer our cherished and familiar anxieties to trust in his gift. Certainly we cling to the old way, the "old Adam," storing up treasures where moth and rust corrupt and erecting bulwarks of superfluous and spurious righteousness against an imagined future! Certainly we resist the new, open-ended way, the way of hope, and turn the church into a sanctuary and hiding place from the world.

But the wrestling Spirit "helps us in our weakness," and we help one another as well. The "dividing walls of hostility" by which our life had been characterized are giving way to mutuality. Alienation, that distorted form of our creaturely solitariness, is giving way to reconciliation. In place of preoccupation with death—the exaggerated consciousness of our finitude—we are finding that our boundaries are less fixed than we had imagined: there is perhaps no boundary to the love that is surrounding us! Not death itself! From that debilitating concern for self which had taken hold of us, being tempted, we are beginning to know what it means to lose ourselves, to become sufficiently nonchalant about our personal condition to see the others with their needs—our neighbors. And though we are by no means free from anxiety, we are less prone to despair; for now our anxiety is challenged by hope, and we do not think this hope will disappoint us in the long run.

We have not finished this course, to be sure; but we are on the way. "We are not yet, but we shall be. It has not yet happened, but it is the way. Not everything shines and sparkles as yet, but everything is getting better" (Luther). We do not know *what* we shall be. But we know already something of the courage to become.

B. Suffering as Participation and Transformation

The second aspect of the suffering of the church is its participation in the suffering of Christ *for the world*. In the preceding chapter we reminded ourselves that the only "answer" that biblical faith provides to the problem of human suffering is the presence of One who shares human suffering, who bears its unbearable consequences, who makes a conquest of its causes from within.[7] At the conclusion of that discussion, however, we linked this suffering of the Christ with the life of the community which through the Holy Spirit he calls into existence. The newer Testament's response to human suffering is not a theoretical response; it is a matter of Christian *praxis*, and as such the foundation and paradigm for all Christian ethics.

To elaborate: The gospel which the church announces, while it certainly does not and must not have the church itself as its subject, nevertheless includes the church as object. It would be a theoretical "gospel" indeed were it simply the proclamation that through the sacrificial grace of God in Jesus Christ the suffering of the human race had been met and dealt with! The truth is, of course, that this is all too close to what empirical Christianity has frequently proclaimed: Jesus is the Answer! In him salvation has been achieved. Accept this message and your problems will be solved!

The classical theories of atonement have lent themselves all too readily to such reductionism. In the earliest of the two older types of atonement theology, as we have seen in the foregoing, the problem of human suffering is identified chiefly with demonic influence in the human sphere. This so-called ransom theory assumes that, since the fall, humanity has been oppressed by supramundane powers of evil over which it has little or no control. The work of the Christ is that of the rescuer or liberator, who (in classical expressions of the doctrine, through trickery) achieves a victory over the demonic, thus establishing a new situation for the human community and human history. It is not necessary to discard every facet of this soteriology; as we have seen, present-day forms of liberation theology are to some extent dependent upon certain motifs within it. But the objectivistic tenor of the theory in its classical expression not only suggests a cosmic struggle between good and evil in which humankind has no part, but it leaves unanswered the question: What then shall we say to the continued presence of evil structures and deeds, and the continuing agony of the race that is their consequence? Modern renditions of the theory which propose that this is merely the residue of evil and suffering are hardly convincing—especially to the victims!

The Anselmic soteriology which grasped the imagination of Western Christendom for nearly a millenium, and is still in all probability the dominant doctrinal presupposition of the Western church's response to human suffering, takes with greater seriousness (as we have seen) the complex relations between human suffering and human sinfulness. The sources of evil and suffering, it finds, are not so readily located outside the human will and psyche; therefore the question that it sets out to resolve is how God could forgive and remedy sin without destroying the sinner. Again, however, the theory opts for a response which virtually eliminates humanity from the scene of the resolution: God the Father accepts the "substitutionary" sacrifice of God the Son in lieu of the guilt incurred by sinful humanity; we then become the inheritors of "the benefits of his passion."

Obviously, the hold of this theory upon Western spirituality must mean that it has been able to speak meaningfully to many. So long as guilt could seem the most flagrant dimension of human suffering, a theory which addressed itself directly to the guilty conscience could achieve a hearing. But it is questionable, despite the obvious continuation of "guilt-complexes" in our society, whether the anxiety of guilt is the principal form of anxiety in our time. Tillich[8] and many others have identified the typical anxiety of our "age of anxiety" (Auden) as that of "meaninglessness and despair." Whether for this or for other reasons, the Anselmic-Calvinistic[9] soteriological response to human suffering has shown up in the 20th century as a highly theoretical one, and probably (for many of our contemporaries) even more remote than the ransom theory.[10] What precisely could it mean that Jesus *substitutes himself* for my sin, unholiness, and guilt?[11] What kind of *theology* (i.e., doctrine of God) does such a concept assume? Is God, then, *that* kind of God, deserving the irony of Dorothy L. Sayers, who in her *Christian Letters to a Post-Christian World,*[12] in answer to the question "What is meant by the Atonement?" answers (with more than a skeptical nod towards Messers. Anselm and Calvin):

> God wanted to damn everybody, but his vindictive sadism was sated by the crucifixion of his own Son, who was quite innocent, and, therefore, a particularly attractive victim. He now only damns people who don't follow Christ or who have never heard of him.

Both of these powerful traditions of atonement soteriology provide background assumptions for answers to the problem of human suffering. Under auspicious historical circumstances (as Christian history has made plain), each of these traditions has its special appeal. But they both remain theoretical-theological, and this comes to the fore as soon as the church emerges from the Constantinian situation. So long as the church functions in society as the primary cultic force and dispenser of spiritual cure, its various ministrations as the representative of such theories as these can seem effective and authoritative. But it is the effect of cult and custom to which they owe their continued life, rather than their internal power to convince. When, in the face of a rampant secularity, respect for cult and religious custom disappears or is greatly diminished, theory, as we can easily detect from a glance around the formerly "Christian" world today, will not stand on its own; and the church, which as purveyor of the theory may have enjoyed a certain prominence under the conditions of legal or cultural establishment, can seem particularly superfluous in the post-Christian world, especially where its soteriology is out of touch with both language and the human problematique.

What this situation raises by way of an inquiry for our present consideration is whether we might not recover something of the original Christian community's sense of *participation* in the sufferings of the Christ. Everything that we read about the suffering of the church in the newer Testament reminds us that the earliest Christians regarded their suffering as the mode and sign of their participation in the suffering of the Christ. Theirs was not a theoretical approach to suffering! Not only did they bear witness to a Messiah who participated fully in the human condition—who "though he was in the form of God. . . emptied himself. . . and became obedient unto death" (Phil. 2:6-8), but they regarded their own being as *soma Christou* as an ongoing participation in the Christ's participatory life.

> Do you not know that all of us who have been baptized into Christ Jesus were baptized into his death? We were buried therefore with him by baptism into death, so that as Christ was raised from the dead by the glory of the Father, we too might walk in newness of life (Rom. 6:3-4).

They understood their corporate life as an *incorporation* into his sufferings, a matter of being "conformed to" his image (Rom. 8:29), made sharers in his destiny as the One who through voluntarily assuming the burdensome suffering of the world would transform it for life. Their "witness" (*martys*) therefore implied their own profound involvement in the pain of the world—a pain which included not only the suffering of human beings but the groaning and travail of the whole creation (Rom. 8:22).[13] Martyrdom in the more literal sense was only an end factor, for some, in a martyriological *process* in which all were necessarily participants. To hear this gospel, to submit oneself for Baptism, to take the bread and the wine, to acknowledge the One head and the many members, to be caught up by the divine Spirit—all of this had for its object an existential identification with the crucified one which is as such also an identification with the world for whose sake he was crucified:

> Because the church is not an elite body separated from a doomed world, but a community placed in the midst of the cosmic community of creation, its task is not merely to win souls but to bear the burdens of creation to which it not only belongs, but to which it must also bear witness.[14]

In this biblical articulation of the relation between the church and Christ (the key doctrinal question of all ecclesiology), there is a strong mystical and sacramental dimension which Protestants are liable to find remote or even suspicious. Is it not possible, however, that as Christians who through half a century of practical ecumenicity have gained new access to the whole ("catholic") tradition, we might develop a greater appreciation for just this dimension? Is it not time for us to admit that much in classical Protestantism, extended beyond the moment of its prophetic impact and altered, as well, through its combination with modern rationalism, has had the effect of gravely undermining this *biblical* sense of the participation of the people of God in the process of divine redemption? It would not, I think, imply a renunciation of the Reformation to admit this. Clearly, the late medieval mishmash of superstition and sacrament, saints' days and indulgences and works-righteousness had to be challenged by a gospel which reasserted the centrality of the Christ and of sheer grace (*sola gratia!*). Moreover, the type of Catholicism which long after the Reformation (and in reaction to it) so concentrated upon the principle of identification in the relation between Christ and the church that it tended to confuse "the body" with "the head"—this, whether it is found in Catholic or reputedly Protestant circles,[15] has still to be challenged from the side of the *sola gratia, sola fide, per Christum solum* of the Reformation.

It is possible, however, to err also on the side of the principle of differentiation, and to make the Christ so transcendent, so discontinuous with his "body," that Christians come to conceive themselves as *recipients of* grace rather than *participants in* grace. While the strategic theology involved in the insistence that salvation is "through Christ alone" remains normative and can never be relinquished by any faith that intends to be biblically based, the danger of such an emphasis must also be kept in mind. It is the danger precisely of "cheap grace"—grace as theory, as principle, as doctrine: a grace which not only implies no inherent praxis but functions exactly to discourage participation.

"When Christ calls a man," wrote Bonhoeffer, "he bids him come and die";[16] and with this one sentence—elevated to the status of prophetic Truth by the life and death of its author—Bonhoeffer charged the church to recover an image of itself which Luther, for all his criticism of the *imitatio Christi* cultus, never lost sight of, namely, the image of itself as a people being conformed to the crucified Lord (*conformitas Christi*).[17] The "concrete mysticism" (Tillich) or "Christ mysticism" which caused Luther to see Christ in the needy neighbor[18] and to *suspect* all extrahuman or supernatural appearances of the divine may have been Luther's legacy from the medieval mystics; and as such it may have seemed quaint and anachronistic to that modern rationalism which already had begun to influence the Protestantism of Zwingli and others. But we have been all the way along the road that was opened up by the rationalists, and at its end many of us are ready to listen again to those of the past and present who know that life is more than food and the body more than raiment. The one-dimensionalism of the technological society has created its own vacuum. The sensitive ask again after transcendence, depth, and mystery. Trees are no longer just trees—or lumber, or paper! Bread is not only bread—in a world where so many die for want of it, and others from a surfeit of it. There is again in our midst the presence of the insistent thought of the ages, that the finite may indeed have some strange capacity for the infinite. Some, even among the practitioners of that discipline which in its infancy determined to confine itself to the finite—the *natural* sciences!—have begun to suspect that the finite is itself inexplicable on its own terms.[19] In such a time, it may be possible also for churches, so long the refuges of a slightly less conscpicuous one-dimensionalism, to recover something of that sense of the sacramental unity of all that is which could expedite their imaging of themselves as participants in a process of redemption which was, truly, "fulfilled" in the suffering of the Christ, but was not *ended* there!

> Now I rejoice in my sufferings for your sake, and in my flesh I complete what is lacking in Christ's afflictions for the sake of his body, that is, the church . . . (Col. 1:24).

It is not necessary, nor would it I think be wise, to appropriate to ourselves all the speculations of those who have promoted the church as the "extension of the incarnation." That, it seems to me, has been an exercise in dogma which, however noble its intentions, has given rise to more ecclesiastical hubris than is either wise or scripturally warranted. But unless we can envisage the people of God in the world as participants in a process of redemption greater than their own human deeds and words, we shall neither save the gospel from the fate of all theory and ideology nor shall we realize fully our own spiritual potential. We are being brought to *live* the representative life of Christ in the world, not merely to announce that such a life has been lived, but ourselves to live within and from that life. The *necessitas* (the "must") under which that one life was lived becomes now for us the ground and direction of our life together.

That is to say, suffering is necessary for the body of Christ—and is the one indispensable mark of its authenticity—because there is still suffering in God's beloved world, and God would still be involved in it. God's involvement in the world's suffering is not a once-for-all matter. It preceded the advent of the Son ("There was a cross in the heart of God long before a cross appeared on Calvary!"[20]), and it succeeds his ascension. As Christians we believe that the Christ achieved a decisive identification with and conquest of human suffering; and we therefore know our own part in this redemptive process to be a matter of "grace alone," the grace of our incorporation into *his* suffering. But we do not offer his suffering in and for the world as if it were "the answer" to human suffering in some doctrinal package. That would be the ultimate in arrogance. The answer, the only answer that we ourselves know and that we are obliged and glad to share with others, is the ongoing presence of the crucified one. That that presence is greater by far than the visible church we are well aware! But in whatever ways God continues to suffer with those who suffer—and they are numberless— we for our part know that this is our vocation. We are part of the response of God to the massive suffering of God's world. In and through the church, visible and invisible, God provides in this world a representative—a priestly—people, a people learning to suffer the becoming of the creature, learning sufficient freedom from self-concern, that they may assume in concrete ways the concerns of their neighbors, their society, their world.

"The doctrine of redemption," writes Nicholas Lash, "does not afford the Christian any licence to substitute a *theory* of reconciliation, of the 'transcendence' of alienation, for its practice." He continues:

> The doctrine of redemption articulates the form of Christian hope, but that hope has to be *enacted*—in individual and social existence, in marriage, technology, art and politics—in the struggle for the "true resolution of the conflict between existence and being."[21]

God's response to suffering is neither just a theory nor a story— "Once upon a time . . . ." Or, if it is a story, it is an unfinished story. The story, as Nicholas Lash says, "has, as yet, *no ending.*" The Christian propensity to give the story an ending—and a very happy one[22]—may well be related to Christian reluctance to *participate in* the story, to tell it as if it were all over and done with, so that their "witness" had simply to be a verbal one—and even that, for the most part, without much struggle of soul or mind! The truth is that the story goes on. It is a tale of the continuing movement of God towards the world, of conquest from within. It involves in a central way a people, grasped by grace and compassion, search-ing out and identifying themselves with other people—especially with history's victims (Matthew 25). Not that this people possesses a special talent for compassion or vicarious suffering! Not that it alone, and under the nomenclature *church*, provides the "comfort" (Isaiah 40) that suffering humanity needs! Whatever capacity the church of Jesus Christ has for being a community of suffering, where the very sharing of the burden can constitute the beginning of the healing process, is a capacity which it is always itself receiving from beyond its own possibilities. It is a case of the comforted comforting, the healed healing, the forgiven showing mercy.

The principle of grace, therefore, is strictly upheld. But what must not be upheld—what Christianity at the end of the Constan-tinian era must at last root out—is the kind of spectator spirituality which, having taken to itself in some domesticated form "the bene-fits of *his* passion," is itself able to exist in a suffering world without either passion or compassion. To repeat the note that was sounded briefly at the end of the preceding chapter on the meaning of re-demption: the Christian faith's manner of addressing the multifold questions implied in the title of this work, "God and Human Suf-fering," will be assessed finally, not on the basis of the adequacy or inadequacy of its theology, but, like all things else, by its fruits, that is, on the basis of the church's deportment of *itself* in a suffering world.

C. We Rejoice in Our Sufferings: Suffering and Hope

> We rejoice in our hope of sharing the glory of God. More than that, we rejoice in our sufferings, knowing that suffering produces endur-ance, and endurance produces character, and character produces hope, and hope does not disappoint us, because God's love has been poured into our hearts through the Holy Spirit which has been given to us (Rom. 5:2-5.).

Paul's bold declaration of joy in suffering, a theme that is not lacking in other writings from this same source, is offensive to many.

This is not surprising, since it runs against the grain of most popular Christianity, whether liberal or conservative in its leanings. It calls in question the bourgeois optimism of the liberals, who do not in any case appreciate paradoxes of this sort; and it secretly annoys the conservatives, who prefer an undialectical happy ending to the story they tell—a return to Paradise through the resurrection from the dead. Against both versions of a finished tale, Paul knows that "the story, as yet, has no ending"—or, to be more accurate, he knows that the ending (*eschatos*) that has been introduced *in medias res* is a matter of hope, not of sight, and as such an ending *out of* and *towards which* we are commanded to live.

Clearly, the apostle has no abiding interest in suffering as such. He gives it a place of prominence, as does Jesus in the Sermon on the Mount, only because it is a sign of something else. His reasoning is obvious, and without either guile or trickery. It is a clear case of that same "logic of the cross" (Niebuhr) of which we have been thinking: The good news of which as Christians we have been made hearers is the *kerygma* of God's entry into the life of humanity through the suffering of the Christ ("I decided to know nothing among you except Jesus Christ and him crucified"). We, as the "body of Christ," are being "conformed to the image of the Son." But given the ambiguity of our own lives, the "war" that is going on within us (Romans 7), how can we be sure of such a new identity? Is it not presumptuous of us to think such a thing? Presumption, Paul knew, was the downfall of many of "our fathers," who counted too uncritically on their status as the elect of God! So his mind moved unerringly towards a thought which simultaneously exercises a critical judgment against all religious boasting and offers an authenticating mark of the new being into which he believed the faithful to be called: *if we suffer with* him we may truly belong to his company. If we suffer with him, we may rejoice, knowing that we are participants in the reconciling work that God is achieving through him, knowing that we are part of the story. Suffering, in short, is both *conformatio* (the mode of our being conformed to the new identify) and *confirmatio* (our confirmation of membership in his body).

In other words, for Paul the *theologia crucis* leads inevitably to an *ecclesia crucis.* A gospel which has at its core the cross of the Christ (*crux sola nostra theologia*) must produce a *koinonia* whose life is marked by suffering. Somewhere along the way, this altogether *logical* thought was lost to Christian view. As Emil Brunner commented, Luther, following Paul,

> contrasts the *theologia gloriae* as a false theology with the genuine theology, the *theologia crucis.* The whole history of Christianity, and the history of the world as a whole, would have followed a different course if it had not been that again and again the *theologia crucis* became *theologia gloriae,* and that the *ecclesia crucis* became an *ecclesia gloriae.* [23]

No doubt it is a human thing to wish to avoid suffering and to regard the lack of suffering as a mark of special favor, or at least good fortune. Conversely, it is also a human and a healthy thing to eschew unnecessary suffering, and to be skeptical of those who go out of their way to find crosses to bear! But once the church confesses faith in a God who through sacrificial identification with a suffering creation heals its brokenness from within, it commits itself to a life in which suffering will have considerable prominence.

There is, however, a very important proviso in all of this. It is not suffering in itself, or suffering of *any* kind, that interests the shapers of the theology of the cross. One can suffer for the wrong reasons, just as one can "do the right thing for the wrong reason" (T. S. Eliot). One can also take a special interest in suffering as an end in itself—and then it must be called what it really is, masochism. The only suffering in which the "church of the cross" can find a reason to rejoice is *his* suffering, the suffering of the One whose cross signifies identification with a suffering God and a suffering world. It is not therefore a special ecclesiastical suffering in which this tradition is interested. The church is not asked to create for itself a special history of suffering, thereby assuring itself of future glory or adding to a treasury of meritorious bloodletting! For all the pathos—sometimes even nobility—of their lives and deeds, the "Acts of the Martyrs" sometimes give the impression that the church was rejoicing because it had been able to add a considerable weight of pain and guilt to an already overburdened world! One hopes that it is more in the telling than in the reality of their often courageous acts, but too many of these examples of Christian suffering seem to miss the point! The object, surely, is not to create more suffering, a special sort of religious suffering which can be recounted afterwards (always to the shame of the wicked world) and celebrated and set down, so to speak, as point for our side! The object, rather, is to identify oneself with the suffering that is already there in one's world, to let oneself be led by the love of Christ into solidarity with those who suffer, and to accept the consequences of this solidarity in the belief—the *joyful* belief—that in this way God is still at work in the world, making a conquest of its sin and suffering from within.

It is just this rethinking and reexemplifying of the nature of Christian suffering in general—martyrdom in particular—that makes the thought and life of Dietrich Bonhoeffer so important for our whole theme. Whoever follows Bonhoeffer's life story carefully will realize that he, too, in continuity with many pious Christian pilgrims of the past, might have understood his own suffering in that category called "saintly," that is, as a special religious or holy suffering, created *by* the world rather than *with* it and *for it*. But along the way to his destiny at Flossenburg, this rather scholarly, disciplined, and pious young man became more and more conscious of the massive suffering of humankind in his age. One can trace in his writings a mental and spiritual movement away from ecclesial and even "Christian" consciousness and towards an ever more committed awareness of the suffering world of which he was part. It was this personal movement of intellect and spirit that made him reconsider Christianity as a whole; and out of that rethinking came, along with a few other jottings that he left us, the following statement:

> During the last year or so I have come to appreciate the "worldliness" of Christianity as never before. The Christian is not a *homo religiosus,* but a man pure and simple. . . . I don't mean the shallow this-worldliness of the enlightened, of the busy, the comfortable, the lascivious. It's something much more profound than that, something in which the knowledge of death and resurrection is ever present.

Later I discovered and I am still discovering up to this very moment that it is only by living completely in this world that one learns to believe. One must abandon every attempt to make something of oneself. . . . This is what I mean by worldliness—taking life in one's stride, with all its duties and problems, its successes and failures, its experiences and helplessnesses. It is in such a life that we throw ourselves utterly into the arms of God and participate in his sufferings in the world and watch with Christ in Gethsemane.[24]

This statement, which is not only courageous but full of untapped wisdom so necessary for the churches in our time, takes the suffering of the church out of the sanctuary and puts it back where it belongs—with Christ in the world. Only if this happens can the suffering *of the church* be regarded as a topic pertinent to the question addressed in this book. Otherwise—that is, if Christian suffering is of a special order, another genre—it has no place in a dissertation on "God and Human Suffering." But if (as I believe) the suffering of Christ's church is indeed a consequence—the only really sure consequence—of our incorporation into his life, then the church's suffering is entirely germane to such a discourse and, in a certain way, the most immediate and specific response that Christians can give to the innumerable questions implied in that discourse. We may *rejoice* in our sufferings, if that be the case, not because they are authenticating marks of *our own* promised redemption but because they point towards a hope for *our world.* That world does not, in our time, give out many tokens of a glorious—or even an acceptable—future. As Nicholas Lash has said:

I see no rational grounds for optimism concerning the future of mankind. But there does exist, with whatever fragility and ambivalence, a form of hope, focused in the death of one man interpreted as resurrection, for which the struggle for humanity is deemed to be worthwhile because not just that one man's death but the entire wilderness of the world's Gethsemane is trusted to be the expression of that mystery whose truth will be all men's freedom.[25]

Strange, paradoxical, and even offensive as it may seem to the world, the presence in it of a community which, without having to, enters into solidarity with its suffering may be a better sign of hope for the world than are the schemes of those who promise paradise.

APPENDIX

Dialog
and Conclusions

In the course of this study, I have introduced a number of themes and subthemes which, as the reader will readily discern, invite further discussion. I am referring not only to the major aspects of the subject as I have treated it but also to a variety of concepts entertained along the way. Most of them, either because they are too complex in themselves or because they are more or less assumptions of mine, could not be treated at any great length in the foregoing text. Like most theology—and especially theological work that seeks to offer a comprehensive statement concerning this particular issue—the contents of these five chapters no doubt leave the reader with many unresolved questions.

What I should like to do now—not in order to resolve all the questions, but to set the stage for their further development and discussion—is to attempt to *focus* some of the primary points that I have made in these chapters. I shall do this by entering into a kind of dialog with five other authors who have written on this subject. In this way I hope not only to sharpen certain aspects of my own approach, but also to encourage the reader to consider the question of God and human suffering as it is treated in a wider theological and religious context.

A word or two is needed to explain my use of the term *dialog* here. It is not my intention to attempt anything so ambitious as either a full resume of these authors' works or an extensive critique of their points of view. Rather, in each instance I shall try to present a sufficiently broad description of their approaches to warrant my own responses to them. Since my purpose is to provide a little more by way of background for the point of view I have expressed in the main text of this book, I shall in most cases concentrate on the *critical* side of my personal evaluation of the five books in question. I would ask the reader in advance, therefore, to believe that my inclusion of these five authors already bespeaks my *basic* appreciation for their work. If I am at times in sharp disagreement with them, it is not to be interpreted as lack of respect. I only wish in this way, through contrast or comparison—through dialog!—to make it a little clearer why, in the main body of this study, I have said some of the things that I have said.

With one exception, all the books to be considered are by Christian thinkers; and I have chosen them, chiefly, out of the many works that could be used in this connection, because of their *popularity*, and because they enable me, in their differing ways, to elaborate certain points that seem to me important.

1. *When Bad Things Happen to Good People,* by Harold S. Kushner (New York: Avon, 1983)

The immense popularity of Rabbi Kushner's book seems to me to be due to two things, one of which has been a major motif of my own work here, namely, the fact that the author takes human suffering very seriously, and therefore steadfastly refuses to offer easy answers to it. In this respect as in many others he is a faithful representative of that "tradition of Jerusalem" about which we have been thinking in this study. Indeed, he is a better representative of that tradition than some of the others whose works we shall consider!

The second obvious reason why this book is widely read by persons of many religious and nonreligious traditions is that it is accessible to a wide readership. The writer manages that most difficult of all combination of literary style, simple language, and profound thought. It is not a "how to" book, though it is eminently practical.

It is in the genuine sense a wise book, and like most human wisdom it has originated in a personal "shaking of the foundations": Kushner was impelled to write it because he himself had to endure what is undoubtedly one of the most excruciating forms of human suffering, the lingering illness and final death of his young son.

There are many points of correspondence between Rabbi Kushner's exposition of this subject and my own. In a way that is refreshing, given the tendency of so many writers on this subject to opt for what I called "the Paradise syndrome," Kushner understands that at least some of what we experience as suffering is a necessary dimension of our creaturehood. "Pain," he writes, "is the price we pay for being alive";[1] and as such it can be "creative,"[2] making people more "sensitive and compassionate."[3] I think that he may have overlooked in this connection the distinction between the "pain" that is part of our human *becoming* and that which is burdensome and *prevents* our emergence into full humanity; nevertheless, his earthy and practical sense of human existence in itself as involving suffering is a healthy antidote both to the religious habit of construing our "original righteousness" (*justitia originalis*) in pain-free terms *and* the luxury assumptions of contemporary North American society.

Again, I am in agreement with Kushner's insistence upon human freedom: "God leaves us room to be human."[4] There is no place here for the kind of divine sovereignty which arranges everything in advance, and therefore ends in the terrible quandary of having to make the Creator personally responsible for the fall! Human beings are both free to go their way (and make dreadful mistakes in the process) and responsible for appropriating what happens to them (including the "bad things"). This is the anthropological correlate of Kushner's main *theological* presupposition, to which I shall draw attention presently.

A third point of sympathy between Kushner's approach in this work and my own is his insistence that it is *not* the business of religion, when treating this or related subjects, to come to the defense of God. Like many other sufferers, Rabbi Kushner found himself deeply offended by many of the things that he read during and after his son's long illness because they "were more concerned with defending God's honor, with logical proof that bad is really good and that evil is necessary to make this a good world, than they were with curing the bewilderment and the anguish of the parent of a dying child."[5] Kushner's work is thus an excellent example of that sentiment, which I insisted belongs to the tradition of Jerusalem, which would stay loyal to the suffering human being even if it meant letting go of cherished beliefs about the divine. Biblical faith has learned from the biblical God that the one who fell among thieves is more important even than our most precious theological assumptions and religious obligations.

The point at which I find myself most engaged by Kushner's argument, however, has to do with his chief theological presupposition—which is at the same time probably the basic contribution of the book. I refer to his refusal to conceive of the deity in power terms. God, for Kushner, is *not* omnipotent. He draws upon the book of Job to demonstrate his meaning. "If God is both just and powerful, then Job must be a sinner who deserves what is happening to him. If Job is good but God causes his suffering anyway, then God is not just. If Job deserved better and God did not send his suffering, then God is not all-powerful."[6] Job's friends assume the first hypothesis: Job must have sinned. Job himself takes the second position: he feels he does not deserve what God has dealt him. But the author of the biblical book, says Kushner, takes the third position:

> The author . . . takes the position which neither Job nor his friends take. He believes in God's goodness and Job's goodness, and is prepared to give up his belief in proposition (a): that God is all-powerful. Bad things do happen to good people in this world, but it is not God who wills it. God would like people to get what they deserve in life, but He cannot always arrange it. Forced to choose between a good God who is not totally powerful, or a powerful God who is not totally good, the author of the book of Job chooses to believe in God's goodness.[7]

This represents Kushner's position throughout his book. Is it one with which Christians can agree?

In my opinion, while there is a rudimentary sense in which Kushner's argument is consistent with biblical priorities, it is not sufficiently nuanced to do justice to biblical faith. In addition, it poses certain difficulties of which I am not sure the author is fully aware. We shall consider the latter first.

One of the difficulties has to do with the use of the adjectives "good" and "bad" which are so important throughout this little book. Naturally we all know what is meant. Everyone uses such distinctions regularly. But our tradition ought to have helped us to correct this rather simplistic habit. For the world is not so easily divisible into good and bad. Are the "bad" things that happen to "good" people so obviously bad always? Remember Joseph's famous line to his brothers: "You meant it to me for evil, but God for good." More important, are the people—including Job—so obviously good? One can certainly concur with Kushner's repeated insistence that "things" do not happen to people because they are bad people; i.e., no simple correlation should be drawn between specific instances of human suffering and real or imagined deeds.[8] Drawing such conclusions is always an obnoxious practice, and it is not only the author of Job who wants to tell us so. Jesus was infinitely more critical of the allegedly "good" people than of the obvious "sinners" at whom the good ones pointed the finger of accusation! "Let him who is without sin cast the first stone!"

Yet Kushner's conception of sin seems strangely truncated, if not moralistic. Morally, Job may indeed be a "good" man. But, as the speech out of the whirlwind indicates, there is a sense in which none of us, no matter how (comparatively!) good we are, can stand before the Holy without guilt. This sense of our own unworthiness is not only a specifically Christian sentiment. The writer of Isaiah's temple vision (Chap. 6) understood it very well; and the modern Jewish author of *The Trial* (Kafka) understood it at least as well as did that ancient Jewish convert to Christianity, Paul, who had to confess finally that "all our *goodness* is as filthy rags."

This is not to diminish the importance of a moral life or to make light of distinctions at the level of deeds and motives; but it *is* necessary to do some sort of justice to the existential sense of "wrongness" that seems inherent in the human psyche at its most sensitive and has no direct correlation with our performance morally. If sin is understood not in terms of being "bad" or "evil" but in terms of a mysterious and fundamental distortion of human freedom; and if, besides, sin is conceived of (as it should be) as corporate and not merely as personal, then there is surely more of a connection between sin and suffering than Kushner appears to recognize. I think that his failure to grasp the deeper connotations of sin within the tradition of Jerusalem weakens his argument considerably. For it means that his book can be read by average "good" middle-class North Americans *without ever causing them to question their fundamental assumptions about themselves and their society.* In sensitive pastoral ways, such a book can comfort people in their personal tragedies, but it will hardly incite them to ask the kinds of questions Job asked of himself—whether he had in fact taken a wrong turn, whether his values were legitimate, whether his way of life were perhaps based on naive or illusory presuppositions, what good his affluence was in the first place, etc. In short, the *contextual* factor—to which I paid attention in the Introduction and elsewhere—is conspicuously absent from this statement. And if there is a *third* reason for its popularity, it may be due to just this fact—that one can get comfort from it without experiencing anything like the judgment that Isaiah felt in the temple, when he knew himself to be "a man of unclean lips, dwelling in the midst of a people of unclean lips."

Another difficulty implicit in Kushner's way of defining God's powerlessness is that it courts a cosmic dualism. We must, as I have argued in the foregoing discussion, grant that the Bible on the whole assumes a kind of *provisional* dualism—though it would be more accurate to say duality. For it depicts the created order as sufficiently independent of God that it is neither an extension of the divine nor predetermined as to its course and destiny. In human beings, where this distinction from the divine is most finely articulated, it takes the form of human freedom. We are not, as Kushner insists, "programmed." The world is other than its Maker, and this otherness, while it is the presupposition of the relationship of *love* between Creator and creature, is also the Achilles' heel of creation, the point at which radical alienation can occur.

There is, then, in biblical thought, a sense of two-ness, over-againstness, or duality; and while it resists adamantly a full-blown dualism it is nonetheless willing to risk *that* danger rather than succumb to a metaphysic in which the principle of absolute unity (monism) renders any thought of *relationship* superfluous or merely poetic.

It is, however, a considerable step beyond such a provisional dualism when Kushner alleges that there is a "randomness" in the world,[9] that many things happen for no reason at all,[10] and that "the facts of life and death are neutral."[11] While he guards against a too blatant statement of the continuing influence of the primeval chaos,[12] his urgent (and, in principle, laudable) desire to avoid making God directly responsible for things like the Lisbon earthquake frequently forces him to accentuate the chaotic element, thus courting a more substantial form of dualism than the tradition will bear. Some of his statements in this connection seem almost frivolous: "But suppose God didn't quite finish by closing time on the afternoon of the sixth day?";[13] or again his interpretation of God's famous whirlwind oration in Job as meaning, ". . . if you think that it is so easy to keep the world straight and true, to keep unfair things from happening to people, you try it."[14]

The basic project in which Rabbi Kushner is involved here is, in my opinion at least, right: representatives of the Judeo-Christian tradition do grave injustice to their sources when they interpret the deity in terms of power. As I have attempted to show in the preceding sections of this study, God in our tradition is a Being far more complex (and more simple—in the profound sense!) than Nero, and we who represent this tradition must simply *stop* attributing to God the things that belong to Caesar! Every responsible attempt to rethink the question of "God and human suffering" (as I shall have occasion to say again before I have concluded this excursion into literature on the subject) must involve in a primary sense a radical reinterpretation of divine omnipotence.

God's "complexity," however, is not sufficiently appreciated if it is cast in terms of a struggle between "goodness" and "power," as Kushner has done. It is in fact not *God's* complexity at all, but a complexity inhering in the nature of the relationship between God and the creation, especially the human creature. How can we speak about this complexity? Of course it is not possible to describe complexity simply! But when there are certain parallels between God's life (as Scripture depicts this) and our own, we can at least have intimations of what may be involved in this relationship from God's side. And in this case there are conspicuous parallels! For every thinking, involved-in-life human being knows something about the complexity of love; and that, precisely, is what is at the bottom of this whole problem!

What I mean, to put it in the most childish way, is that God's problem is not that God *is not able* to do certain things. God's problem is that God loves! Love complicates the life of God as it complicates every life. Without love, the God whom our sources describe obviously *could* behave towards the world in the way that Kushner and many other people seem to think desirable— punishing the evil-doers and rewarding the good (except that then, given the previous discussion about "good" and "bad," we might find a good deal more suffering in the world than we do now!). But "like as a father pitieth his children," the biblical God is prevented from such direct action because of a love which is ready to suffer with and for the beloved before it will give way to strict justice. If God is to "get at" the sources of the deepest human misery (which is certainly related to Sin in the biblical perspective), God *must* (being love!) enter upon a plan or "economy" more complex and indirect than the "simple" meting out of justice. As I have expressed this economy here, it involves an approach which is not only complex but costly; for it means that God's *power* has ultimately to articulate itself in divine solidarity with the sufferer, that is, in the "weakness" of suffering love.

There is, strangely, a conspicuous absence of love in Kushner's discussion of God and human suffering. I say strangely because, unlike *some* of my fellow Christians, I do not accept the idea that love is an exclusively Christian attribute for the divine Being. The whole bent of Israel's theology is informed by the divine *agape* (*hesed*), and while this is undoubtedly more consistently associated with "righteousness" in the older (Judaic) tradition, it should never be reduced to "goodness." For Israel too, the divine love is beyond good and evil as these are regularly interpreted in the human sphere. It is not simply God's "goodness" that prevents God from executing the frequently entertained thought that it would be better, wiser, and more just simply to annul the already sullied covenant, perhaps to annihilate the wicked world! From beginning to end of this story told in the continuity of the Testaments, it is love, sheer love, that constitutes the basis (and the complicating factor!) of the relation between the principal characters.

Because Kushner fails to grasp (or at least to express) this, his response to the fact of human suffering, while full of practical insights, is theologically and humanly unsatisfying. He ends, as do so many liberal Christians, with "religion" being pragmatically useful to sufferers,[15] but it is the sufferer himself or herself who has to derive whatever meaning he or she can from the experience. Because the first (ontological!) principle of biblical theology is missing in this treatment, i.e., that "God is love," the second (soteriological) principle is also missing: grace. It becomes a matter of our wresting from our "bad" experiences whatever "good" we can get from them—of course "with God's help."

> Let me suggest that the bad things that happen to us in our lives do not have a meaning when they happen to us. They do not happen for any good reason which would cause us to accept them willingly. But *we can give them a meaning. We can redeem these tragedies from senselessness by imposing meaning on them. . . .*[16]

Or again:

> The facts of life and death are neutral. We, by our responses, give suffering either a positive or a negative meaning.[17]

Or this:

> How does God make a difference in our lives if He neither kills nor cures? God inspires people to help other people who have been hurt by life. . . .[18]

And:

> To the person who asks "What good is God? Who needs religion, if these things happen to good people and bad people alike?", I would

say that God may not prevent calamity, but He gives us the strength and perseverance to overcome it.[19]

One can certainly appreciate the insights contained in such statements; but they do not reflect the depths of biblical theology. Are they not in fact insights of a postreligious humanism, accessible in differing but related forms to persons out of a great variety of historical religions but mirroring the secular mentality more than the religious faith whose language they still use? As such, they may contain a certain courage—and courage is always admirable. One admires the human being who takes upon himself or herself the search for meaning in the face of meaninglessness, determining to impose purpose where none is present. The question, however, remains: If there is no horizon other than our own determination that historical existence should be purposeful, how can we sustain any faith at all?

Kushner's treatment of the subject seems to me, then, to be a capitulation to modernity. It wants to retain the practical *results* of biblical faith without their ontological foundations. I believe that there are resources of wisdom in the ancient world of the Jews and the Christians which this author has not tapped. The *mythos* of the suffering God—of the God who yearns parentally towards creation; of the God who is not power*less* but whose power expresses itself unexpectedly in the weakness of love: this, I believe, is not only a more *profound* image of God than Kushner's limited deity, it is also more accessible to the human spirit. For every one of us knows, if we've lived and loved at all, something of the meaning of *that* yearning, *that* weak power, *that* powerful weakness.

2. *The Problem of Pain,* by C. S. Lewis (London: Geoffrey Bles, The Centenary Press, 1940)

C. S. Lewis's book about human suffering served something of the same purpose during and immediately after World War II that Kushner's has served at the present time. Lewis, however, writes very self-consciously as an "orthodox" Christian, and his readership has been comprised mainly of Christian intellectuals. Like Kushner, he begins by stating the problem of suffering in terms of the apparent contradiction between the divine goodness and the divine power:

"If God were good, He would wish to make His creatures perfectly happy, and if God were almighty He would be able to do what He wished. But the creatures are not happy. Therefore God lacks either goodness, or power, or both." This is the problem of pain, in its simplest form. [20]

Instead of resolving this seeming contradiction, with Kushner, by opting for the divine goodness and limiting God's power, however, the great British sage takes the more sophisticated route of qualifying *both* of the key concepts. Omnipotence, he firmly believes, *is* appropriately predicated of God; but it does not mean that God can do anything at all. "All things are *possible* with God," as Jesus insisted; but certain things, having been done, exclude certain other things:

If you choose to say "God can give a creature free-will and at the same time withhold free-will from it," you have not succeeded in saying *anything* about God: meaningless combinations of words do not suddenly acquire meaning simply because we prefix to them the two other words "God can." It remains true that all *things* are possible with God: the intrinsic impossibilities are not things but non-entities. It is no more possible for God than for the weakest of His creatures to carry out both of two mutually exclusive alternatives; not because His power meets an obstacle, but because nonsense remains nonsense even when we talk it about God. [21]

The reference to freedom of will in this quotation is not incidental. Lewis shares with Kushner this insistence upon human volition, but unlike the Jewish author he does not link this so much with human responsibility as with sin—for him, the primary cause of our suffering. If God creates a material universe and gives to the human creature freedom of will, God cannot exclude the prospect of suffering: "Try to exclude the possibility of suffering which the order of nature and the existence of free wills involve, and you will find that you have excluded life itself." [22]

As for the second attribute in the couplet, divine goodness, Lewis, in distinction from Kushner, is at pains to explain that it refers principally to God's love. But love applied to God is not *simply* continuous with what we call love. God's love, says Lewis in a finely honed passage,

> is not a senile benevolence that drowsily wishes you to be happy in your own way, not the cold philanthropy of a conscientious magistrate, nor the care of a host who feels responsible for the comfort of his guests, but the consuming fire Himself, the Love that made the worlds, persistent as the artist's love for his work and despotic as a man's love for a dog, provident and venerable as a father's love for a child, jealous, inexorable, exacting as love between the sexes.[23]

This enables the author to conclude that "the problem of reconciling human suffering with the existence of a God who loves is only insoluble so long as we attach a trivial meaning to the word 'love,' and look on things as if man were the centre of them."[24]

With such qualifications of both key terms, it is already fairly clear to the discerning reader what C. S. Lewis intends to do. Kushner, I suspect, would say that Lewis is well on his way to writing a "defense of God's honor." Certainly, the argument is intended to function as a Christian *apologia*, and an "orthodox" one at that. While Kushner's sympathies are quite obviously with the sufferer, Lewis, the convert from atheism to a firm Church of England faith, wishes to speak to those whom Schleiermacher earlier designated religion's "cultured despisers." The names of Huxley and Hardy, among others, appear often enough in this little study to make one aware of that! To a generation that had moved away from official Christianity in large numbers, C. S. Lewis intended here—as in all his works—to say that their rejection of the faith was decidedly premature. And, in a way, that is what most of us who still work at faith and understanding are attempting. It may, however, be questioned whether this is best achieved through an apologetic which is so obviously committed to theological orthodoxy that it must be less than sensitive to the human experiences that have caused so many to defect from the church—experiences labeled meaninglessness, anxiety, or what the existentialists were already in 1940 calling "The Absurd." We shall return to this observation after we have followed Lewis a little further in his argument.

The object of omnipotence is to transform us. Love, in God, is so loving that it wills to alter us. Why do we need altering? Because ". . . we have used our free will to become very bad . . . ."[25] While Kushner seems keen to minimize the connection between sin and suffering, Lewis elevates it to signal prominence. In the original historical situation, Christianity (he says) was preached as good news, because the fear of eternal punishment was great amongst the ancients. "But all this has changed. Christianity now has to preach the diagnosis—in itself very bad news—before it can win a hearing for the cure."[26] It should be remembered that Lewis was writing these words half a century ago, when it was still possible for many people to affirm the essential goodness of the human character and the progress of civilization—though, with World War II under way by the time the book was printed, precisely this belief was already under attack. Lewis was perhaps a little ahead of most of his British contemporaries in sensing the demise of the Age of Progress. Barth and many other continental theologians had been calling for what Lewis describes as "a recovery of the old sense of sin"[27] for more than two decades.

"Christ takes it for granted that men are bad,"[28] Lewis declares, and in that one sentence sets himself in the opposite camp from Kushner. For him, it is not a case of "bad things" happening to "good people" but of things that may from one vantage point be felt to be bad happening to people who are bad. And Lewis makes no bones about the fact that he is speaking about immorality—not exclusively, but very centrally:

> Some modern theologians have, quite rightly, protested against an excessively moralistic interpretation of Christianity. The Holiness of God is something more and other than moral perfection: His claim upon us is something more and other than the claim of moral duty. I do not deny it; but this conception, like that of corporate guilt, is very easily used as an evasion of the real issue. God may be more than moral goodness: He is not less.[29]

As beings intended for eternal felicity, we are in fact gross contra-
dictions of our essence. "Depend upon it, when the saints say that
they—even they—are vile, they are recording truth with scientific
accuracy."[30]

Thus, for Lewis, suffering is in large measure the consequence of
sin. "Our present condition. . .is explained by the fact that we are
members of a spoiled species. . . ."

> I do not mean that our sufferings are a punishment for being what
> we cannot now help being nor that we are morally responsible for
> the rebellion of a remote ancestor. If, none the less, I call our present
> condition one of original Sin, and not merely one of original mis-
> fortune, that is because our actual religious experience does not allow
> us to regard it in any other way.[31]

The fact of our being what we are is in no way to be laid at the
doorstep of our Creator. God did not make us either to sin or to
suffer. "Man, as a species, spoiled himself . . . ."[32] There is a sense
in which pain, according to Lewis, does belong to our creaturely
condition (". . . pain is inherent in the very existence of a world
where souls can meet"[33]); but his emphasis is clearly upon the suffering which issues from our distortion of creaturehood: "When souls
become wicked they will certainly use this possibility to hurt one
another; and this, perhaps, accounts for four-fifths of the sufferings
of men."[34]

When Lewis turns from the analysis of pain to the task of responding to it from the side of belief, his propensity to provide a
satisfactory rationale for suffering, if not to justify all of it, becomes
even more conspicuous. Kushner finds that much human suffering
happens "for no reason at all"; it is random. There is absolutely
nothing of this sort in Lewis's account. His answer to pain is not
easily summarized, because he is a master of subtleties; but for our
purposes we may notice two types of response.

First, suffering is purposeful because it is the occasion through
which God is able to turn us away from our follies and illusions and
towards our true destiny in God. "God whispers to us in our plea-
sures, speaks in our conscience, but shouts in our pains; it is His

megaphone to rouse a deaf world."[35] This is strong medicine, but beings who are very sick need such, in Lewis's view. "No doubt Pain as God's megaphone is a terrible instrument; it may lead to final and unrepented rebellion. But it gives the only opportunity the bad man can have for amendment. It removes the veil; it plants the flag of truth within the fortress of a rebel soul."[36] Since none of us is free from sin, the question is not why some people suffer but why more do not! "The real problem is not why some humble, pious, believing people suffer, but why some do *not.*"[37] With this we are in a milieu not only different from but entirely foreign to the mind of Rabbi Kushner.

Lewis is not insensible to the fact that people may think him callous for justifying pain; he says, however, that he is trying to demonstrate the truth of Christian teaching:

> All arguments in justification of suffering promote bitter resentment against the author. You would like to know how I behave when I am experiencing pain, not writing books about it. You need not guess, for I will tell you: I am a great coward. But what is that to the purpose? When I think of pain—of anxiety that gnaws like fire and loneliness that spreads out like a desert, and the heartbreaking routine of monotonous misery, or again of dull aches that blacken our whole landscape or sudden nauseating pains that knock a man's heart out at one blow, of pains that seem already intolerable and then are suddenly increased, of infuriating scorpion-stinging pains that startle into maniacal movement a man who seemed half dead with his previous tortures—it "quite o'ercrows my spirit." If I knew any way of escape I would crawl through sewers to find it. But what is the good of telling you about my feelings? You know them already: they are the same as yours. I am not arguing that pain is not painful. Pain hurts. That is what the word means. I am only trying to show that the old Christian doctrine of being made "perfect through suffering" (Heb. ii, 10) is not incredible. To prove it palatable is beyond my design.[38]

It is curious that a man as obviously and existentially knowledgable about pain as this passage betokens should think it irrelevant to share this awareness more openly, and with a greater impact

upon his argument. If we were right in claiming that the acknowledgment of the reality of human suffering is one of the two fundamental *biblical* themes in regard to this whole subject, then it is
an odd sort of orthodoxy that intentionally suppresses that reality
in favor of the second major theme of our tradition, the divine
response to suffering. The psalmist apparently did not feel compelled
to be so modest about his pain, nor did Christ on the cross! Lewis's
commitment to the purposefulness of pain appears to blind him to
the very thing that gives rise to the "problem of pain" to begin
with, viz., its seeming inconsistency with our image of the divine.
He bends over backwards to justify the status quo: "If the world is
indeed a 'vale for soul making' it seems on the whole to be doing
its work."[39] Lewis is not ready to say straight out that suffering in
itself is *good*; but he avoids, always, the thought (so central to
Kushner's exposition) that suffering as such is *bad*. Consistently,
Lewis wants to provide the positive explanation. Human beings,
unlike animals, can be "improved by pain";[40] ergo, while "suffering
is not good in itself,"[41] it is decidedly, and in itself, part of the
divine Plan for meeting the *cause* of suffering, i.e., Sin. For "what
is good in any painful experience is, for the·sufferer, his submission
to the will of God, and, for the spectators, the compassion aroused
and the acts of mercy to which it leads."[42]

The second—and, in both the chronological and theological
sense, *final*—aspect of Lewis's response to suffering from the side of
faith is contained *in nuce* in the title of his concluding chapter,
"Heaven." Taking his cue from St. Paul's statement that "the sufferings of this present time are not worthy to be compared with the
glory which shall be revealed in us" (Rom. 8:18 KJV), Lewis writes:

> If this is so, a book on suffering which says nothing of heaven is
> leaving out almost the whole of one side of the account. Scripture
> and tradition habitually put the joys of heaven into the scale against
> the sufferings of earth, and no solution of the problem of pain which
> does not do so can be called a Christian one. We are very shy now-
> adays of even mentioning heaven. We are afraid of the jeer about
> "pie in the sky", and of being told that we are trying to "escape"
> from the duty of making a happy world here and now into dreams of

a happy world elsewhere. But either there is "pie in the sky" or there is not. If there is not, then Christianity is false, for this doctrine is woven into its whole fabric. If there is, then this truth, like any other, has to be faced, whether it is useful at political meetings or no.[43]

Nothing written by this master of English prose is lacking in insight. There are numerous ways in which C. S. Lewis's discussion of pain parallels what I have written here, and also many places where he grapples with aspects of the problem that I have not treated (for example, in his interesting chapter on "Animal Pain"). As my comments along the way will have indicated, however, I find myself at loggerheads with his basic approach. I can perhaps express my disagreement best by discussing briefly three areas of conflict:

First, *about his way of expressing the relation between suffering and sin.* I have criticized Kushner for failing to see connections here; but obviously there are different ways of conceiving of these connections. They are, I assume, rooted in different ways of thinking about sin itself. Despite his protestation of agreement with those "modern theologians" who want a less moralistic Christianity, sin for Lewis is very much a matter of immorality—not in the narrow or in the "bourgeois" sense, but all the same in a rather characteristically Anglo-American manner. What is missing in Lewis's hamartiology is that whole dimension which we have called "the tragic side." European continental theology has always had a better grasp on that dimension than Anglo-Saxon religious thought, which has difficulty both with radical sin and radical grace. With Lewis and against Kushner I believe it to be mandatory for biblical religion to uphold a causative relation between sin and suffering; but if sin is lacking this tragic dimension, and if, besides, its *corporate* aspect is underdeveloped (and in Lewis's work that is the case), then one ends with an inherent necessity of saying that human beings deserve the pain they get. Lewis is too sophisticated a thinker to claim such a thing outright, but it is there as a muffled conclusion throughout his book. In response to it, I am inclined with Kushner to prefer a God who can't do anything much about our suffering to One who actually makes it "His" most effective mode of communication—

"His" megaphone! I cannot imagine what sort of message God (or anyone else!) could communicate through the "megaphone" of the suffering of battered or starving children. To justify Hiroshima or Auschwitz by saying that God had made some people more compassionate through them is, as Emil Fackenheim would say, to give Hitler a posthumous victory—and to add one more supporting argument to the cause of those who are preparing the *future* Hiroshima. If Kushner is squeamish or "liberal" about the connection between sin and suffering, Lewis is all too specific. He might have saved himself from the criticism that he obviously wishes to avoid (too easy justification of pain) had he developed his conception of Sin with more mystery in it, more understanding of the tragic and corporate nature of it, and therefore more compassion for sinners. But this course does not seem compatible with his general mindset, at least as it is expressed in this particular book. Like other pious Christians of this mind-set, Lewis is most at home here when he is being a moralist. His moral indignation is brilliant. Fortunately, he was also a storyteller, and it is hard for a good storyteller, which he was, to be a consistent moralist.

Second, *I object to Lewis's heaven-is-the-answer.* Christians are not obligated to tell people that there is "pie in the sky"—no matter how cleverly that may be said. They are obliged to say, rather, that "nothing can separate us from the love of God that is in Christ Jesus, our Lord, neither life, nor death," etc. There is nothing that can cut us off from *this love which we already experience here and now.* The unknown and awesome "Afterwards," whatever it is—and biblical faith is very cautious, not to say agnostic, in that connection— is not going to be other than what we already now "taste" by way of God's faithful, forgiving, cleansing and healing Presence.

That is a far cry from offering Heaven as a consolation for the sufferings of earth! If anything distinguishes the Judeo-Christian tradition from many, if not all, religions (including empirical Christianity!) it is the abiding insistence of biblical faith that all that God does is done vis-à-vis and for the sake of creation. God's project, the *modus operandi* of which is a series of "covenants" culminating (for Christians) in "the new covenant in my blood," is not to get people into heaven but to make them responsible, grateful, and joyful citizens of earth. It is the sufferings of earth, the groaning of the whole creation, that are addressed by divine revelation; and to offer the gospel of Jesus Christ as a species of "Heaven" is to betray the incarnation and cross of Christ in a blatant manner. It is not necessary to *deny* the reality of "Heaven," but it is high time for Christians to accentuate the other side of the matter, namely, that it is "the kingdoms of this world" that "have become the kingdom of our God and of his Christ." Thinking about "the kingdom of heaven" in supramundane terms does not even do justice to what the newer Testament means by "heaven." And when the message degenerates into a promise that "earth hath no sorrows that heaven cannot heal," then I fear that the Ivan Karamazov in me rises up in righteous human indignation.[44] As Kushner has said, there is nothing more infuriating than when religious bystanders offer heaven to their suffering acquaintances. "To try to make a child feel better by telling him how beautiful it is in heaven. . . is another way of depriving him of the chance to grieve."[45]

Third, and chief, I am greatly disappointed by *the absence of an active and compassionate Christology in this work.* One might have expected something better from the creator of that wonderful Christ figure "Aslan."[46] Throughout *The Problem of Pain* there are some quite conventional ("orthodox"?) allusions to the Christ, mostly along the lines of what one supposes would be a substitutionary theory of the atonement if it were developed; but since it is not, and since, in addition, the *God* whom Lewis presents in this study is so eminently "reasonable," one can only conclude that at this stage in his life Lewis had not reflected deeply on the connection between human suffering and the significance of the cross. The whole notion, so important for the position that I have represented in this book, that God's primary response to human suffering is God's identification, in Christ, with the suffering species and world, is *conspicuously* absent from Lewis's account. Not only is his answer to pain cloaked in terms which do not require an active Christology,[47] for it is just as readily understood theistically or even deistically, but it is an answer which would only be altered, and drastically, if the representative suffering of the Christ *were* seriously introduced into it. For that suffering is representative, not only of

the human condition but of God in response to the human condition. The first "answer" to the "problem of pain" is: "the pain of
God" (Kitamori). It is not only the suffering Christ who is missing
from Lewis's account of things, then, it is also the "Father" to whom
the Christ prayer, the one who "pitieth his children," the "compassionate God" (Song). The God whose case Mr. Lewis is pleading
here is more likely the God that Mr. Huxley and Mr. Hardy did
not believe in.

This brings me to the final criticism of this work. It is, in my
opinion, *a philosophic rather than a theological work.* By this I mean,
among other things, two: first, that it assumes an abstract theism
and an equally abstract human situation. Biblical language and traditional Christian theological terminology are of course employed
throughout; but behind it there stands the god of the philosophers
and not the God of Abraham, Isaac, and Jacob (older Testament
references, incidentally, are almost wholly lacking from the work);
and the human being most visibly present to the author's mind does
not live on High Street but in an Oxford common room. Second,
by philosophic I mean that the whole discourse, while enormously
clever, is lacking passion. There is no sense in which the author
contends with God! Kushner's work, though (as I indicated) perhaps
more humanistic than biblical, is authentically of the tradition of
Jerusalem in this respect, that one never doubts the author is engaged in a struggle; that he knows from the outset that he will not
get a satisfactory answer but will likely have to go away limping,
like Jacob; and that, nonetheless, he will refuse to the very end to
settle for less than a satisfactory answer! Throughout *The Problem
of Pain,* C. S. Lewis appears in the role of God's spokesperson—
not the contender. This is because, in the first place, he is dealing
with a theistic (perhaps even a deistic) construct rather than the
passionate God of Sinai and Golgotha; and in the second place it
is because he does not have the (Jewish) sense of *loyalty to the human.*
I do not doubt that C. S. Lewis suffered as a human being, in his
way, just as Kushner has. But what I do doubt is that, at this point
in his career in any case, Lewis had identified himself deeply with
the human condition. I am not willing to make it a rule, but it is
all the same, I think, very close to the truth of the matter, that

the only persuasive *theology* is articulated by persons who have become so thoroughly humanized that they must struggle with God.

3. *The Traces of God: In a Frequently Hostile World,* by Diogenes Allen (Cambridge, Mass.: Cowley Publications, 1981)

This work of a philosopher of religion at Princeton Theological Seminary announces as its chief purpose "to show that our sufferings, however frustrating, can be put to good use. Through adversity we can begin to discover God's presence, either for the first time or in new and fresh ways, and to receive his help."[48] The book is divided into three parts. Part I ("Our Preparation") is designed to help the reader to "recognize another dimension of our world—a divine one."[49] With many other commentators on our era, Professor Allen believes that the spiritual course of Western civilization during the last 300 years has been such as to "reduce everything to a single plane," with a resulting "loss of a sense of mystery." But the mystery dimension that Allen wishes us to recover is "not to be identified simply with the unknown."[50] Writing as a person of faith—specifically a Christian—the author has reference rather to a dimension of mystery which is part of belief in God. Where the biblical God is concerned, mystery refers not so much to God's unknownness but to God's self-manifestation. As Luther would have put it, the revealing God (*Deus revelatus*) conceals (is *Deus absconditus*) in the revealing. This being so, says Allen, we must be *prepared* if we are to discern the "traces of God" in the ordinary events of our life, particularly in adversity.

Then, in a manner reminiscent of Augustine's famous dictum about our "restless hearts," Allen begins his work of preparation by reminding his readers that there is within all of us an irrepressible quest for happiness. The world, however, cannot satisfy this quest—not when it is earnestly pursued. "Those who have endured the void know that they have encountered a distinctive hunger, or emptiness; nothing earthly satisfies it."[51] It is true that we *attempt* to find satisfaction in mundane things; but those who have resisted this temptation know that the quest for felicity is something transcendent and cannot be reduced by association with inappropriate objects.[52]

The path of resistance, i.e., "the act of forsaking the world, of withholding from it our love, allows us to receive a divine seed";[53] that is, by our refusal to be satisfied with less than the ultimate, we are led to seek intimations ("traces") of the love of God which can and does answer our thirst for happiness. This resistance implies the renunciation of power—and here Allen uses extensively Friedrich Dürrenmatt's radio play, "Nocturnal Conversation with a Despised Person," to illustrate the distinction between the route of power and that of "humility." The latter alternative, he says, "is a commitment to suffer even to the extent of losing one's own life at the hands of that power which seeks to get its own way, rather than to resemble that power in any respect, by any form of self-aggrandizement. Such a response sees with utter clarity the unjust use of power for what it is, and by its humility is joined to a goodness that is otherwise separated from it by a great chasm."[54]

Through the refusal to satisfy our desire with earthly things and our relinquishing of power in favor of the humble acceptance of "our vulnerability to injustice,"[55] we are prepared for understanding and *responding to* the divine love manifested in Jesus (Part II is entitled "Our Response").

> Only if we have suffered and endured the same unjust use of power, in however small a degree, will we come to see the reality of an indestructible goodness in Jesus' suffering.[56]

Apart from some preparatory experience of the nature designated in Part I, "what Jesus *is* will not be properly seen"; the depth of mystery in this (after all) rather ordinary story will elude our grasp.[57] What Jesus "is" for Allen is classically expressed in the *Logos* doctrine: "the incarnation of divine love and goodness." Drawing heavily on the thought of Simone Weil, Allen articulates a theology and Christology along the lines of categories he has already established in the first part. God, too, knows the meaning of self-renunciation, for both creation and cross depict the divine Being as one who eschews power in favor of humility. While creation may seem to us primarily an act of power, it is really one of "profound renunciation"; for it means that God "chooses out of love to permit something else to exist. . . . So the creation of a world means that God renounces his status as the only existent—he pulls himself back, so to speak, in order to give his creation room to exist for its own sake."[58] (The reader may recall Rabbi Kushner's statement that "God leaves us room to be human.")

The cross reinforces and extends this image of God. It is "Jesus' voluntary renunciation of himself. . . . He lays down his life in humility instead of following the way of force, or self-exaltation, and of blind assertion."[59] On the human plane, i.e., apart from our preparation to perceive mystery in the ordinary, the cross is a portrayal of a man "unjustly and brutally executed, who endures death with humility."[60] But when this event is placed within the context of "Incarnation," it is seen as the manifestation of "a unique love," viz., divine *agape:*

> This love enters the creation and bears the destructive effects of creatures whose nature is no longer directed by the Creator's love. Divine love bears this as a creature, and bears it humbly. Such love is divine, a love that allows the creation its own freedom, and is willing to enter that realm as a creature to bear its ill effects.[61]

Those whose "preparation" for the perception of this event has been adequate will receive it as a revelation of ultimate significance. But even they will experience "impediments" to their recognition of the "traces of God" in this life and death. The impediments are in particular our sufferings: the sufferings that we experience through "natural evil," and the suffering that results from "human cruelty."[62] Although the natural world produces "immense beauty,"[63]

> nature's order. . . can at the same time produce intense and brutal suffering. At such times we do not know how to connect our faith in God's goodness with illnesses which cause the death of children, senseless accidents, and natural catastrophes. They do not seem to go together, and when such catastrophes occur we do not know how we can reconcile God's love with intense human misery.[64]

At best, ordinary human courage can only "hang on" in the face of such occurrences; but "if we have the conviction that Christ's response to his own suffering was redemptive," we can accept this suffering "at the hands of nature. . ." as "an opportunity for *contact* with God."[65] Thus, in a way that is somewhat reminiscent of Lewis, Allen finds that the natural sufferings which come our way can help us to discover or rediscover who we really are. But, unlike Lewis, Allen's point is not to accentuate the fact that we are *sinners* ("bad"); rather, through our subjection to natural evils, Allen thinks, we are shown our solidarity with all flesh. We are brought to the realization that we are not special, not exempt from the conditions of creaturehood. We are in fact "material beings, subject to the grinding wear and tear of matter. In facing the hard facts of illness, accidents, decay, and death we can rise above our egotism to discover that we are spiritual beings."[66] If our preparation for faith has been sound, it is possible for us to say yes to "the unavoidable necessities of life."[67] It is not inevitable that we shall do so, but it is possible. And if we do accept such an identity, trusting in God's sovereignty over nature, we can avoid heaping negation upon negation; we can find "redemptive features" in the most negating of experiences.

> The basis for trust in such situations is our knowledge of the suffering Jesus endured on the cross. Even though his affliction was caused by human action, it still happened because he was a vulnerable piece of matter which could be nailed to wood, could bleed and die.[68]

At this juncture Allen introduces an interesting distinction upon which I shall comment later: Jesus, "the Son," is, as the incarnate one, "distanced" from "the Father." "The incarnate Son, while he is in the world, is subject to natural forces; the Father is not. They are separated by the 'distance' of the created world."[69] With the cry of dereliction, Jesus "can be said to have been driven the greatest possible distance from the Father." "The Son," he continues,

> is afflicted by the Father for our sakes; he enters the world, is made subject to it, and is crucified to establish contact between what is

subject to nature and sin, and what is not. All this is brought about through the Father's loving will.[70]

And again,

The Son's great victory is to yield to the will of his Father; thus they are united over the great span of distance, because there is love at each extremity. Their distance from one another thus becomes a measure of the extent of their love, expressed by the very medium of their separation. Christ's pain is real pain; his affliction is horrible. Yet he responds to it as the will of the Father, and this affliction is unable to break the contact between himself and his Father.[71]

Our faithful response to this revelation of the divine love is the basis of our own activity in relation to suffering:

Reflection on Christ's affliction thus gives us a basis for action, for bringing some redemptive element into a negative situation. By humble faith we can actually effect and change the total situation. We can continue to love even when the love of God is veiled by the unpleasant pressure of nature, and the result is a more perfect love of God. There is always a role we can play in our own suffering; not utterly powerless, we can bring a new element to the total situation and make it different from what it would otherwise be. God still provides us with a way to act redemptively. We have not been driven utterly beyond this possibility, but our own action can mitigate the evil of unavoidable suffering.[72]

Turning then from the suffering that results from natural evil to "suffering human cruelty," Professor Allen applies essentially the same insight as in his discussion of the former suffering. God cannot be held responsible for the suffering we receive at the hands of other persons; "he merely permits it by allowing people to be free."[73] People have been able to "experience the love of God even in the most extreme circumstances of human cruelty, and have been driven so close to Christ that he and he alone has become the rock on which they stand."[74] Allen's elaboration of this affirmation is almost wholly cast in the form of a digest of writings by Iulia de Beausobre, one of the victims of Stalin's infamous purges. Through unbearable torture, this woman discovered the gracious capacity of communion with her tormentors, and in the process not only came to know the love of God in Christ more intimately than ever before, but also deeply affected those who persecuted her.

The third and final part of this work ("Our Behaviour") describes the calling of the Christian as participant in the redemptive work of God in Christ. It parallels many of the things that I have said in my discussion of the church as a community of suffering. "Concern for those in severe need," writes Allen, "is not a matter of choice for the Christian; it is to be a Christian."[75] The need we are called to meet is not just "physical needs"[76] but "people's heavenly need through teaching, preaching, and the sacraments."[77] The two needs are inseparable.

> Both a gospel that lacks social concern as a necessary ingredient, as well as a social concern that neglects the needs of the soul as a necessary element in social action, are inadequate. Neither conveys the breadth and depth of the divine love. It is misleading to say, "We must be concerned for the gospel *and* social action," for it is not a question of adding something to the gospel. Only through its desire to alleviate other crushing burdens can preaching amount to a genuine desire for people to know God's love. Otherwise, such proclamation is not a gracious act. It may do some good, just as social action without recognition of people's heavenly need may do some good. But such an approach serves, in the end, merely to trivialize the gospel.[78]

It will be evident enough that I can happily find myself in basic sympathy with most of what Professor Allen has done in this work. In particular, his emphasis upon the centrality of the divine *participation* in human suffering seems to me a refreshing return to biblical faith after the failure of the two previously discussed authors to explore this motif. Although I shall have something critical to say about his presentation of "God the Father," I am particularly grateful for his (and Weil's) insight that creation itself already involves self-renunciation on God's part.

Without in any way qualifying my appreciation for this work, however, I should like for the sake of my own project here to indicate four areas of question:

First, I wonder whether it does not set up an unnecessary and potentially dangerous dichotomy between the Creator and Creation when one presents this world as containing nothing in which our quest for happiness could find satisfaction. Naturally, one knows what is meant, and it is an old and time-honored theological convention to convince people that this world is a poor object of their ultimate orientation, that they should turn from it and towards the One who made it. But this kind of theocentrism has always tended to suggest a denigration of the created order, and at a time when (as Abraham Heschel once put it) humankind and the biosphere may have no friend left other than the Lord God, it is rather vital, it seems to me, that Christian theology should stop indulging in this particular apologetic device. Even when it is sensitively put forward—as with Allen—it lends itself to the creation of a world-negating trend that is already far too pronounced in Christendom. Might it not better be said that we discover the ultimate happiness as we enter deeply into the contemplation of the mystery of creation itself? that we are led *through* the particular to the universal? through time to the eternal—*and back again?* At a moment in history when the means are at hand to have done with a world that cannot require of its inhabitants their ultimate loyalty and gratitude, is it not irresponsible for a faith which professes the *incarnation* of divine love to perpetuate this unfortunate dichotomy, even indirectly?

This leads at once to a *second*—and perhaps more important—question. Professor Allen's book gives very little evidence of its own time frame. His references to various authors, to events like the Stalin purge, and other similar internal textual evidence would naturally make the reader aware of the general period to which the book belongs. But the contextual dimension in its more profound sense, i.e., as containing specific issues with which theology must wrestle if it is to exceed mere doctrine, is at best only implicit. The book might have been written at other times and in other social settings, with only minor changes in the illustrative, literary, and other material. In his final part, Allen insists that "social concern"

is an integral part of the gospel itself, therefore presumably of theology. But this concern does not seem to me to inform in any
conspicuous way his basic approach. He is writing as a citizen of
one of two great superpowers, and in the year 1981, that is, after
Auschwitz, after Hiroshima, after Vietnam, after Watergate, after
"the death of God," after and in the midst of El Salvador, acid rain,
"Future Shock," etc., etc. Ought not such realities—to say nothing
of the internal spiritual conditions they have presupposed and
helped to create—to have informed more explicitly his treatment
of this theological problem in particular?

Third, while Allen's discussion of "natural evil" is illuminating
in many ways, I confess that I find his treatment of suffering inflicted
on account of human "cruelty" to be very limited. He has devoted
almost all of his discussion in this chapter to the analysis of one
type of suffering; and while it is dramatic enough, it is by no means
typical or even representative of the suffering that is the consequence of our distorted use of our freedom. As with the ancient
tales of the martyrs, the extreme suffering of Mme. de Beausobre
at the hands of Stalin's crude henchmen is edifying for all who suffer
human cruelty. But it is one thing to become one with the suffering
Christ and one's tormentors under the conditions of abject and
horrible torture, and something else to find Christ present in the
suffering inflicted upon one by those whom one loves, or by the
impersonal forces of one's society, or by cutthroat business practices
in one's community, or by any number of daily afflictions that for
the most part have no stories written about them. By singling out
this one, dramatic form of suffering under the conditions of sin,
Allen seems to me to have left many ordinary sufferers without a
response from the side of faith. I suspect that this has something
to do with the fact that his understanding of sin, like that of Kushner, is simplistic. "Cruelty" is only one of the myriad manifestations
of that deep-seated alienation which enters into our dealings one
with another.

Finally, I am perplexed by the manner in which Professor Allen
seems to shield "God the Father" from participation in the human
condition. There is no question about the Son and the centrality
of the cross in this whole discussion. But while *Jesus* is caused to

share our lot fully, God remains strangely transcendent. With sentences like, "The Son is afflicted by the Father for our sakes. . . . All this is brought about through the Father's loving will," one even has the impression (which is of course not novel in Christian circles!) that God the Father is orchestrating the scene at Golgotha.

Such an emphasis is not without precedent. Behind it stands the whole Patripassian controversy, supralapsarianism, predestinationism, and the Anselmic-Calvinistic theology of atonement. But (as Peter Abelard also sensed) it leaves one with a very questionable image of the "Father in Heaven." It also seems to me rather exclusively "Christian"—and I do not mean because of the centrality of the crucified One, but because the "Father," who is so very "distant" (and so characteristically paternal!), seems incommensurate with the God of Abraham, Isaac, and Jacob. Jewish believers are frequently heard to ask how it happens that while Abraham, ordered to sacrifice his son, was finally spared that horror, the Christian God goes through with it! Defensively, Christians respond that the comparison is not apt—and it is not. But we miss the point when we respond in that way. What the statement really wants to say to us is that while the Jewish confession of the divine transcendence does not prevent Israel from depicting "Yahweh" as a passionate and compassionate God who is capable of profound identification with us, Christians appear to want a God who not only does not suffer but could require of human beings the most sacrificial acts of suffering!

Must we not seriously consider the possibility that the gospel declaration of Jesus Christ's being "God with us" (Emmanuel!) implies the presence of a great question mark over all Theology which accentuates the distance dimension, especially when it does so at the expense of soteriology? A statement from our earlier discussion can perhaps best convey my meaning:

> When the crucified Jesus is called "the image of the invisible God," the meaning is that this is God, and God is like this. God is not greater than he is in this humiliation. God is not more glorious than he is

in this self-surrender. God is not more powerful than he is in this helplessness. God is not more divine than he is in this humanity.[79]

4. *God, Pain and Evil,* by George A. Buttrick (Nashville: Abingdon, 1966)

The unforgettable preacher of Madison Avenue Presbyterian Church and Harvard University Chapel was a master of allusion, nuance, and illustration. His book on suffering, a rather large one, cannot be summarized in this context. My inclusion of it here is due to its central hypothesis, which is interesting in itself and provocative on account of its contrast with previously discussed works. I shall confine my comments to a brief examination of that hypothesis.

It is announced already in the Preface of the book, where Dr. Buttrick shares with his readers something of his own struggle in trying to come to terms with "the problem of pain." He had written the manuscript of a book on the subject over the course of several years, but for some reason he did not find it satisfying. "Then one day light struck. . .":

I was wont to carry the "problem of pain" on my mind and one day I addressed myself. . . as follows: If pain were a problem, there might be an answer in philosophy or theology; and if pain were a concern in medicine only, there might be an explanation and even a cure in science; but since pain is existential, an event, even if it be no more than a toothache, the only possible answer is another Event set over against it. So now I make confession: I, a preacher of sorts, had never outrightly confronted in regard to pain the focal Event of the New Testament or dared to expose myself to the light shed by that Event on the enigma of man's suffering. I laid aside the books and read and reread the Bible. The light that had pierced a dull mind now broadened into day. Still, I found no neat answer: there is none. But I no longer cared about an answer. Why waste time on rationalistic "reasons" when you have been "surprised by joy."[80]

In the introductory chapters of the book, the author acknowledges "the fact of pain" (his "realism"),[81] its "constitutionality" ("against a confident humanism" which thinks pain can be wholly overcome),[82] etc. He also notes the inadequacy of numerous "answers" to suffering, and discusses in considerable detail three forms of suffering: "natural evil," "historical evil," and "personal evil." It is however not until the sixth chapter ("Dawn Watch: But How Can God Suffer?") that he comes to the heart of his message and leads the reader towards a fuller explication of his basic hypothesis, broached already in the Preface.

Since he shares the opinion—expressed in the present study—that suffering is not only real but in some sense and degree an essential aspect of our *creaturehood*, the mere dissolution of pain might, he says, "rob life of its reality."[83] We do not need a God who *annuls* our suffering but one who "shall break through into our world of pain, so that we can see through the opened door another world, so that the very pain contributes to the new journey into joy. We repeat: that *God* shall break through."[84]

This thought, however, gives rise to what is for Buttrick (as for Allen) an obviously thorny issue: ". . . how can God and suffering be joined?"[85]

> If God enters our suffering to share it, is he not thereby limited and disfigured by evil? On the other hand if he is lifted above our pain in an eternal Passivity, which seems to us an eternal callousness, can he be God? Certainly it would seem that in the latter event, beneath such an unapproachable heaven, our life is "solitary, poor, nasty, brutish, and short." If God shares our pain, it would be "justified," or at least we could wait for the "reasons." Yet pain, we have seen, is incipient death. How can the Godhead be infected with the obscenity of death?[86]

In his elaboration of this ancient problem, Buttrick makes extensive use of Baron von Hügel's renowned essay, "Suffering and God." It is a classical statement of the anti-Patripassianism which both Catholic and Protestant sources have conventionally adopted. (We heard distinct echoes of it in the work of Professor Allen.) " 'There is no Suffering in God,' " writes von Hügel; " 'Sympathy, yes, indeed, overflowing Sympathy . . . but no Suffering; and Suffering, indeed, overflowing suffering, in Christ, but as Man, not as

God.' "[87] As Buttrick responds, however, "We cannot believe in a heartless God. We cannot understand how there can be Sympathy without Suffering. The very word 'sympathy' means to 'feel with'.
. . . The word 'Father' is in the Lord's Prayer. Of course it is 'in heaven', above our poor parenthood, but the word 'Father' still has meaning."[88]

Yet, having thus clearly betrayed his own basic sympathies, Buttrick seems to pull back from the radicality of his incipient Patripassianism. There is a long and rather obtuse section on the nature of paradox, and we are left at last with the declaration that in this matter, too,

> we confront a paradox: If God suffers, he is limited and infected with death, and so is not God; but if he does not suffer, he is both heartless and denied the insights which suffering alone sometimes brings to us, and once again is not God. Yet a paradox is not an untruth or a deception, for both its terms are verified in daily life: we are free, yet under Sovereignty; we are individual, yet social; we are body, yet psyche. If the conviction of a suffering God flatly affronts the mind which God himself has given, we had better forget the whole business.[89]

Having thus satisfied himself (though not, I think, the reader) about the ancient debate over the Father's suffering, the author now turns to his primary statement in a chapter which, he confesses, "obviously . . . should have come first."[90] It is called "Breakthrough: The Event." Echoing sentiments that were found as well in our previous authors, Dr. Buttrick laments that we are so influenced by methods of "science" (Jacques Ellul would have said the great god, Fact!) that we are inhibited from perceiving how truth in the deepest sense normally comes to us "in Event." "We overlook the sharp event in favor of universals such as 'humanity' or 'the absolute.' Intellectual pride dotes on universals."[91] But, he asks, ". . . suppose truth finds us through events. . .," and "suppose there is one Event which gathers all other events into a strange sovereignty."[92] No doubt, hearing such a proposal, the average person would look about for a very impressive occurrence. "If God wishes to make a Breakthrough he should not arrive in 'Galilee of the

Gentiles,' that is, in a region which could not boast even the staunch Hebraism of Judea. He should not choose a town of little note and a craftsman's home . . ."[93] "*unless* . . . his glory is lowliness, and by the same tremendous paradox his power is love."[94]

Why, asks Buttrick, in a style reminiscent of Luther, should "so small an affair" as the story of the Nazarene "be called a breakthrough?"[95] The answer, he hastens to advise us (and here Calvin, not Luther, is his master!) is "*not in the first instance* the cross." Had there been nothing beyond Golgotha, the story should have ended with the disciples returning to their fishnets—and not a soul today would have heard about it. Jesus is "remembered," rather, "*because he rose from the dead.*"

> There is nothing like it. For while it is continuous in one sense with the Old Testament, it is sharply discontinuous: it is the Book of the *New* Covenant which God has made with men through Jesus Christ. It is the good news of the Breakthrough, that is, of the Resurrection and of the present Spirit of Jesus.[96]

Given the resurrection from the dead, the cross (the *second* reason why Jesus is "remembered") is now thrown into a different light. For it means that what was happening at Golgotha concealed a reality of cosmic significance: in and through the death of the "man of sorrows," God was meeting the event of our suffering with the "sovereign Event" of God's participation in our suffering. "Because God was in our pain, suffering for our sins, pain was *purged of judgment and stripped of any final power.*"[97]

> The light of the Resurrection means that God is in the Cross. He is with us in all our pains in both love and power. Surely our time, though perhaps only when a worse brokenness has come upon us, will leave the shallows, and find once more the depth of the New Testament joy.[98]

This event does not by itself and as such, however, constitute the complete "Breakthrough"; for it calls for our response. Without that response the cross-resurrection event is "void."[99] Our response does not *give* the event its significance; but without our faith-response the event does not have meaning *for us.*

Again, however, this poses a problem: Why would one settle upon this particular event (the scandal of particularity)? Why would anyone consider that "Truth," which is "another name for God,"[100] resides just here?

Buttrick tries to prepare us for his answer to this perennial problem by providing, with the help of "Existentialism," three criteria of events which can be properly so called: (1) *"an event comes from the totality,"* i.e., it emerges out of the whole history of a people, as Hitler's invasion of France arose out of and can only be comprehended in the light of the geography and history of Europe; (2) *"an event has its own invasiveness,* its singularity, almost its arbitrary inruption. . . . It . . . walks in without an invitation . . . . It 'takes place' "; and (3) *"an event is a gauntlet thrown down in our path,"* demanding of us a decision: ". . . what will you now do?"[101]

Well and good, but such criteria could be claimed for many actual events—the Dialogues of Plato, the "first thrust of science," "the first school, precursor of an education which billboards proclaim as 'America's Greatest Blessing,' etc."[102] There is, says Buttrick, no externally compelling reason for us to settle upon the Christ event as ultimate. "Each of us must answer for himself."[103] Yet faith, when it is present, knows that this event does indeed meet the above-named criteria: (1) It emerges from *"the totality"*: " 'It came to pass in those days that . . .' '. . . the Word was made flesh. . .' "; (2) it has its own *invasiveness* (self-authentication?): " 'Behold, I stand at the door and knock. . .' "; and (3) it is like a *gauntlet,* a challenge thrown down before us: " 'If any one hears my voice and opens the door . . . .' "[104] To be sure, faith is not certitude. But neither is it entirely arbitrary—or even unusual. "All our life is by faith. . . . Anyone and everyone lives by faith." There is always risk in faith, but it is not without its reasons; and in considerable measure the reasonableness of faith in the Christ event relates precisely to the new perspective that it affords us on the fact of our suffering:

> What comes of our response to the Event of Christ as regards pain and evil? . . . To the New Testament pain is not morbidity or hopelessness or retribution. It is still devil's work, but the devil has been

overcome and the penalty has been cancelled. So pain is now cleansing, illumination, and vocation; not in itself, for pain is incipient death, but because the Event of Christ has changed the bitter waters into a pool of healing.[105]

The remainder of the book is an extensive elaboration of this basic confession.

What seems to me particularly important about this approach, despite certain weaknesses which I shall mention in a moment, is its consistent and imaginative attempt to respond to the reality of human suffering *existentially*. I am of course aware that that is an overworked and still-ambiguous term, but in a Christian context it can be useful nonetheless. In that context, where the primary realities are relational rather than conceptual or substantial, and where, therefore, all the key terms (love, grace, faith, hope, obedience, sin, etc.) presuppose encounter, meeting, engagement, confrontation, it is simply not adequate to treat a question like human suffering as if it were a problem to be solved through ratiocination and logic. It is necessary to get the encounter language of faith into the discussion, and in a central way. Otherwise, a very wrong impression is created from the outset. It was this wrong impression that I sensed in Lewis's study.

Buttrick understands in a manner that is deeply personal (even if it is not always clearly articulated) that a "fact of existence" as profound as is connoted by the word *suffering* can only be met by a reality that can truly *engage* that "fact." The event of our suffering must be encountered, if it is to be encountered at all, by another event. "Answers" to human suffering—as we learn from Job's comforters—are *always* inadequate, no matter how "right" they may be in their way. Interestingly enough, some of the same things that the God of Job says out of the whirlwind have already been iterated by the comforters, especially Elihu! But that does not make the "answers" of the comforters appropriate after all; because it is not *what* God says finally to the suffering Job but *that* God says something that is the answer; and, as I put it earlier in the text, it does not matter that by far the greater portion of the divine "answers" to Job are in the form of questions! The Presence itself is the answer, and the only appropriate and convincing one, for all its elusiveness. The silence is broken (Endo).

Buttrick (the preacher!) understands that suffering is not, finally, a problem. It is a dimension, and a very prominent one, of life itself. The only satisfactory response to it therefore is one that seems to come from the source of our life. Jesus, Buttrick knows, *can* be (for faith) that response, because Jesus is not just a teacher, a prophet, an example, but a compelling representation of the source of life: "I *am* the way, the truth, and the life." Because the word-event of which Jesus is the core does not bypass—nor does it easily resolve—the "fact" of our suffering but goes to the heart of it, accepting its reality, being broken by it, yet hiddenly engaging it with a love that is stronger than death—because of this participation and encounter with suffering humanity which is at the center of the kerygma, it can be experienced by faith as an event meeting face to face the event of our vulnerable existence.

Academic theology, being devoted too exclusively to concepts (and "absolutes"), and feeling too little the pulse of life, may provide helpful insights and guidelines for our comprehension of "the problem of suffering." But until it is able to translate into its medium of communication *the encounter quality* that is at the heart of the *euangelion* it will usually be flat and unmoving. It is perhaps not accidental that the preacher, Buttrick, has sensed this, where more discursive scholars have not. For preachers and pastors, if they are "for real," know that the fundamental issues of human life can be met only by what itself bears about it the taste of life, and not by theory.

There are, of course, certain difficulties associated with this work, as I am able to internalize it. (There is no nonproblematic theology—including the present volume!) One problem is the way in which the author hedges over the question of God's suffering—this once more! He rightly challenges the anti-Patripassianism of von Hügel and others, and it is fairly obvious what he would *like* to do: he would like to say (to use Moltmann's phraseology again) that God is not other than what he is revealed to be in the suffering servant named Jesus! But Buttrick seems fearful of plunging into those waters—and one wonders, as one plows through his rather turgid discussion of paradox: What *is* it in the Christian doctrinal past that makes us all so anxious in this connection? Is it really (what Buttrick claims) a reluctance to depict Almighty God so close to death? Or is it not rather our cultural conditioning, our centuries-long requirement of providing a fitting symbol of imperial splendor, our need to make the sovereign Lord God really *look* like a sovereign! Luther, in this and in other important respects a maverick in Christendom, dared to write about "the crucified God"! It seemed not to threaten or diminish his understanding of God's true dignity and "otherness"—even *total* otherness, if you will! In fact, if it is true (as Buttrick so beautifully said at one point) that God's "glory is lowliness, and . . . his power . . . love," might it not be more consistent with divinity thus understood to come over to the side of the Patripassians?[106]

A *second* difficulty (for me, at any rate) has to do with Buttrick's way of relating cross and resurrection. I can concur with him that in a certain sense the cross is the "second" reason for "remembering" Jesus, if by this he means that the cross becomes meaningful only when faith is able to perceive in and behind it a more eternal and compelling reality than appears on the surface of the crucifixion as such. I understand this "secondariness" of the cross if Buttrick intends, through it, to say that in the first place there must have been (for the first Christians) and must still be (for us) some deeply spiritual awakening, causing us to "think twice" about Golgotha. If this is what he (and others) mean by the primary nature of the resurrection and the advent of the Spirit, then I am willing to agree that the cross could be called "second." But if that is what Buttrick means, he has not communicated it very clearly (and in that respect he is not alone!). Instead, he comes dangerously close, I should say, to making of the resurrection a kind of miraculous table-turning, an astonishment of the first order, and therefore strictly discontinuous with the very ordinariness and simplicity which he (rightly) attributes to the whole event on which he wants to fasten our attention. If, as one gathers from his general approach, the point of the Christ event is that it meets our suffering lives on their own level and thus (as I have put it in my own text) engages them "from within," surely this primary emphasis must not be undone by a resurrectionism which dazzles the mind and spirit with precisely its extraordinariness, leaving us with a heavenly "answer" to what is *not* just an earthly "problem."

A *third* problematic area in this work is the rather unsatisfactory manner in which the author attempts to bridge the gap between faith and reason. It shows up in his structure as well as his content. The central thesis, by his own admission, is contained in his Christological chapters, beginning with the sixth. Yet he tries to prepare for this by drawing upon a variety of generalizations, with the consequence that one feels the presence of unacknowledged leaps of faith, only loosely covered by homiletical nuances. With respect to content, the faith/reason gap grows conspicuous with the discussion about the "why" of choosing this *particular* event. It is not enough to say that all life operates "by faith." The question still persists, Why this particular faith? I do not believe that there is any facile way of overcoming this faith/reason dichotomy. The scandal of particularity remains, after all the arguments are in. But at least Christians ought not to proceed as if they could move between ordinary human wisdom and an explicitly Christian faith without sensing at every point "the folly of what we preach."

Despite these difficulties, however, my appreciation for this work is basic. "The claim of this book," writes George Buttrick in his final chapter, "is that pain and death are events, and that therefore they cannot be answered either by a formula in science or a theory in philosophy, but only by an Event."[107] This, I believe, is fundamental; and if I have not made it perfectly clear that that is where I also stand, especially in my Christological chapter, then I would invite the reader to return to that discussion in the light of the present one.

5. *Salute to a Sufferer,* by Leslie D. Weatherhead (New York and Nashville: Abingdon, 1962)

The renowned preacher of the City Temple in London, England, at the end of 45 years in parish ministry, set for himself a ponderous task: he would write a small book, first offered as the Peake Memorial

Lectures, on the Christian understanding of human suffering. Only, it must be a book which—like Wesley's sermons, read beforehand to a kitchen maid—could be understood by everyone.

> What I have tried to do is to imagine that I am writing this book for a Christian friend of ordinary education and outlook who has suddenly fallen seriously ill, perhaps incurably ill, or whose wife or child has done so.
> I imagine that his mind is in a whirl of confusion about it.[108]

The author's purpose, then, is to clear away some of the confusion, and he does so by posing, in 10 short chapters, an equal number of questions: "Does God want me to be ill?" "But surely it is God who allows my suffering?" "Why should this happen to *me?*" "Where do God's goodness and omnipotence come in?" "If I don't get better, is God's plan defeated?" etc.

Those who know other works of Dr. Weatherhead, especially his *Why Do Men Suffer?*[109] a much earlier work, will not be surprised by the approach taken in this little book. We may summarize the argument as follows:

Certainly God does not "want me to be ill"! In fact, it is clear from what we know of God as God is revealed, especially, in Jesus, that "God's ideal intention for all his sons and daughters is perfect health of body, mind and spirit."[110] But it is true, of course, that God "allows" suffering, because God "allows human sin";[111] it is the consequence of God's not only allowing but willing human freedom. Yet allowing something is not *intending* it. To take "the best illustration of all, the cross of Christ,"[112] it could not be claimed (says Weatherhead) that God *intended* the Son to be crucified, yet God did quite obviously allow it.

> It must be stated fearlessly that the cross was not the will of God in the sense of being God's intention. Jesus did not come into the world to be murdered. He came to be followed. Any opposite view involves the deduction that Judas, Pilate, and the evil, crafty priests were pawns in a divine game and carrying out a divine plan. This is impossible logic. It was wicked men who put Christ to death.[113]

This same primary "illustration" takes us still further along the road to understanding suffering: While God did not positively *will* the death of the Son; while it is the consequence of blind and evil and ignorant human freedom, God is able to cause the cross of Jesus to become "the very center of what we call God's plan of redemption."[114] For nothing "finally and ultimately" is able to defeat God's omnipotence. Thus, while God does not will *any* suffering, God is able to "weave it into a pattern as wonderful as one which left it out."[115]

> God can bring us, not in spite of our suffering, but because of it and his use of it, and our reaction to it, to the same place as we should have reached if suffering had never come our way and with final gain instead of loss.[116]

But "didn't God know that suffering would fall upon me?" Yes, replies our author, because the God who is omnipotent is also omniscient. But again, knowing something does not imply willing it.

> We must admit then that God is responsible for the possibility, nay the probability, of suffering, but he ever seeks to implant the opposite of its causes, that is, knowledge instead of ignorance, wisdom instead of folly, and holiness instead of sin. Further, he knows that where those opposites cannot be established he can still make evil serve his purposes, and this is the justification of its possibility.[117]

At first glance, this may seem callous, since we naturally associate God with kindness. But (an important distinction!) we are not in fact told that God is "kind" but that God "is love." "Love has in it a stern note, something stronger than mere benevolence. Kindness makes us happy, but it has no power to make us improve. Love has."[118] Like C. S. Lewis, Weatherhead has a sharp eye for human assumptions at this point. As Bonhoeffer once put it, the emphasis in the biblical declaration that "God is love" should fall upon the first word: it is God who defines what love means, not vice versa.

> There is a sense in which God is not kind. His relationship with us is bigger and grander and closer. Kindness is often a love substitute

which we offer to people whom we may not love, cannot love, or cannot be bothered to love, and kindness is too poor a thing to express God's relationship to us.[119]

We may *want* a God who is merely kind. "When I think about God I realize that, in weak moments of self-indulgence, I should like to live in a world where 'a good time was had by all,' where God was kind and everybody was happy." But this is a superficial wish; deeper reflection brings the awareness that true happiness is never so easily acquired: ". . . in better moments I realize that it would be asking for a love substitute, kindness" to entertain such a dream. "Our truest happiness is a by-product of our quest for blessedness. . . ."[120]

Blessedness implies, usually, some experience of suffering. When suffering comes our way we do not, of course, feel that it is a blessed thing. Why, the sufferer asks, should this "bad thing" happen to *me?* Weatherhead's way of answering this question is interesting in the light of our discussion of Kushner's thesis: "This world," he says, "is not a finished piece of work. God is still at work on it and in it. It is not yet 'the best of all possible worlds' but it is the world of best possibilities."[121] While this answer comes closer to Kushner's than do the approaches of the other Christian thinkers we have been considering, it is by no means so radical as that of the Jewish thinker. The reason is fairly obvious—and entirely consistent with what we have already observed about *Christian* discourse on this subject generally: Weatherhead, unlike the Jewish thinker, is deeply committed to the profession of the divine omnipotence. Omnipotence may be *qualified* by human freedom (freedom being for Weatherhead as for most other Christian commentators the primary cause of suffering), but it is not defeated. Given the fact that God chose from the outset to create a world in which human beings are both free and mutually interacting, human suffering is certainly (from the outset!) possible—"nay, probable." To the question "Why me?" therefore, part of the answer must be: " 'Because you belong to the human family.' Your suffering is part of the price the team pays in its great struggle toward perfection."[122]

The question is not, in that case, what God can and cannot do, but what God *may* and *must not* do. God must not set aside the laws of nature simply to ensure the happiness of this or that individual;[123] and God must not simply *do for* the human creature what men and women are intended to do for themselves, if they are to become the mature and "perfect" beings God intends them to be.

What precisely *does* the divine omnipotence mean, then? "Is it. . . that God is not as powerful as we thought; that he cannot help the suffering that overtakes us?"[124] Here Weatherhead flatly rejects the Kushner hypothesis: ". . . one fleeting thought of the power of wind and wave, of flashing lightning and tearing hurricane, of volcano and earthquake, apart altogether from the terrifying energy locked up in the atom, convince us that the creator of this universe could fitly be called the Lord of power."[125] Ah, but power in its real sense is not just might! Sheer might could end by wrecking the creation! Power is effectiveness, is "the ability to achieve purpose."[126] No doubt the God who without human aid created Mount Everest *could* do (and does!) any number of things; but would such things as we associate with power in fact achieve God's deepest purposes? If God's purpose is the creation of a world in which human beings, out of freedom and love for life and one another, build a world that is good and beautiful, then such a purpose could hardly be achieved through sheer might. God *must not*, in that case, apply power tactics to the working-out of the divine intention. God *must not* "have favourites," or "achieve an end as though the means did not matter," or perform the *kinds* of miracles that are really just "magic";[127] and God *must not* just give me whatever I ask for, either, since my own experience tells me how frequently what I have asked for has been precisely the wrong thing! All of this means that I shall have to suffer in the process of living; but it does not mean that God's omnipotence is a meaningless concept. God is *"finally* omnipotent," says Weatherhead, because God is able to bring out of all the mistakes and wrong turnings and confusion of the creation what is God's ultimate intention.

We are really so ignorant of that ultimate purpose! Anyone who walked into a theater, watched the first act of a play for a few minutes, and then went off with all kinds of deductions about the author's intention would be deemed foolish. But this is what we do, most of the time, with God's earthly drama. The human race as a whole is such a recent affair, after all. The geologist Gheyselinck has graphically illustrated that by pointing out that "if the whole history of the world from the Archaean Age until today were compressed into a film scheduled to run for twenty-four hours, man would not *appear* until *the last five seconds of the film!*"[128] "Why," exclaims Weatherhead, "the play has hardly started yet, has it?"[129] The one thing of which we can be sure, he believes, is that *ultimately* God's *good* purposes will prevail. "The victory is promised on what Livingstone called 'the Word of a Gentleman,' and our private sorrows and suffering, however sore now, desolating to our present faith, and puzzling to the intellect, will finally form such a glowing part of God's victory, that joy will fill our hearts. So far from everlasting complaining, we shall be saying, 'Fancy God being able to make *that* out of my pain! Blessed be his glorious name forever."[130]

For the present, this (eschatological) awareness of the ultimate triumph of the divine purpose for life expresses itself in a faith which is our best weapon in "fighting illness" and other forms of suffering. Fortunately, Weatherhead (unlike so many contemporary faith healers and peddlars of religion) has retained something of the biblical and Reformation understanding of faith; so he immediately warns his readers against false conceptions. Faith is an overworked and misused word. "In regard to faith a lot of misunderstanding is current. We are told by some to 'have faith,' as if one could do so like turning on a tap."[131] Faith rightly understood (Luther also understood it so!) is *trust:* it means "quietly trusting the God who is like Jesus *whether one is healed or not.* . . ."[132]

In the final chapter, Dr. Weatherhead returns to the theme which has obviously exercised his spirit throughout this work (and, I suspect, his life): God's omnipotence. "If I don't get better, is God's plan defeated?" asks the chapter head, and the author responds with "a triumphant 'No!' "

The very idea of omnipotence is not that everything that happens does so because God wills it in the sense of intending it. The truth about omnipotence is that nothing that does happen, even though it springs from man's misused free will, or from the human family's mass ignorance, or from folly or sin can *finally* defeat God.[133]

Suffering is against the divine will; yet through the power of grace and faith we may discover the divine omnipotence at work also *in* suffering: ". . . it can never be too emphatically stated that there is an opportunity in suffering which it is God's will that we should take and turn to our own, and the world's, high advantage. . . . There is an alchemy which turns all things into spiritual gold, and that alchemy is the right attitude to them."[134] We may not in this way *understand* everything that happens to us, but we may sense enough of the mystery of it to believe that it is purposeful. Hence, "we may rise above" our suffering and so "rob it of its power to quell us."[135]

In the closing paragraphs of the book, Weatherhead returns to the cross. "I cannot," he reiterates, "myself avoid the conclusion that the Cross was no more the will of God than any other brutal murder. It was the work of wicked men." Jesus' agony in Gethsemane and on Golgotha was his fear "lest God's plan should be defeated." He had hoped to persuade the world of his message about the divine "Fatherhood" and human cohumanity; but now it seemed hopeless. Yet, while God did not *intend* the cross, it meant in the long run "that far more spiritual power has been released into the world than if Jesus had lived to a ripe old age and died in quiet retirement. And:

> God can weave our lesser sorrows and sufferings into a plan which will leave us with no sense of loss at last. God can flash to us code messages by means of lamps which we did not light. Jesus might have said to Caiaphas and those who plotted his death what Joseph said to his brethren, "You meant evil against me; but God meant it for good" (Gen. 50:20).[136]

There is, in my opinion, a wealth of Christian wisdom in this slim volume, reflecting the experience of a pastor and preacher over many years. Though its language and some of its concerns may reflect, in a measure, another epoch, it is still eminently worth reading, and useful, I should think, in pastoral situations. The simplicity of the style, and the fact that it is addressed to Christians "of ordinary education and outlook," should not, however, deceive us! This is a highly sophisticated little study. It does, in my opinion, a much better job of handling some of the difficult concepts we have considered in these pages than do most works that are advertised for their erudition! The reader may thus surmise that I have left this book to the last because, of the five, I think it the best.

That does not mean that it is without problems, of course. Let me mention them first, and leave for last what I think is right about this statement—because in that way I shall also be able to express whatever concluding word I have, at this juncture in my life, on this unconcluded subject!

For one thing, Weatherhead manifests what is probably a characteristically Methodist ambiguity about the relation between "faith and works." On the one hand he wants to tell us that it is God who takes all the confusion and chaos and ignorance and evil of the world and transforms it into an unheard-of affirmation of existence. It is sheer grace! But then he will turn, in the course of a sentence, and put the onus on us: it is all a matter of "attitude"—this is the "alchemy" that makes gold out of dross.[137] Now, in defense of Methodist and other forms of ambiguity on this subject, I for one would like to go on record as being of the opinion that it is a subject in relation to which it is extremely difficult if not impossible to *avoid* ambiguity! Some of the seemingly clear-headed thinkers who *have* avoided ambiguity in relation to this couplet have ended by giving us blatant and dangerous heresies. The "cheap grace" that Bonhoeffer had to take on at the outset of his brief witness was a consequence precisely of an *un*ambiguous reading of Reformation teaching on the subject. The lack of a social dimension, particularly, in much of the Christianity stemming from the Reformation is another consequence of the same one-sided emphasis upon the *sola gratia.* From the other side, so is liberal Christianity's overemphasis upon human potentiality.

Still, as Buttrick would have said, paradox is not a synonym for confusion or contradiction. There is a paradoxical—or at least dialectical—relation between grace and obedience, gospel and law, faith and works; and if we are to avoid saying two mutually exclusive things then we Christians have to become more adept at articulating that dialectic. We cannot (must not!) say to suffering people, either in the pastoral setting or in the wider social context of our suffering world: (1) God is able to make it all come out right, and (2) It's entirely up to you! The first message leads to ethical passivity—and in a nuclear age we know what that means! The second, in such an age, probably leads the sensitive to despair. Their combination leads to a dismissal of the message!

Second, and in a subtle and related way, Weatherhead's manner of discussing the cross leaves one unsatisfied and unconvinced. For one thing, one wants to ask him whether the term "illustration" is adequate here. It was a concept heavily relied upon by theological liberalism, and it is by no means without significance: something is illustrated, demonstrated, *revealed* in the cross of the Christ. And indeed if that aspect—illumination, or whatever we may call it— is left out of our atonement theologies, they easily degenerate into sheer myth and magic, as Abelard also knew. But one wants to ask the liberals what some of Abelard's contemporaries (e.g., Bernard of Clairvaux) asked him: Does anything *happen* in this "event"? Is anything *changed*? Is anything *new* introduced? Do we, should we, look around in the environs of Golgotha for anything like a new "indicative" (gospel) upon which the old "imperative" (the law of love) might find a foundation, a *fundamentum in re?*

This aspect of Weatherhead's soteriology is, of course, connected in a rudimentary way with his repeated insistence that the cross was not *intended* by God. Now, I have already (in connection with my discussion of Allen's book) expressed my own abhorrence of the notion of a Father-God who orchestrates the scene on Golgotha. I believe this to be a misunderstanding, not only of the scriptural witness to the passion of Christ but also (in its best expressions) of the doctrine of the Trinity. It is born of the desire to preserve the aseity of God, and frankly I doubt very much if human beings need to be so worried about that! I might say, facetiously, that God is probably capable of looking after his own aseity! What *we* have to attempt, in the most serious and credible way that we can, is to say how the high and holy One of Israel, who "inhabits eternity," dwells "with him also that is of a contrite and humble spirit, . . . to revive the heart of the contrite ones" (Isa. 57:15).

It will be evident enough, I think, from the earlier sections of this study, that I believe the best (i.e., most scripturally sound, most contextually significant, and most communicable) way of achieving such a goal is through reflection upon and rethinking of the minority tradition that Martin Luther designated *theologia crucis*. The "theology of the cross," unlike every sort of *theologia gloriae*, is free of cultural images of the divine which commit us to soteriological positions that rule out in advance God's personal and total involvement in the cross of the Christ. If God *is* who God is revealed to be in this event, then God's holiness, glory, wisdom, goodness, love, and power, along with every other "perfection" of deity, must be interpreted in the light of this revelation, and not as if they were attributes whose meaning we could derive through sources independent of this event![138] If God has chosen to express the meaning of aseity through engagement, of immutability through *kenosis*, of transcendence through solidarity, of holiness through servanthood, of love through suffering-with, then why should we continue to treat the deity in Christian faith and theology as if "He" were *personally*, so to speak, above all that, and could only permit "Himself" to enter into proximity with "all that" in a once-removed manner—through "the second person of the Trinity"?

Naturally, if we insist upon keeping God-Father "up there and out there" (Robinson), we shall either have to depict the first person of the Trinity as directing the proceedings that led to the Place of the Skull (as Allen does), or else (with Weatherhead) demonstrate the Father's skill at the a posteriori rearrangement of events! If that is our choice, then let us by all means choose Weatherhead's way! The notion of a father (*any* father!) actually planning the murder of his son (any son!) is just gruesome, and we should admit it openly! It is not made less gruesome by the weight of sacred *doctrina* that has been superimposed upon this scenario. But if the event in question is one which in some profound sense involves God's own "death," God's own "acquaintance with grief," God's own proximity to "pain" (as it does for Endo, Kitamori, Moltmann, and other representatives of the *theologia crucis* tradition) then it *can* be meaningful to speak of a divine "plan" in which the cross of the Christ is central; for, as I have tried to show in the main text of this work,

the whole movement of God (God personally, not just God's representatives!) in the story that is told in the continuity of the Testaments is towards identification with sinful, suffering humanity.
Israel's story is already the story of a people "hastening towards
Golgotha." We shall be able to sustain the high significance of *that*
transcendence—the transcendence of the One whose "weeping" is
what elevates him "beyond such things"—only if we are bold enough
to proclaim that *God* was "in Christ," *in* this event, not only par-
tially, or by proxy, or poetically and illustratively, but really and
fully: Emmanuel, "God with us," and not only in our glory but in
our humility, not only in our power but in our vulnerability, not
only in our life but in our death.

If what the cross of Christ means is that God—God's own Self—
has here entered into the kingdom of death with which the kingdoms of this world have continuously covenanted (Isaiah 28), to
conquer the power of death *from within*, then *something really has
happened* at Golgotha. It is not only an "illustration" of something
eternal, but the *fundamentum* of a new situation, the seed of a new
beginning; and we may participate in it, not only as those whose
minds have been illuminated, but whose lives have been and are
being transformed by this new reality.

To speak finally about what I consider right about this book, let
me say in one word that it is its *eschatology*. I did not include in
the major part of this brief study a chapter on eschatology, and this
may be regarded by some as a fault in a book which purports to
think about God and human suffering comprehensively within the
framework of the basic Christian doctrines. By way of explanation,
let me say that this omission is entirely intentional. For I do not
consider eschatology a separable aspect of Christian faith and theology, such as could be (and traditionally was) assigned a chapter
(usually at the end of the exposition!). Eschatology is, rather, a
dimension of *every other* aspect of our tradition, and it is as such
that it must be incorporated into every theological statement. I
believe that I have done this—though to do it really well is next
to impossible, because of all the motifs of our faith this one is the
most difficult to articulate.

What I particularly appreciate about Weatherhead's little work is that he has expressed an eschatological posture in relation to this subject which is not only sensitive but graspable by Christians "of ordinary education." He has done this, primarily, in connection with the great struggle of his book, which is his attempt to comprehend what could be made today of the divine omnipotence—the theme to which he returns continuously.

Rightly and carefully, he refuses to engage in a defense of divinity either by straightforwardly upholding God's omnipotence *or* by denying or limiting it. Unfortunately, he does not explore the paradox of divine power being "made perfect in weakness," and this, as I have already said, weakens his case. But he does the next best thing—and a thing that is in fact closely allied to the theology of the cross: he depicts a God who, being personally involved in and committed to the historical project, must not superimpose upon it a finality that is wholly discontinuous with its course. Not *can* not, but *must* not! To do so would be in effect to cancel creation, to count it a failed experiment, to start over again. Omnipotence must wait! That is, if it is the omnipotence of love.

The futurism of this eschatology will be disturbing to all who require consummation here and now. Realized eschatologies abound, in which they can have their consummations! But remember: *La theorie c'est bon, mais ca n'empeche pas d'exister!*[139] Weatherhead (again, perhaps significantly, a pastor and preacher) is too keen an observer of the human condition to settle for comfortable theoretical endings which fail to take into account the fact "things exist" despite our theoretical exorcisms. At the same time, he is not ready (with Kushner) to buy into the modern conclusion that many things happen "for no reason at all." Is it a compromise to say that the One who is in charge is still in the process of executing the reason (*telos*), that "finally" God's good purposes will emerge? It could be, of course—and especially if that message were accompanied by an *ethical* "wait and see." But in Weatherhead's case there is little danger of ethical passivity, I think; and if the kind of thing that he says about God's godhood is compromise it is only the compromise of faith, which is willing in the meantime to live in the tension between expectancy and experience, and to believe

198 God and Human Suffering

that what it hopes for, though not "seen" (Heb. 11:1), is on the
way to meet us, even if now it is "hidden beneath its opposite."

> The believer is bound to be agnostic about the form which the ul-
> timate state of God's creation will take. He can only trust in the love
> of God which he believes to have been revealed and, in the light of
> his present experience of God, affirm with Julian of Norwich that
> "all shall be well, and all shall be well, and all manner of thing shall
> be well."[140]

Notes

Introduction

1. Both optimism (with which Christian hope is regularly confused in New World Christianity) and pessimism (the favored resort of those who, quite legitimately, reject "Christian" optimism) are finally "childish categories" (Heidegger) because they succumb to the adolescent need to force existence into a uniform and predictable mold, thus sacrificing both its mystery and its variety. "Optimism and pessimism," writes Karl Jaspers, "are equally unfounded and inadequate. As knowledge they are delusive; in practice they distract from the task of man. They do not lead to the high road of humanity. Do not calamity and opportunity both lie in the course of events? Is it not only when man does his best and is ready for whatever happens, beyond optimism and pessimism, that he is rational and truly human?" (*The Future of Mankind* [Chicago and London: University of Chicago Press, 1961], p. 324).

   For another discussion of optimism and pessimism as they relate to this theme, see John Cowburn, S.J., *Shadows and the Dark: The Problems of Suffering and Evil* (London: SCM, 1979).

2. I have discussed what I understand of the importance of the contextual factor in two essays: "Contextuality in Christian Theology," *Toronto Journal of Theology* 1 (Spring 1985), and "Die Vielgestaltigkeit christlichen Zeugnisses im Spannungsfeld zwischen Wortgebundenheit und Kontextbezug," in *Oekumenische Erschleissung Martin Luthers*, ed. Peter Manns and Harding Meyer (Paderborn: Bonifatius-Druckerei; Frankfurt: Otto Lembeck, 1983), pp. 293ff. (English translation in *Luther's Ecumenical Significance*, ed. Peter Manns and Harding Meyer [Philadelphia: Fortress, 1984], pp. 247ff.).

3. In the light of the most painful (and alas most formative) events of our epoch—events like Auschwitz and Hiroshima, whose occurrence cannot be separated from the influences of fixed Christian doctrinal conventions which shielded their adherents from the realities of their world—only the most intransigent forms of Christianity can sustain conceptions of "the gospel" which preclude this struggle with the "here and now." A concrete, poignant, and still timely statement of the reason why the good news can be heard only by those who submit themselves to the world's "bad news" is given, implicitly, in this incident from the memoirs of Sir George MacLeod:

"When I was in South Africa, just prior to a big public meeting in Durban, an unknown ulsterman approached me and said, 'I hope you are going to give them the Gospel red hot.' 'Yes,' I replied, 'I am speaking of its social implications here in Durban.' 'Social implications?' he repeated in an acme of suspicion, 'what is wanted is the Gospel red hot.' 'But is it not of the Gospel,' I asked, 'that by the right of Christ all men have an equal dignity?' 'Yes,' he said, 'That is of the Gospel.' 'Then what,' I said, 'are you Gospellers doing about the 10,000 Africans and Indians who have not got a decent shelter in Durban this cold night?' 'Them?' replied the hot Gospeller, 'I wish the whole damn lot were sunk in the harbour.' Yet that man could have recited the whole Christian offer immaculately, and his own engagement to be in Christ" (*Only One Way Left* [Glasgow: The Iona Community House, 1956], p. 54).

4. *Nihilism: Its Origin and Nature—With a Christian Answer* (London: Routledge and Kegan Paul, 1961), pp. 176-177.

5. See *Pedagogy of the Oppressed* (New York: Seabury, 1972); also, by the same author, *Education for Critical Consciousness* (New York: Continuum, 1980).

I am indebted for these insights to Robert and Alice Evans and other organizers of a conference on "Pedagogies of the Non-Poor" at Claremont, Calif., in 1983, attended by Friere. What becomes clear when one compares situations in which human suffering is manifest and acknowledged with situations in which it is unknown or repressed is that in the latter "pedagogies" must begin with a "conscientization" aimed at awakening the mind and spirit to a negative reality that people in such societies (naturally?) are at pains to avoid; hence there is no easy translation of either method or content from the situation of the oppressed to that of "the oppressor."

Chapter 1   The Reality of Human Suffering

1. For example, "The modern experience belongs in the category of pathos or irony rather than tragedy, because contemporary culture has no vantage point of faith from which to understand the predicament of modern man. It is therefore incapable either of rising to a tragic defiance of destiny, as depicted in Greek drama, or of achieving a renewal of life through a contrite submission to destiny, as in Christian tragedy" (*Faith and History: A Comparison of Christian and Modern Views of History* [New York: Scribner, 1951], p. 9).

2. J. E. L. Newbigin, *Missions under the Cross*, ed. Norman Goodall (London: Edinburgh House, 1953; distributed in U.S.A. by Friendship Press, N.Y.), p. 109.

3. Mary Baker Glover Eddy's religious community was established in 1866, and the chief document of the movement, the founder's *Science and Health, with Key to the Scriptures*, was first published in 1875.

   For an interesting and sympathetic account of Christian Science see Robert Peel, *Christian Science: Its Encounter with American Culture* (New York: Henry Holt, 1958). Peel quotes Count Hermann Keyserling, who believed that Christian Science is "the prototype of American religiousness" (ibid., p. 200).

4. See George P. Grant, *Philosophy in the Mass Age* (Toronto: Copp Clark, 1959).

5. *Soldiers: An Obituary for Geneva*, trans. Robert David MacDonald (New York: Grove, 1968), p. 56.

6. *Perspectives on 19th and 20th Century Protestant Theology* (New York: Harper and Row, 1967), p. 92.

7. New York: Bantam Books, 1949.

8. Quoted by Richard Shickel in *Time*, April 9, 1984, p. 104.

9. Both quotations are from Shickel's review of the 1984 production of the play in *Time* magazine (ibid.).

10. *The Courage to Be* (New Haven and London: Yale University Press, 1952), p. 39.

11. *The Denial of Death* (New York: The Free Press, 1973), p. 178. I regard Becker's work as one of the most profound analyses of our society, combining insights of individual and social psychology, anthropology, history, and—not *very* far in the background—the ancient wisdom of the Jews.

12. Robert Lifton and Richard Falk, *Indefensible Weapons: The Political and Psychological Case against Nuclearism* (Toronto: CBC Publications, 1984), p. 103.

13. It could of course be argued that contemporary life is even more frank and open about the negating element. Our children are subjected to media displays of death and violence far surpassing anything accessible to young people prior to World War II! There is, however, a significant difference between the two periods. The violence displayed in much contemporary "entertainment" is so fantastic as to foster the propensity to regard the Nihil as unreal; moreover, precisely because it is "entertainment"—and may be so regarded even when it is actual news!—it does not call forth the same emotions as do stories or works of art. Romantic and dated as they now seem, Anderson's "The Little Match Girl" and Longfellow's "Evangeline" can still put us in touch with deep emotions left untouched by "Rambo."

14. Jean-Francois Beaudet, "Making Theology in the Contexte Quebecois: Towards a Revolutionary Theology of the Cross."

15. At the height of this transition to modernity, it was planned to take as the motto of the Montreal hosting of the World Fair (Expo 67) the phrase "Man against Nature!" Fortunately for later ecological consciousness, this was altered to "Terre des Hommes" (the phrase popularized by Ste. Exupéry).

16. Although the English word sympathy has been reduced to the status of a synonym for mere pity, its etymology points to something far deeper: pathos (from the verb paschein) with the prefix sym denotes literally "to suffer with."

17. In this connection, see my discussion of "Feindbilder" in Christian Mission: The Stewardship of Life in the Kingdom of Death (New York: Friendship Press, 1985).

18. The Denial of Death, p. 187.

19. See Lighten Our Darkness: Towards an Indigenous Theology of the Cross (Philadelphia: Westminster, 1976).

20. Does God Exist? trans. Edward Quinn (New York: Doubleday, 1980), p. 694.

Chapter 2   Creation: Suffering as Becoming

1. Quoted by Martin E. Marty, Righteous Empire: The Protestant Experience in America (New York: Harper, 1970), p. 256. Marty makes the interesting point that today even those "evangelists" who follow in Moody's footsteps, like Billy Graham, assume that something can be done about this world.

2. See Robert McAfee Brown, *Making Peace in the Global Village* (Philadelphia: Westminster, 1981), p. 12.
3. *The Courage to Be* (New Haven: Yale University Press, 1952).
4. *God and the Rhetoric of Sexuality* (Philadelphia, Fortress, 1978).
5. Paul Tillich was and is often criticized (by Reinhold Niebuhr amongst others) for coming too close to the equation of creation and fall. I realize that this is a difficult line to walk, but it is surely just as questionable to make an absolute distinction and discontinuity between creation and fall as to merge them. If the conditions necessary for falling are not already present in creation, then "the fall" must be regarded in a strictly supralapsarian way.
6. See Dietrich Bonhoeffer, *Temptation* (London, SCM, 1955).
7. See my discussion of this conception of being in *Imaging God: Dominion as Stewardship* (Grand Rapids: Eerdmans, and New York: Friendship Press, for the National Commission on Stewardship of the National Council of Churches, 1986).
8. Peter Shaffer, *Equus* (New York: Avon Books, 1974-75), pp. 122-123.
9. Paul Tillich, *The Courage to Be*, p. 39.
10. Introduction to the Signet Book edition of *A Streetcar Named Desire* (New York: New American Library, 1947), introduction unpaginated.
11. Act III, 5, 32-33.
12. Johannes Baptist Metz, *Poverty of Spirit*, tr. John Drury (Paramus, N.J., and New York: Paulist, 1968).
13. Grand Rapids: Eerdmans, 1962.
14. The Jewish author Elie Wiesel raised just this question in a television interview some years ago. Wiesel has dedicated most of his life to keeping alive the memory of the Holocaust; so the question, when asked by such a one, cannot be dismissed as if it were the concern of those who refuse to admit the reality of suffering (Chapter 1).
15. Albert Camus, *Caligula and Three Other Plays*, trans. Stuart Gilbert (New York: Knopf, 1966), p. 8.
16. See my book *The Steward: A Biblical Symbol Come of Age* (New York: Friendship Press, for the Commission on Stewardship of the National Council of Churches, 1982).

Chapter 3 The Fall: Suffering as Burden

1. Trans. Everett R. Kalin (Philadelphia: Fortress, 1973), p. 22.
2. Ibid., p. 23 (the quotations are from Calvin's "Forms of Prayer for the Church").

3. The adjective *Christian* should never be taken at face value! As Hans
   Küng has written, "The word 'Christian' today is more of a soporific
   than a slogan. So much—too much!—is Christian: churches, schools,
   political parties, cultural associations. . ." (*On Being a Christian* [Glas-
   gow: Wm. Collins, 1979], p. 119).
4. See *Systematic Theology*, vol. 2 (Chicago: University of Chicago Press,
   1957), pp. 29-44, esp. 36-39.
5. See, e.g., *The Irony of American History* (New York: Scribner, 1952),
   especially Chapter 8.
6. "The Dreamers," in *Seven Gothic Tales* (Harmondsworth: Penguin,
   1963), p. 308.
7. *Weimarer Ausgabe*, vol. 7, p. 337 (trans. Prof. E. Furcha).
8. Karl Barth has a beautiful passage on this theme in *Church Dogmatics*
   3/3, trans. G. W. Bromiley and R. J. Ehrlich (Edinburgh: T. & T.
   Clark, 1960), pp. 240-243.
9. Iris Murdoch, *The Sea, The Sea* (Frogmore St. Albans: Triad/Panther
   Books, 1980), p. 502.
10. *The Gospel of Suffering*, trans. David Swenson and L. M. Swenson
    (Minneapolis: Augsburg, 1948), p. 36.
11. Writing this on the 40th anniversary of the bombing of Hiroshima,
    I cannot forebear mentioning how essential something like the dogma
    of original sin is for understanding and articulating what it means to
    live in a world which has discovered and already, in a small way,
    employed the means of its own annihilation. It is to the credit of one
    of the Bomb's chief inventors that he could still express the sense of
    sin, and in a way which incorporates both its tragic and its moral
    dimensions: " 'In some sort of crude sense which no vulgarity, no
    humor, no overstatement can quite extinguish,' said Robert Oppen-
    heimer in a lecture to his fellow scientists, 'the physicists have known
    sin; and this is a knowledge which they cannot lose' " (*Time*, July 29,
    1985, p. 51).

Chapter 4   Redemption: Conquest from Within

1. *Faith and History* (New York: Scribner, 1951), p. 22.
2. C. S. Song, *The Compassionate God* (Maryknoll, N.Y.: Orbis, 1982),
   pp. 109f.
3. New York: Atheneum, 1971, p. 247.
4. *Christus Victor: An Historical Study of the Three Main Types of the Idea
   of Atonement*, trans. A. G. Hebert (London: SPCK, 1953).

5. . . . And, not incidentally, to Satan's earthly emissaries—frequently identified in Christian history as the Jews.
6. "Cur Deus Homo?" in A Scholastic Miscellany, ed. Eugene R. Fairweather, Library of Christian Classics, vol. 10 (London: SCM, 1956), pp. 100ff.
7. See "Exposition of the Epistle to the Romans," in A Scholastic Miscellany, pp. 276ff.
8. For a more detailed discussion of this theme, see my book Has the Church a Future? (Philadelphia: Westminster, 1980).
9. Mount Fuji and Mount Sinai: A Pilgrimage in Theology (London: SCM, 1984), p. 241.
10. The Crucified God (London: SCM, 1973), p. 72.
11. In the context of a discussion about Nietzsche's rejection of Paul's theology, Eberhard Jüngel makes the important point that it is only in connection with love that power and weakness are not antithetical. "For Paul, the Crucified One is weak, subject to death. But Paul does not celebrate this thought with melancholy, but rather thinks of it as the gospel, as a source of joy. What is joyful about the weakness of the Crucified One? The weakness of the Crucified One is for Paul the way in which God's power of life is perfected (II Cor. 13:4). Weakness is then not understood as a contradiction of God's power. There is, however, only one phenomenon in which power and weakness do not contradict each other, in which rather power can perfect itself as weakness. This phenomenon is the event of love. Love does not see power and weakness as alternatives. It is the unity of power and weakness, and such is certainly the most radical opposite of the will to power which cannot affirm weakness. Pauline 'theology of the cross' (theologia crucis) is, accordingly, the most stringent rejection of all deification of self-willing power" (God as the Mystery of the World: On the Foundation of the Theology of the Crucified One in the Dispute between Theism and Atheism, trans. Darrell L. Guder [Grand Rapids: Eerdmans, 1983], p. 206).
12. See Faith and History: A Comparison of Christian and Modern Views of History (New York: Scribner, 1959), p. 128.
13. Earlier I made a passing reference to the Virgin Birth, in which I contrasted an ontological (or metaphysical) with an "historical" approach to the dogma. I believe the Virgin Birth to be an important symbol of precisely the point being expressed here. It does not have to do with the possibility or impossibility of a woman producing a baby without the cooperation of a male, however metaphorically

suggestive that may be! It has to do with the nature of grace, or with grace and nature. It speaks of the *receptive* capacities of nature and history while denying their *redemptive* capacities. (See Karl Barth's treatment of the subject in *Dogmatics in Outline*, trans. G. T. Thompson [London: SCM, 1949], Chapter 14: "The Mystery and the Miracle of Christmas," pp. 95ff.)

14. *The Crucified God*, p. 205.

15. "The Crucified God," in *Theology Today* 31 (1974): 18.

16. In this connection it may be remarked that the combination of iconoclasm and fideism in the more doctrinaire forms of Protestantism produced peculiarly stilted versions of the gospel, especially at the point of their atonement theology. By comparison with medieval mysticism, German pietism, and (especially) Luther's "picture of Christ," the Christological and soteriological utterances of many of the Reformed divines (including Calvin) are pervaded by a kind of rationalism which, as soon as it gets beyond the bounds of 16th- and 17th-century European scholasticism, holds little for the mind and less for the heart. Theology cannot *depend upon* art—and indeed it could be argued plausibly that great Western art, even into our own secular age, has relied very heavily on faith and theology (consider Rembrandt and Rouault). But theologies that imagine they can be *independent of* art (not *kitsch*, but real art) should take warning from the fate of Protestant Orthodoxy!

17. There is in fact no limit here, because all human experience, when it is truthfully represented, illuminates the breadth and meaning of the experience of the One to whom Pilate pointed, saying, *Ecce, homo!*

18. Trans. William Johnston (Tokyo: Sophia University, in cooperation with Rutland, Vt., and Tokyo: Tuttle, 1969).

19. Trans. Richard A. Schuchert, S.J. (New York: Paulist, 1973).

20. I have used this way of designating the theology of the cross tradition in my *Lighten Our Darkness: Towards an Indigenous Theology of the Cross* (Philadelphia: Westminster, 1976)—a work in which I have discussed this tradition in much greater detail than is possible here, and with special reference to its applicability to our own sociological and historical context.

21. It is an interesting and provocative fact that the most compelling *artistic* treatments of the *theologia crucis* seem to come from Roman Catholic and Jewish authors. Among these I would name particularly Georges Bernanos's *Diary of a Country Priest*, Graham Greene's *The Power and the Glory*, and the works of Elie Wiesel, especially *Night*

and *The Town beyond the Wall*. It seems possible, if not probable, that this is related to the observation, developed in an earlier note, that while a Protestantism distrustful of art tended to degenerate into rationalism and conceptualism, both Catholic and Jewish faith permitted and encouraged a wider exploration of the human terrain for analogies to revelation.

22. *Theology of the Pain of God* (Richmond: John Knox, 1965), p. 46.
23. *Life of Jesus*, p. 71.
24. See my article, "Rethinking Christ: Theological Reflections on Shusaku Endo's *Silence*," in *Interpretation* 33 (1979): 254ff.
25. *The Compassionate God*, p. 115.
26. *Poverty of Spirit*, trans. John Drury (Paramus, N.J., and New York: Paulist, 1968), p. 27.
27. Thornton Wilder, *The Angel That Troubled the Waters* (New York: Coward-McCann, 1928), p. 148.
28. Perhaps it is even more the case in triumphant cultures sensing decline! There is a spirit abroad in our society today (it is very evident in the public response to films like *Rambo*) which cries for ever more bizarre displays of "winning."
29. *Mount Fuji and Mount Sinai*, p. 242.
30. J. Christiaan Beker, *Paul's Apocalyptic Gospel: The Coming Triumph of God* (Philadelphia: Fortress, 1982), p. 19.

Chapter 5 The Church: Community of Suffering and Hope

1. This theme is present everywhere in Luther's writings. The following quotation from "On the Councils and the Church" (*Luther's Works* 41 [Philadelphia: Fortress, 1966], pp. 164-165) is typical: "The holy Christian people are externally recognized by the holy possession of the sacred cross. They must endure every misfortune and persecution, all kinds of trials and evil from the devil, the world, and the flesh (as the Lord's Prayer indicates) by inward sadness, timidity, fear, outward poverty, contempt, illness, and weakness, in order to become like their head, Christ. And the only reason they must suffer is that they steadfastly adhere to Christ and God's word, enduring this for the sake of Christ, Matthew 5[:11], 'Blessed are you when men persecute you on my account.' They must be pious, quiet, obedient, and prepared to serve the government and everybody with life and goods, doing no

one any harm. No people on earth have to endure such bitter hate; they must be accounted worse than Jews, heathen, and Turks. In summary, they must be called heretics, knaves, and devils, the most pernicious people on earth, to the point where those who hang, drown, murder, torture, banish, and plague them to death are rendering God a service. No one has compassion on them; they are given myrrh and gall to drink when they thirst. And all of this is done not because they are adulterers, murderers, thieves, or rogues, but because they want to have none but Christ, and no other God. Wherever you see or hear this, you may know that the holy Christian church is there, as Christ says in Matthew 5 [:11-12], 'Blessed are you when men revile you and utter all kinds of evil against you on my account. Rejoice and be glad, for your reward is great in heaven.' This too is a holy possession whereby the Holy Spirit not only sanctifies his people, but also blesses them."

2. *Church Dogmatics*, 2/2, trans. G. T. Thompson and Harold Knight (Edinburgh: T. & T. Clark, 1957), p. 53.

3. Many of the passiontide hymns of the church are no-longer sung in fashionable North American congregations because they are too "mournful."

4. Jürgen Moltmann, *The Crucified God* (London: SCM, 1973), p. 1.

5. Paul Tillich, *The Courage to Be* (New Haven and London: Yale University Press, 1952), p. 39.

6. *The Living Thoughts of Kierkegaard: Presented by W. H. Auden* (Bloomington: Indiana University Press, 1966), p. 30.

7. Cf. Dorothee Sölle, *Suffering* (Philadelphia: Fortress, 1973), pp. 145 ff. ("Within Jewish religious thinking the answer given [to human suffering] is understood in terms of the *shekinah*, the 'indwelling presence of God in the world.' . . . 'His glory itself descends to the world, enters into it, into "exile", dwells in it, dwells with the troubled, the suffering creatures in the midst of their uncleanness—desiring to redeem them.' In his emptied, abased form God shares the suffering of his people. . . .")

8. Especially in *The Courage To Be*, but implicitly in all of his works.

9. Calvin's "penal theory" must, I think, be regarded as a variation on the same theme of substitutionary sacrifice.

10. I am not forgetting that substitutionary atonement theology is one of the five "fundamentals" of Christian fundamentalism, and therefore to this day a powerful religious force, on this continent especially.

This, however, is related to the subsequent discussion of cultural religion in the text.

11. See Dorothee Sölle, *Christ Our Representative: An Essay in Theology after the Death of God* (London: SCM, 1965), pp. 19ff.

12. *Christian Letters to a Post-Christian World* (Grand Rapids: Eerdmans, 1969), p. 98.

13. In this connection, see H. Paul Santmire, *The Travail of Nature: The Ambiguous Ecological Promise of Christian Theology* (Philadelphia: Fortress, 1985), especially Chapter 10 ("Ecological Reading of the Bible").

14. J. Christiaan Beker, *Paul the Apostle: The Triumph of God in Life and Thought* (Philadelphia: Fortress, 1980), p. 364.

15. The most consistent example of this of which I am aware is the encyclical *Mystici Corporis Christi*, promulgated by Pope Pius XII. Liberal Protestantism, however, in its more sentimental version of Jesus' relation to the church, frequently ends in a similar confusion of head and body.

16. *The Cost of Discipleship*, trans. R. H. Fuller (London: SCM, 1948), p. 73.

17. See, e.g., Jaroslav Pelikan's comments in *Luther the Expositor*, Companion Volume to *Luther's Works* (St. Louis: Concordia, 1959), pp. 169-171 (on Luther's concept of Baptism).

18. An example of Luther's extraordinary sense of the *internality* (conquest from within) of God's redemptive work in Christ: "When God wants to speak and deal with us, he does not avail himself of an angel but of parents, of the pastor, or of my neighbor. This puzzles and blinds me so that I fail to recognize God, who is conversing with me through the person of the pastor or father. This prompts the Lord Christ to say in the text [the incident of the woman at the well]: 'If you knew the gift of God, who it was that is saying to you, "Give me a drink," then I would not be obliged to run after you and beg for a drink' " (quoted by John M. Todd in *Luther: A Life* [New York: Crossroads, 1982], p. 351).

19. The American scientist Loren Eiseley is one of many modern and contemporary scientists who are rediscovering the dimension of mystery *in* and *through* their science, and therefore find it necessary to express their discoveries in forms of thought and language sharply distinguished from the kind of "objectivity" still popularly associated with scientific disciplines. A recent commentator on Eiseley's work has written: "Contemplation is a kind of human activity in which the

mind and spirit and body are directed in solitude toward some other. Scholars and critics have not yet taken the full measure of contemplation as an art that is related to the purpose of all scholarly activity—to see things as they really are. Therefore most scholarship is a carefully crafted veneer of rationalistic activity, helpful perhaps on its own level, but not usually leading to genuine insight.

"Scholars like Eiseley confront us with the impoverishment of our understanding. . . . Eiseley was a contemplative who gazed into and *through* the otherness of reality. One discovers through contemplation that reality consists of various encounters with an other without which we ourselves are incomplete. Finding that otherness is almost always a matter of vision, a way of knowing that we have forgotten" (Richard Wentz, "The American Spirituality of Loren Eiseley," *The Christian Century*, April 25, 1984, p. 432).

20. C. S. Dinsmore, *Atonement in Literature and Life* (Boston and New York: Houghton and Mifflin, 1906), p. 232.
21. *A Matter of Hope: A Theologian's Reflections on the Thought of Karl Marx* (Notre Dame, Ind.: University of Notre Dame Press, 1982), p. 193.
22. "Christians have always been tempted to transform the tragedy of Jesus into comedy by supposing that resurrection gives to his story a 'happy ending'. But no story has an ending until it is fully told. The context that gives meaning (or fails to do so) to the history of each individual (including Jesus) is the history of the human race" (ibid.).
23. *The Mediator*, trans. Olive Wyon (Philadelphia: Westminster, 1948), p. 435.
24. *Letters and Papers from Prison* (London, SCM, 1953), pp. 124-125.
25. Nicholas Lash, *A Matter of Hope*, p. 292.

Appendix: Dialog and Conclusions

1. P. 64.
2. P. 63.
3. P. 64.
4. The title of Chapter 5, pp. 72ff.
5. P. 4.
6. P. 38.
7. Pp. 42-43.
8. "Some medieval and Victorian thinkers saw the eruption of Vesuvius and the destruction of Pompeii as a way of putting an end to that

society's immorality. Even today, the earthquakes in California are interpreted by some as God's way of expressing His displeasure with the alleged homosexual excesses of San Francisco or the heterosexual ones of Los Angeles" (p. 53).

9. P. 52.
10. Cf. Chapter 3.
11. P. 138.
12. "The world is mostly an orderly, predictable place, showing ample evidence of God's thoroughness and handiwork, but pockets of chaos remain. Most of the time, the events of the universe follow firm natural laws. But every now and then, things happen not contrary to those laws of nature but outside them. Things happen which could just as easily have happened differently" (p. 52).
13. P. 52.
14. P. 43.
15. Cf. Chapter 8.
16. P. 136 (emphasis added).
17. P. 138.
18. P. 139.
19. Ibid.
20. P. 14.
21. P. 16.
22. P. 22.
23. P. 35.
24. P. 36.
25. P. 43.
26. Ibid.
27. P. 45.
28. Ibid.
29. P. 53.
30. P. 56.
31. P. 73.
32. P. 76.
33. P. 77.
34. Ibid.
35. P. 81.
36. P. 83.
37. P. 92.
38. P. 93.
39. P. 96.

40. P. 117.
41. P. 98.
42. Ibid.
43. Pp. 132-133.
44. In this connection, see Brian Hebblethwaite's *Evil, Suffering and Religion* (New York: Hawthorn Books, 1976), which has a more sympathetic ear for Dostoevsky's famous character.
45. Kushner, p. 98.
46. *Chronicles of Narnia* (Harmondsworth: Penguin, 1956).
47. See again my summary of the two principal "responses" Lewis offers to "the problem of pain," supra, pp. 162-165.
48. P. 8.
49. Ibid.
50. P. 7.
51. P. 19.
52. P. 20.
53. P. 21.
54. Pp. 27-28.
55. P. 33.
56. Pp. 33-34.
57. P. 33.
58. P. 35.
59. P. 42.
60. Ibid.
61. Ibid.
62. P. 43.
63. P. 45.
64. P. 46.
65. P. 47.
66. P. 49.
67. P. 51.
68. P. 53.
69. P. 54.
70. P. 55.
71. Ibid.
72. P. 56.
73. P. 59.
74. Ibid.
75. P. 93.
76. P. 93.

77. P. 96.
78. P. 97.
79. Jürgen Moltmann, *The Crucified God* (London: SCM, 1973), p. 205 (supra, p. 112).
80. P. 8.
81. Pp. 14f.
82. P. 17.
83. P. 84.
84. Ibid.
85. Ibid.
86. P. 85; see note 106.
87. P. 90.
88. P. 96.
89. Ibid.
90. P. 110.
91. P. 99.
92. Ibid.
93. P. 100.
94. P. 101.
95. P. 104.
96. P. 106.
97. Pp. 107-108.
98. P. 110.
99. P. 122.
100. P. 116.
101. Pp. 118-119.
102. P. 120.
103. P. 121.
104. P. 121.
105. P. 125.
106. I am of course aware of the difficulties associated with the term *Patripassianism* as such. My point here and in the earlier discussion of Buttrick's position, however, concerns what appears to me an inordinate cautiousness on the part of the theologians throughout the centuries with respect to the divine aseity.

 Patripassianism is the nomenclature (according to some, it is a term of derision or a nickname) assigned to the doctrinal position of the modalistic monarchians of the 3rd century C.E., Sabellius being chief amongst them. Since, in their desire to maintain the ontic unity of the godhead against the dangers of tritheism, they failed to distinguish between the *personae* of the Trinity, their doctrine ended in the insistence that "the Father" (*Pater*) suffered (*passion-em*) in and as "the Son."

The rejection of this position by trinitarian orthodoxy, however understandable and justifiable within its own terms of reference, has left Christianity with a conception of God that is, to say the least, ambiguous. On the one hand, Christians are counseled by the guardians of trinitarian orthodoxy against regarding "Almighty God" as being capable of suffering. On the other hand, they are assured that Jesus, the crucified, fully and supremely reveals God: "He who has seen me has seen the Father" (John 14:9). This ambiguity is hardly clarified by the theological sophistry which argues that while Jesus "suffered," as the Creeds declare, God the Father *had compassion;* for, as Tertullian observed long ago, what is compassion if it is not suffering-with?

Yet the desire to shield "the Father" from overt suffering is very deeply entrenched in Christian thought and piety. There are echoes of it, for instance, in Paul Tillich's *Systematic Theology.* "God himself," writes Tillich, "is said to participate in the negatives of creaturely existence. This idea is supported by mystical as well as by christological thought. Nevertheless, the idea must be stated with reservations. Genuine patripassianism (the doctrine that God the Father has suffered in Christ) rightly was rejected by the early church. God as being-itself transcends nonbeing absolutely" (vol. 1 [Chicago: University of Chicago Press, 1951], p. 270). As Tillich goes on to notice, however, the immediate consequence of this theological decision is that it introduces serious doubts concerning the extent of God's involvement with the world—in his own words, concerning the "participation of the divine life in the negativities of creaturely life" (ibid.). Later (vol. 3, published in 1963), when Tillich returns to this question, it appears to be the latter aspect of it that occupies his mind. While again insisting that "the so-called patripassionist doctrine" had to be rejected because it "contradicts too obviously the fundamental theological doctrine of God's impassibility," he continues: "But the rejection of patripassianism does not solve the question of the negative in the blessedness of the Divine Life. Present-day theology tries—with very few exceptions—to avoid the problem altogether, either by ignoring it or by calling it an inscrutable divine mystery. But such escape is impossible in view of the question's significance for the most existential problem of theodicy. People in 'boundary-situations' will not accept the escape into the divine mystery on this point if it is not used on other points, for example, in the teaching of the church about God's almighty power and his ever-present love, teaching which demands interpretation in view of the daily experience of the negativity of existence. If theology refuses to answer such existential questions, it has neglected its task" (p. 404).

The "answer" that I have been attempting to unfold in these pages begins, if I may put it this way, with a question: Why is it so mandatory for a theology that is biblically based and Christocentric to be so protective, not to say defensive, when it comes to God the Father? Is "God's impassibility" really "*the* fundamental theological doctrine?" If we are rooted in the faith of Israel then—as Abraham J. Heschel has so ably demonstrated in his classical study of *The Prophets* (New York: The Jewish Publication Society of America, 1962, p. 224)—the truly *fundamental* teaching about God in this source is not the divine impassibility or aseity but the divine *pathos*: "God is concerned about the world, and shares its fate. Indeed, this is the essence of God's moral nature: His willingness to be intimately involved in the history of man." The same conclusion, a fortiori, must surely be the outcome of all serious Christological reflection. If it is really God who is revealed in and through the crucified one, then how can we continue to speak about the divine "impassibility" at all, or at least without subjecting it to a thorough Christological overhaul!

What we are dealing with here, I think, is a classical instance of the intrusion of a metaphysic foreign to the spirit of the tradition of Jerusalem into the midst of evolving Christian doctrine. So long as one begins in one's theological reflections with a theism typical of the high philosophic traditions of Athens, one quite naturally has to defend Deity against a too intimate relationship with creation—with matter, with the flesh, with life's "negativities." I do not think, however, that the alternative to this theistic/deistic position is to insist, with the Sabellians, on an ontic unity of Father and Son which is so undifferentiated as to end not only with a god who is born and suffers but also with a *Christos* who is no longer truly human. The truth is, the monarchian heretics were starting from the same metaphysical presuppositions as their detractors; they simply applied to the second person of the Trinity the ontological presuppositions applied by their opponents to the first person.

The alternative, rather, is to *return the whole discussion of "the*

godhead" to Jerusalem! What this would mean is beyond the scope of
an endnote (though I trust that its meaning is at least implicit
throughout the present study). At bottom, it would entail eschewing
the substantialistic frame of reference in favor of a relational/repre-
sentational understanding of the Christ. The important message of
the church is not to demonstrate that the *being* of God and the *being*
of Jesus are identical (with distinctions!), but to present Jesus as
God's mode of *being-with* us: *Emmanuel.* The crucified one is then
an authentic and ultimate representation of the divine, and the medium of God's communication with us and ours with God.

Something like this, I believe, is what Dorothee Sölle has done
in her book, *Christ the Representative: An Essay in Theology after the
"Death of God"* (trans. David Lewis; London: SCM, 1967). In her
conclusion she writes, ". . . The God who is arraigned because of
the suffering of the innocent is really the omnipotent God, the king,
father, and ruler, who is above the world. Modern man rightly indicts
this God. And none of the theological devices used to silence this
indictment can suppress the truth of this questioning of the almighty
God. Certainly no dogmatic positing of a God who reduces us to
silence because he alone has the right to speak.

"If we refuse to drop this question, and do not piously suppress it,
we are led to abandon the theistic God. The open-eyed, deliberate
atheism of modern times has not drawn its strength from the wells
of scientific rationalism and historical criticism. Its existential argument . . . has been the pain, injustice and suffering endured by
the innocent. In all religions, a question mark has been set against
the omnipotent and serene gods by the sufferings of men. But only
in Christ does the concept of a suffering God appear" (pp. 150-151).

107. P. 229.
108. P. 8.
109. Nashville: Abingdon, 1936.
110. P. 13.
111. P. 17.
112. P. 18.
113. Ibid.
114. P. 21.
115. Ibid.
116. Ibid.
117. P. 24.
118. P. 27.

119. P. 28.
120. P. 29.
121. P. 37.
122. P. 33.
123. Interestingly enough, it was Weatherhead who led opposition to spiritualistic healing, culminating in 1952 with the Methodist Conference barring public healing services from Methodist churches in Britain. (See his appendix to Chapter 9 on "Healing Missions," pp. 81ff.)
124. P. 47.
125. Pp. 47-48.
126. P. 49.
127. P. 52.
128. P. 57.
129. Pp. 57-58.
130. P. 74.
131. P. 78.
132. P. 79.
133. P. 87.
134. P. 89.
135. P. 92.
136. Pp. 92-93.
137. Supra, p. 268.
138. Perhaps the greatest contribution of Karl Barth to the doctrine of God was his correction of Calvin at just this point. The divine "perfections" (attributes) are, in the *Church Dogmatics*, brought under the aegis of Christology. See vol. 2/1, trans. T. H. L. Parker et al. (New York: Scribner, 1957), Sections 29, 30, and 31.
139. "Theory is fine, but it doesn't prevent things from existing"—Charcot.
140. Hebblethwaite, *Evil, Suffering and Religion*, p. 105.

Indexes

Scriptural References

Genesis 2   69, 85
2:18   54
2:23   55
3   64, 69, 81, 85
3:7   81
50:20   153, 192

Job   24, 28, 62, 76, 152,
   155, 183

Psalm 102   31
130   59

Proverbs   127

Ecclesiastes   21

Isaiah   125
6   153
28   196
40   19, 48, 142
57:15   194

Lamentations   28

Hosea   125

Matthew 5   207

5:3-11   126
6:5   132
6:25   133
6:25f.   79
6:27   132
6:28   21
6:34   132
7:14   128
10:30 (par)   75
16:23 (par)   117
18:12-14   21
19:23   128
19:26   128
25   142

Luke 15:1-10   21

John 1   109
9:10   76
10:10   66
13:17   92
21:15f.   117

Romans 5:2   142
5:3   66
6   132
7   143

8:18   164
8:22   68, 138
8:29   124

1 Corinthians 1:2   106
1:21-25   105
15:55   56

2 Corinthians   123
1:19-20   128
12:9   106
13:4   205

Philippians 2   56, 137

Colossians 1:24   140

Hebrews 2:10   124, 163
11:1   198

James 1:17   128

1 Peter   123
4:12   124

Revelation   128
21:4   75

Names

Abelard, Peter, 32, 101,
   177, 194
Allen, Diogenes, 169ff.,
   179, 194, 195
Anderson, Hans Christian,
   202
Andre, Brother, 44
Anselm of Canterbury, 78,
   92, 101, 135-36, 177

Aristotle, 108
Auden, W. H., 136, 108
Augustine, 169
Aulen, Gustav, 99

Barth, Karl, 77, 107, 109,
   126, 161, 204, 206, 217
Beausorbre, Iulia de, 173,
   176

Becker, Ernest, 42, 46
Beker, J. Christian, 207
Bernanos, Geroges, 206
Bernhard of Clairvaux, 194
Bonhoeffer, Dietrich, 28,
   35, 57, 113, 133, 139,
   145f., 188, 193
Brown, Robert McAfee,
   203

Brunner, Emil, 144
Buechner, Frederick, 99
Buttrick, George, 178ff.

Calvin, John, 76, 136, 177, 206, 208
Camus, Albert, 64
Charcot, Jean-Martin, 41
Constantine, 126-27
Cowburn, John S.J., 199

Dineson, Isak (Karen Blixen), 79
Dinsmore, C. S., 210
Dostoevsky, Fydor, 74, 212
Dürrenmatt, Friedrich, 170

Eddy, Mary Baker, 36f.
Einstein, Albert, 50
Eiseley, Loren, 209
Eliot, T. S., 144
Ellul, Jacques, 180
Endo, Shusaku, 114ff., 184, 195
Evans, Robert and Alice, 200

Fackenheim, Emil, 166
Fairweather, Eugene, 205
Feuerbach, Ludwig, 91
Fox, Terry, 39
Freud, Sigmund, 41
Friere, Paulo, 26
Furcha, Edward, 204

Graham, Billy, 202
Grant, George P., 40
Greene, Graham, 206
Guder, Darrell, 205

Hardy, Thomas, 160, 168
Hebblethwaite, Brian, 212, 217
Heidegger, Martin, 61, 128
Heschel, Abraham J., 175
Hitler, Adolph, 63, 166, 182
Hochhuth, Rolf, 40
Huxley, Aldous, 160, 168

Irenaeus, 66

Jaspers, Karl, 199
Johnson, William, 206
Julian of Norwich, 198
Jüngel, Eberhard, 205

Kafka, Franz, 85, 153
Kalin, Everett, 203
Keyserling, Count Hermann, 201
Kierkegaard, Søren, 26, 71, 86, 129
Kitamori, Kazoh, 114, 168, 195
Knight, Harold, 208
Koyama, Kosuke, 105
Küng, Hans, 48, 204
Kushner, Harold S., 149ff., 158, 160-68, 171, 176, 189-90, 197

Lash, Nicholas, 141, 146
Lewis, C. S., 158ff., 172, 183, 188
Lifton, Robert, 43
Longfellow, Henry Wadsworth, 202
Luther, Martin, 77, 80, 105, 107, 123-124, 134, 139, 144, 169, 181, 185, 191, 195, 199

Manns, Peter, 199
Marty, Martin, 202
Marx, Karl, 91, 210
McLeod, Sir George, 200
Metz, Johannes, 62
Meyer, Harding, 199
Miller, Arthur, 41f.
Moltmann, Jürgen, 105, 111, 184, 195, 208, 213
Moody, Dwight L., 50
Murdoch, Iris, 204

Newbigin, Leslie, 201
Niebuhr, Reinhold, 33, 77, 78, 95, 107, 119, 143, 203
Nietzsche, Friedrich, 205

Oppenheimer, Robert J., 204

Parker, T. H. L., 217
Peel, Robert, 201
Pelikan, Jaroslav, 209
Pius XII, Pope, 209
Plato, 182

Rembrandt, 206
Rouault, Georges, 206

Saint-Exupery, Antoine de, 202
Santmire, H. Paul, 209
Sayers, Dorothy L., 136
Schleiermacher, Friedrich, 160
Schuchert, Richard, S.J., 206
Segundo, Juan Luis, 50
Shaffer, Peter, 60
Shakespeare, William, 51, 61
Skinner, B. F., 98
Socrates, 89
Sölle, Dorothee, 76, 208-9
Song, C. S., 96f., 168
Stalin, Joseph, 173, 175
Swenson, David, 204

Thielicke, Helmut, 23
Thomson, G. T., 206, 208
Thompson, Francis, 128
Tillich, Paul, 41, 42, 57, 77, 78, 131, 136, 139, 203, 208
Trible, Phyllis, 54

Von Hügel, Baron Friedrich, 179, 184

Weatherhead, Leslie D., 186ff.
Weil, Simone, 170, 174
Wesley, John, 187
Whitehead, Alfred North, 21
Wiebe, Rudi, 63
Wiesel, Elie, 203, 206
Williams, Tennessee, 60f.
Wyon, Olive, 210

Zwingli, Huldreich, 139

Subjects

"Absurd, the," 161
Acid rain, 176
AIDS, 76
Alienation, 130, 134

"American/Canadian Dream," 39, 42

Animal pain, 164, 165

Anti-Semitism, in Christian theology, 205
Anxiety, 55, 59f., 65, 73, 81, 129f., 134

Apocalypticism, 37
Art, 127, 206
Aseity, 194
"Aslan," 167
Atonement theories, 99f.,
135f., 167
Auschwitz, 74, 166, 176

Babel, 56
"Bad" people (Lewis), 161
Baptism, 132
"Becoming," 79-80, 151,
178ff.
Behaviorism, 98

Change, 79, 84, 89f., 103,
119
Chaos, 155
Christian Science, 36ff.
Christology, 167f.
Christus Victor, 99
Church, 30, 121, Chap. 5
(passim); as community
of compassion, 90; marks
of the church, 123; as
participant in Christ's
suffering, 137; relation
between Christ and the
church, 138; as "exten-
sion of the incarnation,"
140; as response to hu-
man suffering, 141; visi-
ble and invisible, 141; as
priestly people, 141; as
community of suffering,
142; "church of the
cross," 144; solidarity
with sufferers, 147
Club of Rome, 59
Communio viatorum, 80
Communism, 76
"Complexity" of God, 155
Conformitas Christi, 139
Constantinian captivity,
104f., 136
Constantinian era, 142
Contextuality, 22f., 49,
154, 175
Cosmogony, 51
Courage, 128ff., 158, 172
Covenant, 112, 157, 166,
181
Creation, 28, 29, Chap. 2
(passim); creation sagas,
54; extrahuman, 68;
goodness of, 129; groan-
ing of, 167
Creaturehood, 131, 133,
179
Creeds, 33

Credulity, 20-21; 27, 52
Cross, the, 27-28, 34, 101,
104ff., 111, 118, 123,
125, 127, 132, 167,
171f., 181, 187f., 192,
194, 196; "logic of the
cross," 107, 128, 143; in
the OT, 140; and resur-
rection, 185
Cynicism, 20-21, 53

Death, 43, 52, 56, 61f.,
119, 129, 134
Death camps, 87
Deism, 167-168
Demonic, the, 87
Dereliction, cry of, 172
Despair, 134; and meaning-
lessness, 136
Determinism, 88f.
Deus loquens, 70
Deus revelatus/deus
absconditus, 169
Discipleship, 131-33
Divine passivity, 179
Docetism, 35
"Dominion," 70
Drugs, 98
Dualism, 55, 62, 154

Easter, 126
Ecclesia crucis, 144
Ecclesia gloriae, 144
Eden, Garden of, 54
El Salvador, 176
Empire, 46, 105
"The Enemy," 46; see also
Feindbilder
Enlightenment, 38
Environmentally caused
disease, 119
Eschatology, 142f., 191,
196
Ethical passivity, 103
"Event" (Buttrick), 181f.
Evil, 100, 110
Evolution, and creation,
60-61; 63
Existentialism, 182

Faith, 20, 28, 94, 106, 111,
182, 191; and doubt,
118, 127; and rationality,
104, 186; and works, 193
Fall, the, 29f., Chap. 2 (pas-
sim)
Feindbilder, 102
Feminist theology, 25, 95
Fideism, 206
Finitude, 80f.

Finitum capax infiniti, 111
"First World," 24f., 78, 86,
102-3
"Fitness," 120
Free will, 83, 98
Freedom, 70f., 98f., 151,
154, 159, 173, 187, 189
Fundamentalism, 208
"Future Shock," 45

Glory, 185
Golden Age, 53
Good Friday, 126
Gnosticism, 36
"Good"/"bad," 153, 156
Gospel and law, 132
Grace, 142, 193f.; common
grace, 42, 58; and nature,
111; "cheap grace," 193
Gratitude, 58, 130
Grieving, 167
Guilt complex, 136

Hamartiology, 29, 69, 90,
165
Handicapped persons, 120
Happiness, 169, 175
"Heaven" (Lewis), 166f.
Hiroshima/Nagasaki, 43,
166, 176, 204
History, 110-11
"Historical evil" (Buttrick),
179
Holocaust, the, 203; see also
Auschwitz
Holy Spirit, 92, 132, 134,
185
Homo religiosus, 145
Homoousios/homoiousios,
108
Homosexuality, 211
Hope, 22, 25, 27, 28, 35,
47, 59, 133f., 142ff.
"Human cruelty," 171,
173, 176f.
Humanism, 158
Humility, 170
Hymns, passiontide, 208

Iconoclasm, 206
Ideology, 39, 41
Imitatio Christi, 139
Immorality, 165
Immortality, 82
Immutability (of God), 79
Incarnation, 34, 107f.,
113, 170-71, 175
Individualism, 83
Industrial Revolution, 38

Jesus Christ, suffering of, 33f., 42, 56, Chap. 4 (passim); Jesus' "distance from the Father" (Allen), 172ff.
Joy, 144ff., 178, 191
"Justification by works," 77
Justitia originalis, 213

Karamazov, Ivan, 167
Kenosis, 131, 195

"La Revolution Tranquille," 44
Lament, language of, 32
Last Judgment, 77
Liberalism, 75-78
Liberation theology, 25, 100, 135
Limits/limitations, 55-56, 58, 73, 79, 81, 120, 129f.; of suffering, 64f.
Lisbon earthquake, 155
Liturgy, 27
Logos, 107, 170
Loneliness, 54, 57-58, 73, 81, 119, 129f.
Love, of God, 99, 114, 145, 156, 158, 160, 166, 171, 185, 188

Martyr complex, 124
Martyrdom, 144f.
Martyriological process, 138
Marxism, 109
Masculine mystique, 96
Masochism, 66, 124, 127, 144
Melancholy, 129
Messianic expectation, 124
Miracle, 110; and magic, 190
Mitleid, 61
Mitsein, 57, 109
Modernity, 37f.
Monarchianism, 112
Moral Influence theory, 101
Moralism, 75f., 77f., 83
Morality, private, 82f., 85
Mystery, 169
Mysticism, 139

Narrative theology, 113
"Natural evil" (Buttrick), 171, 179
Nature, 171f.
Necessitas, 125, 140
Neo-Orthodoxy, 49

Neoplatonism, 36
Nihil, the, 41, 45
Nuclearism, 43, 76, 87

Omnipotence, 95, 114, 152, 155, 158, 161, 188, 189f.
Ontology, 51, 53
Oppression, 86, 102f.
Optimism, 21, 47, 143, 199
Original sin, 86, 162
Orthodoxy (Christian), 75f.

Pain, 151, 162f., 178
"Pain of God" (Kitamori), 114, 126
"Paradise Syndrome," 54, 151
Paranoia, 46
Passion, predictions of, 33f., 109
Pathos, 85
Patripassianism, 177, 213ff.
Peace, 98
Per Christum solum, 139
"Perfections," Divine, 217
Pessimism, 22, 199
"Positive thinking," 35f., 40
Power, 82, 95, 104f., 152, 155, 158, 170, 185, 190, 195; and love, 180; and weakness, 197
Power language, 95f.
Praxis, 134
Prayer, 84
Pride, 69, 133
Prisons, 119
Progress, 37, 40, 92, 109f., 161
Prometheanism, 67
Providentia Dei, 111
"Psychic numbing," 43

Quebec Catholicism, 44

"Rambo," 207
"Randomness" (Kushner), 155
Ransom theory (of atonement), 99f.
Rationalism, 138-39f., 178
Reconciliation, 134, 141
Redemption, 29, 48, 141, 146
Reformation theology, 138f.
Relational categories (of biblical faith), 183

Renaissance, 38
Repression, 42f.
Resignation, 52
Resurrection, 119, 132, 143, 181, 185

Sacraments, 174
Satan, 100
Scandal of particularity, 182, 186
School of Alexandria, 114
School of Antioch, 114
Science (Natural), 140
Scripture, 22
"Second World," 24f.
Sexual morality, 78
Sexuality, and original sin, 87
Shekinah, 208
Sin, 56, 87, 152-53, 161; and suffering, 165; corporate dimension of, 165
Sloth, 69, 133
Social concern, 174
Sola fide, 139
Sola gratia, 138-39, 193
Soma Christou, 139f.
Soteriology, 107, Chap. 4 (passim)
Sovereignty of God, 180, 185
Stewardship, 40; humanity as steward, 67f.
Stoicism, 47, 52f.
Sub contraria specie, 110
Substitutionary soteriology, 136
Suicide, 74, 120
Suffering, passim; problems of (conventional statement of), 97; of the church, Chap. 5 (passim); and the Beatitudes of Jesus, 126; and hope, 142ff.; as confirmatio/conformatio, 143; and sin, 165; participation of God in human suffering, 174
Supralapsarianism, 177
Sympathy, 45, 202

Technology, technologism, 38, 40, 50, 139
Teleology, 51, 53
Temporality, 79
Temptation, 55-56, 59, 64f., 73, 81, 125, 129
Terminal illness, 43
Theo-anthropology, 109
Theocentrism, 175

Theologia crucis, 105ff.,
114, 143-44, 195 (pas-
sim)
Theologia gloriae, 105, 114,
144, 195; *see also* Trium-
phalism
Theology, 94, 120, 168-9,
184; as suffering, 23
Theory, 120, 197
Theotokos, 108
"Third World," 24f., 39,
85, 120
Todestreib, 131
Torture, 174, 176
Totaliter aliter, 112

Tradition, 22
"Tradition of Jerusalem,"
15 n., passim
Tragedy, 32, 40, 47
Tragic dimension (of sin),
78, 82ff.
Transcendence, 112
Trinity, 111f., 194
Triumphalism, 105-6, 126;
see also Theologia gloriae
Trust, 79, 81, 130, 172
Truth, 182

Unemployment, 120
Utopia, 38

Vere Deus/vere Homo, 112
Victorian morality, 127
Victory (God's), 191
Vietnam, 89, 176
Violence, 87f., 103
Virgin Birth, 108, 205-6
Vocation (human), 67f.
Voluntarism, 89

War, 76, 103
Watergate, 176
Westminster Catechism, 51
Word-Event, 183f.
World renunciation, 170-1
"Wounded healer," 125